KB080984

Strategic Psychology for CEOs: Mastering Minds and Markets

Unlock the Power of Psychology in Leadership with
"Strategic Psychology for CEOs: Mastering Minds and Markets"

Issue Date | May 31, 2024
Author | Ryan Kim
Editor | Han Geon-hee
Published by | Bookk Co., Ltd.

Publisher Registration | 2014.07.15. (No. 2014-16)
Address | 119, Gasandigital 1-ro, Geumcheon-gu, Seoul, SK Twin Towers A-305
Phone | 1670-8316
Email | info@bookk.co.kr
ISBN | 979-11-410-8577-3
Website: www.bookk.co.kr

Table of Contents

Introduction

Chapter V: Collaboration and Psychology /263

Chapter VI: Alliance Strategies and Psychology /318

Chapter VII: Financial Management and Psychology /377

Introduction

1. The Intersection of Management and Psychology: Starting with Essential Insights

The modern business landscape is characterized by rapid change and escalating competition. Organizations not only need to survive but also thrive amid these shifting dynamics. Success in this competitive market requires more than technical proficiency or financial acumen; it demands a deep understanding of human behavior and psychology, and the effective integration of these insights into business strategies.

"Strategic Psychology for CEOs: Mastering Minds and Markets" explores how management and psychology interact, illustrating how this interdisciplinary approach can catalyze positive transformations in organizational success. This book directly applies psychological principles to business challenges, empowering readers to make informed decisions and gain a deeper understanding of both employee and customer behaviors.

Psychology has long been a tool for interpreting and predicting the complexities of human behavior. For example, consider a scenario where a lack of employee motivation leads to diminished productivity. By applying Maslow's Hierarchy of Needs and Herzberg's Motivation-Hygiene Theory, one can uncover the root causes and devise strategies to foster an environment where employees are more engaged and satisfied.

Moreover, understanding the psychological factors influencing consumer decision-making is crucial for crafting effective marketing strategies. Implementing principles like Cialdini's Principles of Persuasion can shape advertising campaigns that effectively drive consumer behavior.

This book offers practical solutions by applying psychological principles to tangible business problems across each chapter, bridging the gap between theory and practice. This approach not only aids readers in addressing the diverse management challenges they may encounter but also serves as a valuable resource for enhancing their leadership effectiveness and maximizing their team's potential.

2. Purpose and Structure of the Book

The primary aim of "Strategic Psychology for CEOs: Mastering Minds and Markets" is to provide business leaders with insightful and actionable psychological principles that can be integrated and applied within various facets of management. This book addresses complex and multifaceted issues that arise in key areas of management—ranging from human resources and marketing to organizational change and leadership—demonstrating how psychological insights can be applied effectively.

The objective is also to equip leaders with the psychological tools and techniques necessary to understand and manage the complexities of human relationships within their organizations, thereby enhancing productivity and efficiency—an essential aspect of fostering motivational work environments, resolving conflicts, and shaping organizational culture and change.

In each chapter, the book covers critical management domains comprehensively, explaining how psychology can be applied within these realms. This approach not only facilitates a deeper understanding but also provides leaders with practical measures to implement.

3. Benefits of a Psychological Approach in Management

Imagine entering a meeting room where every participant has a clear grasp of your mood, thoughts, and needs. While this may seem like an unattainable ideal, it is a scenario that can be realized through the strategic application of psychological principles in management. Psychology transcends mere understanding of human behavior; it offers a robust toolkit for predicting and influencing actions, revolutionizing internal communication, and enhancing comprehension of employee reactions.

For instance, Steve Jobs harnessed psychological principles to build Apple into a global brand. His focus on user experience, guided by the psychological principle of 'minimal cognitive load', enabled users to interact with complex technology intuitively, reinforcing Apple's market dominance. Similarly, Walmart's founder, Sam Walton, utilized psychological reinforcement strategies to foster a positive work environment, significantly boosting employee motivation and loyalty, which in turn propelled Walmart to become the world's largest retailer.

These examples underscore the practical applications of psychology in organizational settings, illustrating how leaders can leverage these insights to analyze complex situations, strategize effectively, and drive necessary organizational changes. Moreover, this book not only discusses theory but also offers tools necessary for leaders to become more effective and to enhance organizational performance through psychological understanding.

Further Advantages

1. Enhanced Decision-Making: Psychological insights enable leaders to make more informed and empathetic decisions that consider the emotional and psychological well-being of their employees and customers.

2. Improved Communication: Understanding psychological principles can lead to more effective communication within teams, between managers and employees, and with customers, enhancing overall organizational efficiency.

3. Conflict Resolution: Psychology provides tools for better understanding and resolving conflicts, which can lead to a more harmonious work environment and improved team dynamics.

4. Increased Innovation: By understanding the psychological factors that drive creativity and innovation, managers can foster an environment that encourages innovative thinking and problem-solving.

5. Effective Change Management: Applying psychological theories helps in managing organizational change more effectively, facilitating smoother transitions and better adaptation among employees.

6. Leadership Development: Psychological principles can be used to develop stronger leadership skills, helping leaders to motivate their teams better, inspire loyalty, and drive performance.

By integrating these psychological insights, "Strategic Psychology for CEOs: Mastering Minds and Markets" equips business leaders not only to tackle current challenges more effectively but also to build foundations for sustained success and growth in an ever-evolving business landscape.

Chapter I:
Human Resources and Psychology

The Heart of the Organization: Human Resource Management

If the success of an organization depends on how its members are managed, motivated, and satisfied, then human resource management is the heart of that organization. Just as a healthy and vigorous heart is crucial for the vitality of the human body, effective human resource management is vital for energizing an organization and performing key functions such as motivating employees, enhancing job satisfaction, and resolving conflicts. So, how can we regulate each heartbeat within the organization? This is the most important question facing HR managers, and psychological theories provide the key to answering it.

Human resource management goes beyond mere rules and procedures; it encompasses a depth that is essential for understanding and resolving the complexities of human relationships within an organization. Theories such as Edgar Schein's Culture Theory, Abraham Maslow's Hierarchy of Needs, and Fred Fiedler's Situational Leadership Theory can fundamentally transform HR strategies. This chapter aims to explore in depth how to optimize an organization's most valuable asset—its human resources—using these theories.

Abraham Maslow's Hierarchy of Needs provides insights into motivating employees to reach their full potential. This theory describes various stages of needs individuals experience, and how satisfying each level influences behaviors and attitudes. This understanding allows managers and HR professionals to pinpoint the current needs of each employee and develop strategies to support their progression to the next level.

Frederick Herzberg's Motivation-Hygiene Theory differentiates between factors that enhance job satisfaction and those that, if unaddressed, lead to dissatisfaction. This theory helps managers understand that improving job satisfaction is not merely about addressing dissatisfiers but also involves enhancing motivators such as challenging work, recognition, and personal growth opportunities.

Victor Vroom's Expectancy Theory, which posits that employee performance is influenced by their expectations of achieving desired rewards, underscores the importance of clear communication about performance goals and outcomes. It highlights the necessity of aligning rewards with these goals to effectively motivate employees.

B.F. Skinner's Reinforcement Theory, focusing on the role of reinforcement in shaping behavior, finds practical application in performance appraisals and feedback systems. Positive reinforcement can encourage desirable behaviors in employees, thereby improving performance and job satisfaction.

Kurt Lewin's Change Model, describing the process of organizational change in three stages—unfreezing, changing, and refreezing—provides a psychological framework for managing change. This model emphasizes the need to prepare the organization for change, implement the change, and then stabilize the new practices to ensure sustainable impact.

By examining these aspects of human resources through the lens of psychology, leaders can better understand and implement strategies that enhance employee engagement, satisfaction, and productivity, ultimately leading to a more effective and successful organization.

1. The Importance of Employee Motivation and Maslow's Hierarchy of Needs

Unlocking Potential: Maximizing Employee Motivation Through Maslow's Hierarchy of Needs

Employee motivation transcends mere task completion; it is a critical component linked directly to the success of an organization. When employees engage passionately and actively with their work, the resulting productivity and creativity positively impact the entire organization. The key is to go beyond simple pay raises or temporary rewards, and deeply understand and satisfy the fundamental needs and expectations of employees.

In this context, Abraham Maslow's Hierarchy of Needs offers invaluable insights to organizational managers and HR professionals. This theory lays out a variety of stages, from basic human needs to self-actualization, helping organizations tailor motivation strategies to meet the specific needs of each employee. By applying Maslow's theory, you can understand the unique motivational drivers of each employee and develop strategies that enhance overall satisfaction and performance in the organization.

This approach not only helps organizations more clearly understand the challenges and opportunities they face but also aids in developing effective strategies to respond to them. Capturing the hearts of employees is akin to an art form, where the alignment of individual expectations with organizational promises must be harmoniously blended to achieve true motivation. In this process, Maslow's Hierarchy of Needs provides direction on how organizations can satisfy the individual needs and expectations of their employees.

For example, ZYX Technology, a company known for its rapid growth and innovation, faced unforeseen internal challenges that led to serious difficulties. Continuous delays in major projects diminished client trust, and notably, the increasing turnover rate among high-performing employees significantly derailed the company's growth strategies.

The CEO, deeply concerned about the situation, focused on addressing these issues. Delays in projects affected not just schedules but the company's reputation and brand value, leading to potential losses in new client contracts. Additionally, the departure of talented employees caused a drain of knowledge and experience, increasing the burden and stress on remaining team members.

This situation also had a negative impact on the internal work environment and culture. Increasing anxiety and dissatisfaction among employees led to a general decline in employee satisfaction. The pressure and uncertainty felt by employees stifled creative thinking and teamwork, adversely affecting the company's capacity for innovation. Recognizing that these internal issues posed a significant risk to long-term growth, the leadership decided to undertake fundamental changes to enhance employee motivation and satisfaction. These efforts were crucial as the first steps towards systematically resolving internal issues, restoring trust with employees, and enhancing the organization's stability and productivity.

An internal investigation at ZYX Technology identified unclear job objectives and a lack of a rewarding system as major issues. Employees felt that their work was disconnected from the overall goals of the organization and that their contributions were not adequately recognized. This lack of clarity and recognition demotivated employees and diminished their passion, directly affecting their daily performance and leading to issues like project delays.

Furthermore, employees felt limited opportunities for career advancement, particularly younger staff members, which they perceived as restricting their potential for growth. This perception fueled widespread dissatisfaction and distrust within the organization, ultimately leading to high turnover rates. The reasons employees left were not merely due to salary or working conditions but stemmed from a lack of identity within the organization and insufficient opportunities for career advancement.

Additionally, the company's communication system was revealed to be flawed. Poor communication between employees and management led to feelings of exclusion from changes and decision-making processes within the company. This lack of communication prevented employees from fully understanding and empathizing with the company's vision and strategies, negatively impacting their engagement and motivation.

In summary, ZYX Technology's issues were rooted in employees' unclear role perception, limited opportunities for career advancement, and an inefficient communication structure. These issues demotivated employees and adversely affected overall organizational performance. Now, let's explore how these issues were addressed and what strategies were developed using psychological theories.

Abraham Maslow's Hierarchy of Needs, introduced in 1943, has been widely applied in the fields of psychology and organizational management. Maslow proposed that human needs form a hierarchical structure, and lower-level needs must be satisfied before moving on to higher-level needs. The most basic level of needs according to Maslow is physiological needs, which include essentials for human survival such as breathing, food, water, sex, and sleep. Once these needs are met, people seek to fulfill their needs for safety and security, which include physical and employment security as well as a stable environment that covers resources, health, and property.

Maslow also emphasized the needs for belongingness and love. People desire to feel a sense of belonging and to be loved within their social relationships, which include family, friends, and colleagues. Only after these needs are met can people pursue needs for esteem, where they wish to be recognized and respected by others. The final stage, self-actualization needs, involves the desire to achieve one's full potential, often through creative activities or personal growth.

Maslow's theory is particularly significant in the workplace. When employees feel stable and valued in their jobs, recognize their contributions, and have opportunities for self-realization, they exhibit higher job satisfaction and loyalty to the organization. In the case of ZYX Technology, the failure to meet these needs led to reduced motivation among employees, which in turn caused issues like project delays and high turnover rates. Now, let's take a closer look at how this theory was applied to resolve the company's issues.

To address the decline in employee motivation at ZYX Technology, the management decided to implement a strategy based on Maslow's Hierarchy of Needs. The core of this strategy was to accurately understand and address the needs of each employee.

Firstly, the company confirmed that employees' basic physiological and safety needs were already being met. However, the needs for belongingness, esteem, and self-realization were not adequately satisfied. Based on this, the company explored ways to improve job design so that employees could feel their roles were significant within the organization.

The company redefined the roles and responsibilities of teams and individuals, setting clear objectives and expectations to help employees better understand how their contributions were linked to the success of the company. During this process, a system was established to regularly provide feedback to each employee about how their work contributes to the overall objectives of the organization and how their efforts are recognized.

Additionally, to strengthen employees' sense of belonging, the company increased team-building activities and internal events. These efforts helped enhance camaraderie among team members and fostered a culture of mutual understanding and respect. The company also expanded training programs and promotion opportunities to support personal growth and self-realization for each employee. These opportunities provided a platform for employees to discover their potential and experience personal growth.

Furthermore, the company developed motivational strategies that allowed employees to feel a greater sense of responsibility for their work and to recognize the value and impact of their efforts on the organization. This approach encouraged employees to place more value on their work, enhancing job satisfaction and commitment.

This comprehensive approach effectively applied Maslow's Hierarchy of Needs, focusing on satisfying employees' needs at various stages while motivating them. As a result, this strategy significantly improved employee satisfaction and productivity, bringing about positive changes in the overall performance of the company. These changes enhanced employee loyalty and became a crucial element in strengthening the company's competitiveness over the long term.

In addition to strategies related to employee motivation, there are other psychological theories that can be applied, such as Deci and Ryan's Self-Determination Theory (SDT). This theory posits that people experience greater motivation when they act voluntarily and autonomously. Self-Determination Theory focuses on three basic psychological needs—autonomy (the feeling of controlling one's own behavior), competence (the ability to act effectively and achieve), and relatedness (the feeling of being connected to others). The theory explains that employees experience higher motivation and satisfaction when these three needs are met in their jobs, which can enhance personal growth, well-being, and contributions to the organization.

Furthermore, Skinner's Behaviorism can also be effectively used in workplace motivation. B.F. Skinner believed that rewards and punishments shape behavior, and applying this principle in the workplace can enhance employee productivity and commitment through a proper reward system. For example, by encouraging desirable behaviors through positive behavior reinforcement, an organization can foster a positive behavioral culture.

These theories offer different approaches and can be selectively applied and combined according to specific situations and needs within an organization. Understanding the diverse psychological needs and motivational factors of employees and integrating these into the organization's strategies is crucial for successful operations and sustainable growth.

2. Herzberg's Motivation-Hygiene Theory and Employee Satisfaction

Beyond Satisfaction: Innovating Employee Satisfaction with Herzberg's Motivation-Hygiene Theory

Employee satisfaction is not just a part of the job; it is a core driver within an organization. When employees are satisfied with their work, they go beyond merely completing assigned tasks, exhibiting dedication to the organization and creative energy. This boosts overall productivity and innovation, ultimately strengthening the company's competitiveness. Satisfied employees feel deeply connected to their organization, playing a crucial role in reducing turnover and retaining talent over the long term. Conversely, low employee satisfaction can negatively impact not just individual issues but the entire organizational culture and performance. Dissatisfied employees often lose passion for their work, see a decline in creativity and productivity, and may ultimately leave the organization.

For this reason, it is vital for organizations to effectively develop and implement strategies to enhance employee satisfaction. This process involves deeply understanding the issues employees face and finding ways to meet their needs, going beyond mere monetary rewards to help employees recognize the value and meaning of their roles. When organizations meet employee expectations, employees experience greater satisfaction, increasing their attachment and commitment to their work.

Strategic management of employee satisfaction is essential for the successful operation of an organization. Organizations must continually survey employee expectations and needs, introducing appropriate changes and improvements. This process strengthens organizational culture, enhances employee engagement, and boosts overall performance. Organizations that take employee satisfaction seriously and actively take steps to improve it can become more competitive in the market and achieve sustainable growth through positive relationships with their employees.

XYZ Retail Company, a large retail chain with employees from diverse cultural backgrounds, recently faced significant challenges with increasing turnover rates and decreasing satisfaction. Despite its efforts to maintain competitiveness in the rapidly changing retail market, internal dissatisfaction was building among the staff. Particularly, there was a noticeable decline in job satisfaction among employees, leading to decreased performance across the organization.

To address this issue, the management decided to conduct a comprehensive internal survey focused on diagnosing employee satisfaction and identifying specific problems. Feedback collected from various departments revealed key issues such as inadequate work environments, opaque compensation systems, and limited career advancement opportunities. Many employees expressed a lack of clear direction in their roles, which significantly dampened their passion and commitment to their work.

This situation was particularly pronounced in the sales department, where high-performing employees felt their efforts were not adequately recognized, leading to high turnover rates. As turnover increased, the company lost experienced talent, which negatively affected customer service quality and sales, impacting the company's reputation and market position, and ultimately leading to a decline in overall organizational performance.

This problem extended beyond internal operations. Employee grievances and dissatisfaction were undermining the organizational foundation, directly affecting customer experiences and the company's financial health. Therefore, improving employee satisfaction was not just a concern for the HR department but a critical issue for the company's management. Understanding the problems and their causes faced by employees and finding appropriate solutions became a priority for the organization, essential for its survival and sustainable growth. To overcome these challenges, XYZ Retail Company introduced Herzberg's Motivation-Hygiene Theory to explore solutions for enhancing employee satisfaction.

In-depth understanding of employee motivation and satisfaction is critical, and Frederick Herzberg's Motivation-Hygiene Theory plays a vital role. Developed based on research conducted by Herzberg in the late 1950s, the theory identifies and analyzes factors that lead to satisfaction and dissatisfaction in the workplace. Herzberg's research differentiated between factors that motivate employees and those that lead to job dissatisfaction.

Herzberg's theory is divided into two key elements: motivators and hygiene factors. Motivators directly enhance job performance and satisfaction, including achievement, recognition, the intrinsic interest of the work, responsibility, and opportunities for growth and advancement. These factors encourage employees to engage more deeply with their work, positively affecting performance.

In contrast, hygiene factors contribute to reducing job dissatisfaction but do not necessarily increase job satisfaction when improved. These include salary, company policies and administrative practices, working conditions, supervision style, and relationships with colleagues. These factors meet the basic needs of employees, and their absence can cause dissatisfaction.

Herzberg argued that these two elements act independently; even if one is well-managed, deficiencies in the other can still negatively affect employee satisfaction. His theory provides clear direction for managers and organizational developers on which areas to focus on to enhance employee satisfaction.

By applying Herzberg's theory, XYZ Retail Company was able to understand the root causes of declining employee satisfaction and introduce appropriate improvement measures. The application of the theory enabled the company to strengthen both motivators and hygiene factors, enhancing employee satisfaction and, through this, improving overall organizational performance.

XYZ Retail Company developed a comprehensive strategy to improve employee satisfaction and work environments based on Frederick Herzberg's Motivation-Hygiene Theory. The company initially focused on enhancing employees' sense of accomplishment and autonomy in their roles, educating each employee on how their role is crucial to the organization's bigger picture. These efforts encouraged employees to feel greater responsibility and satisfaction with their work, creating a motivating environment.

Furthermore, the company approached fulfilling employees'

need for self-actualization by supporting career development. It activated mentoring programs and provided suitable training opportunities, helping employees develop professional skills and achieve their career goals. This strategy made employees feel that there were ample opportunities for growth within the organization, inducing long-term commitment.

Improvements in the physical work environment were also a key focus. The company restructured the workspace to create a more open and collaborative environment, facilitating easier communication and cooperation among employees, which enhanced work efficiency and teamwork. Additionally, introducing flexibility in working hours allowed employees to more effectively balance their personal lives and work.

A comprehensive review of the salary structure and compensation system was also conducted. The company strengthened performance-based incentive schemes and established a fair and transparent evaluation system, ensuring that employees felt their efforts were adequately recognized and rewarded. These changes positively impacted employees, contributing to increased loyalty and satisfaction with the company.

Lastly, through regular feedback sessions and employee engagement programs, the company ensured that employees' opinions and ideas were reflected in the decision-making process. This interaction reinforced employees' sense of playing a significant role within the organization, which was a crucial factor in increasing overall satisfaction and commitment. Through this comprehensive approach, XYZ Retail Company was able to improve employee satisfaction and enhance overall organizational performance.

This review of XYZ Retail Company's case through the application of Herzberg's Motivation-Hygiene Theory also allows for additional insights through other psychological theories on employee motivation and satisfaction.

For example, the Self-Determination Theory (SDT) by Deci and Ryan explains that individuals reach the highest state of motivation when three basic psychological needs are met: autonomy, competence, and relatedness. Autonomy gives individuals the feeling of controlling and choosing their actions, competence provides a sense of being able to successfully accomplish tasks, and relatedness means feeling connected to others. By strengthening these elements in an organization, employees' intrinsic motivation can be boosted, leading to more sustained and positive work attitudes.

Another significant theory is Adam's Equity Theory, which describes how job satisfaction and motivation levels are influenced by individuals feeling that their work contributions and corresponding rewards are fair compared to those of their peers. When employees perceive their contributions and rewards as equitable compared to their colleagues, they experience higher satisfaction and motivation. This emphasizes the need for managers to ensure the transparency of the compensation system and apply it fairly across all employees.

Further exploring and understanding these theories can aid organizations in designing and implementing more effective employee satisfaction and motivation strategies. Each theory addresses different motivational factors within an organization, providing ways to optimize productivity and minimize employee turnover.

3. Vroom's Expectancy Theory and Performance Management

Redefining Performance: Innovating Performance Management Strategies with Vroom's Expectancy Theory

Performance management is a strategic tool crucial to organizational success, transcending mere goal setting and evaluations to align individual goals with organizational objectives, thereby optimizing resources, maximizing efficiency, and securing a competitive edge. Effective performance management is essential for assessing how well employees are performing across various levels within the organization and identifying areas for improvement.

An effective performance management system plays a pivotal role in setting clear goals and developing specific strategies to achieve these goals. It provides clear guidelines to employees, helping them understand how they can contribute to achieving organizational objectives. Regular performance evaluations also clarify how their efforts contribute to the overall success of the organization.

The impact of performance management extends beyond improving job performance; it also plays a crucial role in enhancing employee motivation and job satisfaction. When employees feel their work significantly contributes to the organization, their job satisfaction naturally increases, boosting overall organizational productivity. Additionally, continuous communication about issues and improvements identified during the performance management process allows organizations to respond more flexibly to changes and continually make enhancements.

This process benefits both the organization and its employees, elevating performance management from a mere tool of assessment and reward to a core element of strategic organizational development. To this end, organizations must continuously update their performance management systems, adapting them to market changes and internal conditions, and actively encourage employee feedback and participation. This comprehensive approach will enable organizations to effectively meet challenges and changes, ensure stable growth, and support employees in adapting proactively to changing market conditions.

DEF Software Development Company, a rapidly growing firm in the technology sector with strengths in cloud-based solutions and mobile application development, has experienced impressive growth thanks to its creative and dedicated staff. However, as the projects increased in complexity and scope, the pressure on employees intensified.

In recent years, as the company expanded into various international markets and began handling global projects, this expansion brought new opportunities but also significant challenges in team collaboration and communication. Working across different time zones, employees sometimes faced inefficient communication and project management issues, leading to missed crucial deadlines.

The lack of consistency in project management emerged as a significant internal problem. With multiple teams managing multiple projects simultaneously, each adopted its own project management approach, leading to a lack of a unified performance management strategy across the company. This caused confusion in resource allocation and priority setting.

This situation particularly burdened new employees and middle managers, who faced conflicting guidelines and expectations, sometimes resulting in unstable project outcomes. High stress and job dissatisfaction among employees increased, ultimately leading to a decrease in productivity. As this started to directly impact the company's performance, management recognized the urgent need to reevaluate and improve the performance management system.

Against this backdrop, DEF Company's management acknowledged the critical need to systematize and standardize performance management across the organization. To provide clearer guidelines and support for employees, the company decided to establish and implement an effective performance management strategy. This aimed to restore employee motivation, enhance work efficiency, and strengthen the overall organizational culture.

DEF Software Development Company's management undertook a deep dive into the issues affecting organization-wide performance management. This process revealed several critical issues.

First, management recognized the lack of consistency in project management as the major problem. Each team managing its projects independently resulted in the absence of a unified performance management strategy across the company. This led to confusion in resource allocation and priority setting, with redundant efforts or excessive resources being allocated to certain projects, ultimately decreasing overall organizational efficiency.

Second, poor communication and collaboration between teams, particularly those working in different time zones on global projects, were identified as major issues. Inefficient information exchange affected project schedules and quality, creating distrust among team members and worsening the work atmosphere, ultimately reducing overall job satisfaction.

Third, a significant drop in employee motivation and job satisfaction was recognized. Employees felt their efforts were not adequately recognized, and their performance was not fairly evaluated. This reduced personal investment in work, even among high-performing employees, who began to lose loyalty to the company.

Finally, management recognized concerns about the lack of career advancement opportunities among employees. Many employees felt their career paths were unclear, which acted as a long-term detriment to their commitment to the company.

Having identified these issues, management felt a pressing need to overhaul the organization's performance management system and establish specific strategies to enhance employee motivation. This plan aimed to secure organizational stability and promote sustainable growth.

Victor Vroom's Expectancy Theory, developed in the 1960s, is a motivation theory that explains the process of individuals choosing specific behaviors based on three key elements: expectancy, instrumentality, and valence. This theory provides an effective framework especially for designing organizational performance management and motivation strategies.

Expectancy is the extent to which an individual believes that their effort will lead to successful outcomes. It emphasizes the importance of the employee's confidence that their efforts will directly lead to performance outcomes.

Instrumentality is the perception that successful performance will lead to desired outcomes or rewards. It stresses that the rewards or recognition received for good performance should be predictable and consistent.

Valence refers to how attractive the rewards are to the individual. This includes not only the value of the reward itself but also how well it aligns with the individual's goals and desires. It is crucial that the rewards received by employees are genuinely meaningful and valuable to them.

Victor Vroom argued that motivation is maximized when all three elements are positively aligned. This theory emphasizes that motivation is not solely driven by external rewards but is deeply influenced by an individual's internal expectations and values. When designing performance management, it is important to consider these psychological factors.

Based on this theoretical framework, organizations should clearly define the expectations for each employee's role and performance and ensure that the rewards for expected performances are transparent and consistent. Additionally, designing rewards that truly align with individual needs and goals is necessary to ensure employees value them genuinely. By doing so, organizations can enhance employee satisfaction and motivation, ultimately improving overall organizational performance.

DEF Software Development Company actively applied Victor Vroom's Expectancy Theory to address its performance management issues. The goal was to build expectations that each employee's efforts would lead to successful outcomes and that these outcomes would, in turn, be linked to meaningful rewards.

The company first conducted training programs for all employees to clearly understand their roles and how their performance contributes to the organization. The training detailed how their efforts contribute to achieving company goals and how their performance links to personal rewards. This process was a crucial first step in building expectancy.

To strengthen instrumentality, the company reformed its reward system to ensure a direct link between performance and rewards. It revamped the reward system for high-performing employees to ensure that all performances are fairly and transparently evaluated and lead to appropriate rewards. Rewards were diversified to include not only financial incentives but also opportunities for promotion, additional training for personal skill development, and recognition within the company.

Regarding valence, the company conducted employee surveys to understand what rewards were genuinely valued by employees. This allowed for the establishment of customized reward plans that reflected individual preferences and needs. For example, some employees valued flexible working hours or remote work options more than monetary rewards, and the company reflected these preferences by introducing more flexible work policies.

Lastly, the company regularly conducted performance reviews to evaluate employee performance and actively gathered feedback during these processes. This provided opportunities for employees to self-assess their performance and request necessary support, helping to build trust between the employees and the organization and continuously improve the effectiveness of the performance management system.

This approach enhanced employee motivation and efficiently improved the organization's performance management processes, contributing to increased overall productivity and satisfaction. This was a significant change for DEF Software Development Company and greatly aided in achieving its strategic objectives.

In addition to applying Victor Vroom's Expectancy Theory for performance management and employee motivation at DEF Software Development Company, the organization can explore other psychological theories to enrich its employee management and motivation strategies. Here, we introduce a few psychological theories that differ from traditional approaches.

First, Self-Determination Theory (SDT) provides deep insights into employee motivation. This theory distinguishes between intrinsic and extrinsic motivations, explaining that people experience higher motivation and satisfaction when they choose and control their actions independently. Applying this theory in an organization can help employees understand the significance and importance of their work and create an environment where they can exercise greater autonomy over their choices and actions, thereby enhancing their intrinsic motivation.

Second, Goal Setting Theory focuses on the impact of clear and specific goals on performance. Developed by Edwin Locke, this theory argues that people perform better when they set specific and challenging goals. By utilizing this theory, organizations can set clear and challenging goals for employees, increasing their engagement and sense of accomplishment in their work.

Lastly, Cognitive Evaluation Theory explores how external rewards affect intrinsic motivation. This theory explains that excessive rewards can diminish an individual's intrinsic motivation. By adjusting the way rewards are provided, organizations can find a balance that maintains employees' voluntary participation and passion for their work.

By exploring and applying these diverse psychological theories, organizations can diversify their approaches to employee motivation and performance management, facilitating employee and overall organizational growth. This is crucial for maintaining competitiveness and achieving sustainable development in a changing market environment.

4. Performance Appraisal and Feedback: B.F. Skinner's Reinforcement Theory

The Power of Feedback: Revolutionizing Performance Appraisal with B.F. Skinner's Reinforcement Theory

Performance appraisal and feedback are fundamentally crucial processes within organizations, aimed at accurately assessing employee performance and providing the necessary support and improvements to achieve strategic organizational goals. This process goes beyond merely recording numbers and results; it plays a crucial role in fostering long-term growth and development of employees and enhancing overall productivity and efficiency of the organization. Effective feedback not only shows employees how their performance contributes to the bigger picture of the organization but also motivates and instills confidence by offering concrete ways to improve.

This process must be closely linked with the organization's performance management system and should consider not just individual performance but also personal growth and development. B.F. Skinner's reinforcement theory can be incredibly useful in this context. Based on the principle that human behavior is regulated by its consequences, this theory provides reinforcement techniques to increase desirable behaviors through positive outcomes. For example, positive feedback and recognition can reinforce beneficial behaviors, establishing desirable behavioral models within the organization.

When designing performance appraisal and feedback systems, organizations need to understand and enhance each employee's motivational factors. Feedback should transcend its function of merely communicating performance; it should enable employees to recognize the value and significance of their work, feel personal achievement, and appreciate their contribution to the organization. Therefore, performance appraisal and feedback processes must be managed delicately, providing a customized approach to meet the characteristics and needs of each employee.

The aim of these systems is not just to evaluate performance and identify issues, but to help employees gain a deeper understanding of their work, thereby fostering opportunities for them to voluntarily grow and develop. This process not only influences employee performance but also induces positive changes in their behaviors and attitudes, leading to a constructive development in organizational culture and supporting the long-term success of the organization.

GHI Healthcare Company faced a decline in customer satisfaction and inconsistent performance among employees. Despite rapid growth in the complex healthcare service industry, internally, there was an increase in employee dissatisfaction and performance decline. Particularly, the absence of a feedback system increased uncertainty and anxiety among employees, negatively impacting their daily work.

The issue began with employees not receiving clear guidance and recognition for their roles. Many employees experienced irregular feedback, often irrelevant and focused only on negatives. This type of feedback undermined the foundation for employees to proceed confidently with their tasks, leading to increasing doubts about their roles and positions within the company.

This situation led to greater problems of poor communication and information asymmetry among employees. There was a lack of understanding about how their job performance was connected to organizational goals and how their contributions were being evaluated and recognized. This made it difficult for employees to feel responsible for their work, adversely affecting team motivation and productivity.

As a result, teamwork weakened, and individuals became increasingly isolated, escalating tensions among team members and further degrading work efficiency. With performance declining, the quality of customer service also dropped, directly affecting customer satisfaction and significantly harming the company's reputation and growth. This chain of issues emerged as a critical challenge that GHI Healthcare urgently needed to address.

The core issues GHI Healthcare faced stemmed from several factors, but centrally from the flawed feedback and performance appraisal system. Inconsistent feedback, sometimes indifferent or overly negative, amplified confusion and dissatisfaction among employees. This situation prevented employees from understanding their roles and contributions clearly, leading to decreased confidence and negatively impacting their daily performance.

The irregularity and irrelevance of feedback denied employees the opportunity to adequately reflect and improve on their job performance. Employees felt that consistent standards were not applied in evaluating and recognizing their work, which demotivated them, leading to decreased performance both individually and at the team level. Additionally, the tendency to focus on negative feedback prompted employees to concentrate on failures rather than potential improvements, increasing stress and anxiety within the work environment.

These issues also manifested as weakened communication within the organization and a lack of trust between employees and management. Employees felt their opinions were not sufficiently considered, and they began to doubt the direction and support provided by management. This exposed a lack of clear direction within the organization, resulting in weakened motivation to achieve strategic goals.

The dissatisfaction and performance issues among employees also impacted customer satisfaction, delivering a severe blow to the company's overall growth and competitiveness. When employees were not satisfied with their roles and did not recognize their value, this directly reflected on the quality of service and customer experience, creating a vicious cycle that negatively impacted the company's profitability and market position. Recognizing the severity of these issues, the management at GHI Healthcare sought fundamental changes to boost employee motivation and performance.

To address the problems faced by GHI Healthcare, B.F. Skinner's reinforcement theory was chosen. Burrhus Frederic Skinner, one of the most influential psychologists of the 20th century, made significant contributions to the development of behaviorist psychology. His theory focuses on the concept that behavior is regulated by its consequences, developing techniques to increase desired behaviors or decrease unwanted ones.

Skinner's reinforcement theory operates through two main elements: reinforcement and punishment. Reinforcement occurs when a consequence

following a behavior makes that behavior occur more frequently or more strongly, and it can be positive or negative. Positive reinforcement involves providing a pleasant outcome after a desired behavior to strengthen it, while negative reinforcement involves removing an unwanted situation to reinforce the desired behavior. On the other hand, punishment is used to decrease unwanted behaviors and can also be positive or negative.

Skinner particularly emphasized the effectiveness of positive reinforcement, exploring ways to induce behavioral changes in individuals or groups through this method. His research has been applied in various fields, including education, mental health, and organizational management, significantly influencing performance management systems within organizations.

With this background, GHI Healthcare applied Skinner's reinforcement theory in their feedback and performance appraisal processes to promote positive behaviors among employees and reduce undesirable ones. This approach focused on motivating employees to act more actively and productively through the anticipation of positive outcomes, allowing the organization to expect effective performance management and enhanced employee satisfaction.

GHI Healthcare decided to actively apply B.F. Skinner's reinforcement theory in their performance appraisal and feedback processes to improve employee motivation and performance. In this process, the company initially adopted methods to actively reinforce employees' positive behaviors, following the basic principles of reinforcement theory. Particularly, they provided immediate and specific positive feedback when employees performed their tasks successfully to reinforce their behaviors.

To facilitate this, GHI established standard procedures for managers to provide feedback and trained them accordingly. Managers praised employees for successful work performance with specific examples and publicly recognized these achievements through team meetings or internal newsletters, further reinforcing positive behaviors. This positive reinforcement significantly boosted motivation by signaling to employees that their success was positively recognized and valued throughout the organization.

Additionally, when providing negative feedback, GHI applied Skinner's theory by offering specific and constructive feedback on areas needing improvement, instead of merely critiquing. For example, instead of just pointing out the lack of performance, they provided specific action plans for improvement and resources to support employees in achieving success. This approach helped employees internalize the need for improvement by providing clear directions and motivation to enhance their behaviors.

Furthermore, GHI introduced regular feedback sessions to ensure that employees experienced consistent positive reinforcement. These sessions reviewed not only individual performance but also team performance, discussing ways to enhance collaboration and mutual support among team members. This approach enhanced positive reinforcement for both individuals and teams, contributing to improved organizational performance and increased employee satisfaction.

This reinforcement-based approach to feedback and performance appraisal played a crucial role in improving employee performance and satisfaction at GHI Healthcare. Employees felt that their performance was evaluated fairly and transparently, and they recognized that they were supported in their growth and development. This increased employee motivation and led to enhanced productivity and efficiency throughout the organization.

If you are interested in employee motivation and performance management, various psychological theories can be applied in addition to reinforcement theory. These include approaches related to motivation, decision-making, and organizational behavior. Below are some additional theories and concepts that can help in managing and enhancing employee performance:

1. Goal Setting Theory: Developed by Edwin Locke, the Goal Setting Theory emphasizes the importance of specific and challenging goals in enhancing performance. This theory explains the impact of the clarity and difficulty of goals on

employee performance and provides strategies for setting goals and achieving them within an organization.

2. Self-Determination Theory: Developed by Edward Deci and Richard Ryan, the Self-Determination Theory argues that motivation is influenced by three basic needs: autonomy, competence, and relatedness. This theory explains that employees experience higher motivation and satisfaction when they feel greater control over their work, are able to demonstrate their capabilities, and maintain positive relationships with their colleagues.

3. Equity Theory: Developed by John Stacey Adams, the Equity Theory explains that employees are motivated by fairness when they compare their contributions and rewards to those of others. This theory emphasizes the importance of a fair compensation system and explores how employees respond and adjust to perceived injustices.

4. Emotional Labor Theory: Developed by Arlie Hochschild, the Emotional Labor Theory deals with the management of emotions that employees are expected to display during interactions with customers, particularly in the service industry. This theory analyzes how the expression and experience of emotions affect employee well-being and performance, providing strategies for supporting employees in roles where emotional management is crucial.

By understanding and appropriately applying these theories, managers and HR professionals can develop more effective personnel management strategies and maximize employee satisfaction and performance.

5. Organizational Change and Lewin's Change Model

Leading Change: Mastering Organizational Transformation with Kurt Lewin's Change Model

Organizational change is inevitable and essential in today's dynamic business environment. To respond to rapid technological advancements, shifting market demands, and competitive pressures, it is crucial for organizations to embrace and adapt to change flexibly. However, managing change successfully is a challenging task that directly impacts the organization's efficiency and long-term success. Employee resistance, instability, and uncertainty about change can complicate the change process, potentially hindering organizational growth and development.

In this context, the necessity for an effective change management model becomes evident. A change management model helps organizations overcome challenges they face and facilitates smooth transitions, supporting employees in adapting to new environments and conditions. Particularly during the change process, garnering employee participation and support is crucial as it allows employees to take ownership of the change, thus minimizing resistance.

To manage change effectively, it is essential for organizations to set a clear vision and purpose for the change and communicate this effectively to all employees. Simultaneously, organizations need to listen to employee feedback and incorporate it into the planning process, providing opportunities for employees to actively participate in the change process. It is also important to demonstrate how the process and outcomes of change are directly connected to employees' daily tasks and to clarify how the change can positively impact each individual.

This strategic approach enables organizations to manage change successfully, helping achieve organizational goals through transformation. This goes beyond mere implementation of change to improving organizational culture, enhancing employee satisfaction, and ultimately strengthening the organization's competitive edge, laying the foundation for effectively addressing future challenges.

The digital transformation journey at JKL Financial Institution has been dramatic, moving from traditional paper-based operations to digital platforms, anticipated to offer substantial benefits. However, this shift required more than just technological upgrades; it deeply affected organizational culture and the day-to-day operational methods of employees.

In the initial months, employee reactions were mixed. Younger, tech-savvy employees showed excitement and anticipation for the new system, while many veteran employees, accustomed to traditional methods, found it difficult to accept the change. Particularly as new software and digital tools were introduced, some employees feared exposing their lack of tech skills and resisted the change.

This wave of change posed significant challenges for front-line managers and team leaders as well. They had to enhance their team members' technical skills and provide training on the new systems while maintaining continuity in daily operations. Additionally, technical issues in the early stages of digital tool implementation slowed project progress, impacting overall work efficiency.

Anxiety and stress among employees increased, leading to reduced productivity. As dissatisfaction with the new system and processes grew, communication within the company broke down, and conflicts between teams began to emerge. Uncertainty about the change and concerns about job security made the situation even more difficult for employees.

In this challenging context, the leadership team at JKL Financial Institution needed to intensify efforts to alleviate employee anxiety and effectively communicate the benefits of digital transformation. Recognizing the turbulent nature of the change process, it became more important than ever to enhance communication with employees, clarifying the necessity of change and its long-term benefits.

The problems encountered during the digital transformation process at JKL were varied. One of the major issues was employee resistance. Many employees felt inadequately trained and prepared for the new technologies and processes, experiencing anxiety and stress. Concerns about job security due to the changes led to resistance.

Another issue was the technical problems encountered during the initial implementation of the new systems and tools. These issues delayed project progress and ultimately affected overall work efficiency. Initial technical glitches and instability in the systems caused confusion in daily operations, making some employees skeptical about using the new tools.

Communication breakdown within the organization was also a serious problem. Due to insufficient information and support during the change process, many employees did not fully understand why the change was necessary and how it was being implemented. This increased mistrust among employees and led to conflicts between teams.

The anxiety and stress among employees led to decreased productivity, negatively impacting the organization's overall performance. The spread of negative attitudes towards the change caused employees to cling to old ways rather than embracing the new systems and processes.

Addressing these issues required a deep understanding of employee concerns and providing appropriate support and training to help them accept the change. Developing effective communication strategies to clearly articulate the benefits of the change was also crucial. In this process, JKL Financial Institution applied Kurt Lewin's change model to manage change incrementally and systematically within the organization.

Kurt Lewin, a psychologist who began his work in Germany, laid significant foundations for modern organizational and behavioral psychology through his research into social and psychological processes. Often hailed as the "father of modern social psychology," his theory explores how individual and group behaviors are influenced by their environments.

Lewin's change model describes organizational change in three basic stages: unfreezing, changing, and refreezing. This model provides a systematic guide for organizations and individuals to embrace and adapt to change.

In the unfreezing stage, the goal is to dismantle existing practices or mindsets and recognize the need for change. This stage involves enhancing communication with employees to clarify why change is necessary and its benefits, refreshing their perception of change, and challenging the status quo.

During the changing stage, new skills and processes are introduced, and support is provided to help employees learn and apply them. This involves training sessions and mentoring programs that allow employees to experiment with and experience the new systems, gaining confidence and the necessary skills to embrace the change.

In the refreezing stage, the new methods are solidified as standard procedures within the organization, applying them to everyday tasks to stabilize them. This stage focuses on ensuring that the new changes remain sustainable and stable within the organization. JKL made the new processes and technologies a part of the organizational culture, facilitating natural acceptance by employees.

Lewin's change model provides a crucial framework for change management, offering a systematic approach for successfully managing change within organizations. By applying this model, JKL Financial Institution was able to overcome initial challenges and resistance, engaging employees at each stage of the process and integrating change naturally within the organizational culture. This ultimately enhanced organizational efficiency and strengthened competitive positioning in the market.

For further exploration in change management, John Kotter's 8-step change model is a significant psychological theory. This model outlines specific steps for effectively leading organizational change, detailing necessary actions and strategies at each stage. Kotter's model provides more detailed solutions to various issues that may arise during actual change implementation, compared to the three-step model previously discussed.

Another important theory is the ADKAR model, which centers on managing individual change. It constructs change based on five elements: Awareness, Desire, Knowledge, Ability, and Reinforcement. The ADKAR model is designed to systematically understand and support individual change processes, facilitating successful organizational change by focusing on these key elements.

Additionally, the theory of psychological ownership is also critical in organizational change. This theory discusses how individuals' sense of ownership over their work or part of the organization can reduce resistance and enhance active participation in change. By fostering psychological ownership, employees are more likely to engage deeply in the change process and value the outcomes personally, aiding internal acceptance of change.

These models can be applied differently depending on the specific situations and needs of organizations, providing in-depth understanding and effective strategies for planning and executing organizational change. Understanding the characteristics of each model and adapting them to fit the organization is crucial for the success of change management.

6. Conflict Resolution and the Thomas-Kilmann Model

Beyond Conflict: Innovating Conflict Resolution Strategies with the Thomas-Kilmann Model

Conflict is an inherent aspect of any organization, sometimes causing unexpected problems. However, when managed properly, it can transform into a crucial element that promotes innovative growth within an organization. One primary reason conflicts arise is the diversity of backgrounds and expertise among individuals who bring different perspectives and goals to their roles. While this diversity can foster creative ideas and solutions, if not managed properly, it can impede organizational goals and lead to internal divisions.

A classic example of organizational conflict is intense discussions in the boardroom. For instance, when one team insists on adhering to traditional marketing strategies while another advocates for innovative approaches using digital technologies, these conflicting views can escalate into significant disputes. If not effectively managed, simple disagreements can expand into broader organizational divisions. Unresolved conflicts can lead to decreased motivation and efficiency, negatively impacting overall productivity.

Moreover, conflict plays a crucial role in the decision-making processes within organizations. Through conflict, various viewpoints are expressed, leading to more balanced decisions. Solutions derived from effective communication and negotiation during conflicts can often bring about positive changes within an organization. It is important during these conflicts for team members to understand and respect each other's positions while moving towards a common goal.

Managing such conflicts can be systematically approached using the Thomas-Kilmann Conflict Resolution Model. This model offers five primary styles of handling conflicts, enabling organizational leaders to choose the most appropriate strategy for each situation. Each style can be applied differently depending on the effectiveness required by the situation, allowing for a customized approach that considers the complexity and diversity of conflicts.

For example, the competing style may be useful in situations where urgent and important goals need to be achieved, but it can negatively affect long-term teamwork and relationships. On the other hand, the collaborating style is effective in deriving sustainable and stable solutions by attempting to meet the needs of all stakeholders involved. These varied approaches play a crucial role in resolving conflicts while promoting cooperation and mutual understanding within an organization.

Thus, conflict management is an essential process for organizational growth and innovation. Leaders and managers play a significant role in accurately identifying conflicts and presenting appropriate resolutions. By effectively managing conflicts, organizations can harmonize diverse opinions and strategies, achieving their goals more efficiently.

An example of internal conflict can be seen at PQR Consulting Company, where typical clashes occur between the IT and Marketing departments due to fundamentally different objectives. The IT department prioritizes technological stability and security, while the Marketing department focuses on responding swiftly to market trends and driving rapid changes. These conflicting priorities can sometimes lead to tension and conflict.

For instance, when the Marketing department pushes for the quick introduction of new digital tools for a campaign, the IT department may express concerns about the potential security impacts on existing systems. The IT department's insistence on thorough testing and validation can naturally conflict with the Marketing department's goals of quick market entry. Such situations can easily lead to breakdowns in communication, where each team feels its expertise is not adequately recognized.

When conflicts escalate, they can lead to project delays and unnecessary stress among team members. Each team is convinced that its strategy is most beneficial for the company, potentially oversimplifying or misunderstanding the other's approach. This communication failure can decrease project efficiency and negatively impact the company's overall performance.

However, internal conflicts, while often chronic issues within organizations, can also present significant opportunities for innovation and improvement if managed correctly. Balancing the needs and goals of different departments and striving for mutual understanding and respect are essential. In this process, effective conflict resolution strategies play a crucial role.

In the case of PQR Consulting, the conflict between the IT and Marketing departments highlighted several deep-seated issues. The core of the conflict was the difference in objectives and priorities between the departments. While the IT department focused on the technical stability and security of the company's systems, the Marketing department aimed for rapid response to market changes to maintain a competitive edge. This fundamental conflict in goals led to friction and tension in daily operations, affecting both team performance and the overall company outcome.

The IT department advocated for a cautious approach to new technology implementations, requiring extensive testing and validation to ensure seamless integration and secure operation of all new systems and software. This was crucial to prevent technical issues and ensure long-term system stability. Meanwhile, the Marketing department felt pressured to seize and utilize market opportunities quickly, viewing the IT department's cautious approach as a barrier to responding swiftly to market demands. This perception could lead to a weakened cooperative relationship between the departments.

Additionally, the absence of communication is a common source of conflict. When each department emphasizes its perspective and priorities without adequately trying to understand the other's position, communication breaks down, and misunderstandings are amplified. This focus on only addressing immediate issues rather than resolving the underlying causes of conflict can lead to persistent problems.

What is needed in such situations is for each department to recognize the needs and constraints of the other and to find ways to collaborate towards a common goal. This requires a more complex process that goes beyond addressing the superficial symptoms of conflict, involving a reconsideration of the organization's fundamental culture and approaches. Leadership plays a crucial role in this process, requiring a comprehensive improvement in the organization's overall conflict management and communication strategies.

The psychological approach to conflict resolution is particularly highlighted in the Thomas-Kilmann Conflict Resolution Model, developed by Kenneth Thomas and Ralph Kilmann. This model systematically analyzes various behavioral patterns that can appear in conflict situations and suggests the most appropriate solutions for each. This theory is especially useful in organizational settings where conflicts are inevitable, offering ways to constructively manage conflicts and enhance cooperation and efficiency within the organization.

Kenneth Thomas, a renowned psychologist in the field of conflict resolution, provides deep insights into how individuals and organizations perceive and respond to conflict situations. Ralph Kilmann, an expert in organizational change and conflict management, played a significant role in developing conflict resolution strategies with Thomas. Together, they emphasize that conflict should not be viewed merely as a problem to be solved but as an opportunity to foster organizational growth and improvement.

The Thomas-Kilmann model identifies five key styles of conflict resolution: competing, avoiding, compromising, collaborating, and accommodating. Each style is more suitable for certain situations, allowing for selective application based on each team's circumstances and needs.

The leadership at PQR Consulting chose to focus on a collaborative approach to resolve conflicts. This approach sensitively handles conflicts, ensuring that all parties involved can adequately reflect their needs and goals. The company organized workshops and team-building sessions to facilitate understanding and cooperation between departments on a foundation of mutual respect. These activities helped to alleviate tensions and align the goals and concerns of each team through mutual understanding and trust.

Additionally, the management appointed an internal mediator to manage and mediate discussions between teams from a neutral standpoint, offering fair and objective conflict resolution proposals. This process was crucial for allowing each team to effectively communicate their needs and address the root causes of the conflicts.

Through these measures, PQR Consulting successfully managed and resolved inter-departmental conflicts, enhancing the collaborative atmosphere and creative energy within the organization. The company learned from this experience how to transform conflict into a tool for organizational innovation and prepared a robust conflict management and resolution framework for future similar situations.

For a deeper understanding of conflict resolution, several psychological theories and related fields are suggested for further exploration:

1. Emotional Intelligence (EQ): Daniel Goleman's theory of emotional intelligence is highly applicable to conflict resolution. This theory emphasizes an individual's ability to recognize, manage, and respond to their own emotions and those of others. Individuals with high emotional intelligence are better at understanding others' perspectives in conflicts and finding effective ways to mitigate emotional disputes.

2. Negotiation and Mediation Skills: Negotiation and mediation are essential skills for conflict resolution. William Ury and Roger Fisher's book "Getting to Yes" provides negotiation techniques for finding mutually acceptable solutions in conflicting situations. These skills focus on structuring conflicts and conducting fair negotiations to reach agreements.

3. Organizational Behavior: Knowledge of organizational behavior is vital for understanding conflicts within organizations. This field studies the behavior patterns of various members within an organization and how these affect organizational culture, leadership styles, and communication methods, all of which can influence conflicts.

4. Systems Thinking: Introduced in Peter Senge's "The Fifth Discipline," systems thinking offers another approach to handling organizational conflicts. It views organizations as complex systems and focuses on understanding how different elements interact within these systems. This perspective helps identify the root causes of conflicts and find solutions that harmonize with the entire organization.

By understanding and applying these theories and approaches, one can gain a deeper insight into conflicts and manage them effectively. Each theory enables a more careful and effective approach in conflict situations, contributing to the long-term success of organizations.

Chapter 7: Organizational Culture and Edgar Schein's Culture Theory

Decoding the Code of Culture: Innovating Organizational Culture through Edgar Schein's Culture Theory

Organizational culture is akin to the heart of an organization, influencing the behavior and thinking of all members, and directly affecting the overall success of the company. A positive organizational culture motivates employees, strengthens teamwork, and enhances productivity. Conversely, a problematic organizational culture can lead to internal conflicts, increased employee turnover, and reduced performance. Thus, improving and changing organizational culture is a crucial task.

The case of RST Technology Company illustrates the importance and necessity of changing organizational culture. As the company grew from a startup to a mid-sized enterprise, it faced significant cultural challenges due to rapid expansion and the integration of new employees from diverse cultural backgrounds. The performance-oriented management style introduced by the new leadership clashed with the existing friendly and autonomous work environment, leading to serious cultural conflicts within the organization. These conflicts increased tension among employees, led to communication problems, project delays, and a high turnover rate.

To effectively address these issues, RST Technology Company applied Edgar Schein's theory of organizational culture, which describes culture at three levels: artifacts (visible cultural phenomena), shared values (the organization's goals and standards), and basic assumptions (the fundamental beliefs and values of the organization). Through this theory, the organization was able to manage cultural conflicts and resistance, and develop strategies to guide the organizational culture in a more positive and productive direction.

RST engaged the entire organization in regularly scheduled cultural workshops and introduced cultural adaptation programs to help new employees effectively integrate into the existing culture. Additionally, by establishing open communication channels, all employees were able to freely exchange opinions, managing cultural conflicts and enhancing understanding and cooperation within the organization. These measures played a crucial role in reestablishing organizational culture, continuously assessing the effectiveness of changes, and making necessary adjustments.

Through this process, RST Technology Company successfully managed the change in organizational culture, reduced internal conflicts, and significantly improved the overall harmony and efficiency of the organization. The positive change in organizational culture played a decisive role in increasing employee satisfaction and productivity, leading to the long-term success of the organization.

The transformation of RST Technology Company was rapid and inevitable, resembling a swiftly flowing river. The company evolved rapidly from a small, friendly startup to a mid-sized enterprise, experiencing significant internal and external changes. As it expanded into international markets, a large number of new employees from various cultural backgrounds joined, complicating and diversifying the previously established team culture. The new management's preference for a performance-oriented style contrasted with the existing autonomous and collaborative work environment, presenting significant cultural and adaptation challenges for the existing employees.

These changes were particularly pronounced between the technical and marketing departments. While the technical department prioritized stability and security, maintaining existing systems, the marketing department sought to introduce new tools and strategies to respond quickly to market changes. The conflicting goals and priorities between these two departments intensified, with each side strongly advocating their position, leading to increased confrontation, project delays, and communication breakdowns, ultimately heightening tension and anxiety among employees.

These cultural conflicts and the anxiety of the employees led to unnecessary stress and conflicts within the organization, prompting some top talent to leave the company. The increased turnover rate caused more anxiety and dissatisfaction, negatively affecting the company's overall performance. The gap between the new management and the existing employees widened, highlighting the urgent need for significant cultural readjustment.

To address these challenges, RST decided to actively use Edgar Schein's theory of organizational culture. Based on this theory, the company developed strategies to overcome cultural differences and integrate the organization. Regularly scheduled organizational culture workshops encouraged all employees to participate, helping each individual understand and respect their own and others' cultural backgrounds and explore how existing and new cultural elements could be harmoniously integrated.

Furthermore, the company introduced a cultural adaptation program to help new employees quickly adapt to the organization. This program included mentoring, team-building activities, and regular feedback sessions, assisting employees in understanding the organizational culture and contributing as team members. The establishment of open communication channels allowed all employees to freely share their opinions and constructively resolve cultural conflicts.

This multifaceted approach enabled RST Technology Company to successfully manage cultural changes and significantly improve the organization's stability and efficiency. Through this process, employees understood the importance of their roles and contributions within the organization, leading to enhanced overall performance and satisfaction. This experience demonstrates the significant impact organizational culture can have on the success of an organization, providing important lessons for other organizations.

Further exploration of theories and approaches related to organizational culture change can deepen understanding and application in improving and managing organizational change effectively. These theories provide profound insights and practical assistance in efforts to enhance and manage organizational culture change. Each theory offers unique perspectives and tools that can be adjusted and applied according to the specific circumstances and needs of the organization.

1. Geert Hofstede's Cultural Dimensions Theory: Widely used to describe cultural differences between nations, this theory is also useful for understanding diversity and cultural differences within organizations. Hofstede analyzes culture through various dimensions such as power distance, uncertainty avoidance, individualism versus collectivism, masculinity versus femininity, and long-term orientation. This theory is particularly applicable in global companies or multicultural organizations.

2. Cliff Ovio's Organizational Identity Theory: This theory focuses on how members of an organization perceive and define their organization. Organizational identity can help members understand how they are connected to the organization's purpose and values. This theory is effective in strengthening organizational culture and enhancing pride and belonging among members during the process of managing change.

3. Rogers' Diffusion of Innovations Theory: This theory explains how new ideas or technologies spread over time within an organization. The diffusion of innovations curve identifies different groups such as innovators, early adopters, early majority, late majority, and laggards. This theory is useful for predicting the responses of organizational members when implementing innovative changes and developing appropriate strategies.

4. John Kotter's 8-Step Change Model: This model outlines specific steps to successfully manage organizational change, including creating a sense of urgency, building a powerful coalition, and establishing a vision and strategy. Kotter's approach provides a very practical guide for planning and implementing organizational culture change initiatives.

These theories and models offer in-depth insights and practical assistance in efforts to improve and effectively manage organizational culture change. Each theory provides unique perspectives and tools that can be tailored and applied to fit the specific circumstances and needs of the organization.

8. Managing Stress at Work: Lazarus' Stress Theory

Thriving Under Pressure: Mastering Workplace Stress Management with Lazarus' Stress Theory

Workplace stress often exists like a shadow within organizations and is considered one of the greatest challenges modern organizations face. Such stress impacts not only the health of individuals but also deeply affects organizational productivity and employee welfare. If not properly managed, stress can lead to decreased job satisfaction, increased turnover, and a deterioration of organizational culture. Therefore, it is essential for organizations to develop strategies to effectively manage and mitigate the stress experienced by their employees.

Richard Lazarus' stress theory offers valuable insights into addressing these issues. According to his theory, stress varies depending on how an individual perceives and evaluates a situation. The stress response is not simply a result of stimulus-response but is based on how threatening an individual perceives the situation to be and how they assess their own ability to handle it. This perspective suggests that managing stress involves changing individuals' perceptions and evaluations, not just adjusting external conditions.

Organizations can establish various strategies to better understand the situations causing stress and help employees cope with them. For instance, regular stress management training can be provided to help employees identify the sources of their stress and learn positive coping methods. Such training helps employees better understand the situations that cause stress and acquire skills to manage their emotions and responses in those situations.

Additionally, offering flexibility in work can allow employees to better balance work and personal life. Such flexibility contributes significantly to managing stress effectively and enhancing job satisfaction. HR teams can assess the needs and circumstances of individual employees to offer tailored support, including mentoring programs, professional counseling, and health programs, to better manage stress.

These measures play a crucial role in helping organizations manage workplace stress effectively and improve overall employee health and organizational productivity. Through these efforts, organizations can create an environment where employees can collaborate effectively and grow individually and as a team, even in stressful situations.

UVW Communications Company faced sharply rising levels of stress among its employees as it sought to solidify its position in the rapidly changing telecommunications market. Particularly, the marketing department and customer service teams were under intense pressure to meet the timelines for new product launches and the ever-increasing expectations of customers. This work pressure heightened tensions among team members, significantly reduced work efficiency, and exacerbated the psychological and emotional stress experienced by employees.

As the situation deteriorated, some team members began to neglect their duties in response to the overwhelming workload, leading to delays in projects. Moreover, ongoing stress impaired communication among employees, negatively affecting team cooperation and atmosphere. Employees began to express dissatisfaction with the company due to the constant pressure and shifting demands, leading to issues like diminished quality of customer service. Ultimately, all these problems impacted the company's overall performance and started to manifest in increased employee turnover.

The stress experienced by the marketing and customer service teams at the company stemmed from the broader pressures of market expansion and increased competition in the industry. This market environment is constantly changing, and the company faces the pressure of continually developing and launching new technologies and services. This pressure imposes excessive workloads and time constraints on employees, naturally leading to stress when performance expectations are high and resources are insufficient.

In particular, the marketing department often found itself in urgent situations to meet deadlines for product launches, causing employees to lose work-life balance and experience psychological fatigue under constant work pressure. For the customer service team, dealing with continuous and sometimes unreasonable demands from customers isolated team members and intensified their stress. Customer issues and demands are often unpredictable and challenging to manage, requiring employees to provide immediate and effective solutions.

Additionally, communication issues within the team also increased stress. In a high-pressure work environment, communication among team members is often insufficient, which can lead to misunderstandings and heighten tensions within the team. Inadequate communication results in inefficiencies in work processes, ultimately leading to decreased team performance and employee satisfaction.

These issues indicate that workplace stress is not merely a personal problem but deeply intertwined with organizational structure and culture, as well as work processes. Therefore, stress management strategies need to go beyond providing solutions for individuals and include improvements in the organization's overall approach, culture, and work processes.

Ultimately, the stress related to employees' roles directly affected their ability to perform tasks. The complexity and frequent changes in work were overwhelming for employees, becoming a primary factor in reducing operational efficiency across the organization. Recognizing these issues, the company needed to find ways to manage stress effectively in a constantly changing work environment. In this process, the necessity to introduce new approaches to understanding and managing stress through Richard Lazarus' stress theory became apparent.

Richard Lazarus' theory of stress occupies a significant place in psychology, asserting that stress is experienced differently depending on how an individual perceives and interprets situations. Lazarus argued that stress responses are not automatically triggered by external situations but are determined by an individual's subjective evaluation. His theory focuses primarily on two components: 'cognitive appraisal' and 'coping.'

Cognitive appraisal is how an individual perceives their situation, which is divided into two types. The first, 'primary appraisal,' determines whether an individual interprets a situation as a threat, loss, or challenge, influencing the likelihood of experiencing stress. The second, 'secondary appraisal,' involves assessing one's ability to manage the situation, influencing the choice of coping strategies.

Coping refers to the psychological and behavioral strategies that an individual uses when faced with stress. Lazarus differentiated coping strategies into 'problem-focused coping,' which involves efforts to solve the problem causing the stress, and 'emotion-focused coping,' which involves efforts to manage the emotions caused by stress.

The practicality of this theory provides a deep understanding of how individuals interpret and respond to stressful situations, enabling organizations to develop strategies to more effectively manage and mitigate stress. Particularly in designing workplace stress management programs, Lazarus' theory provides crucial benchmarks to improve how employees experience stress and develop healthier coping mechanisms, ultimately contributing to the enhancement of employee welfare and overall organizational productivity.

UVW Communications Company utilized Lazarus' theory on stress and coping to strengthen its strategies for managing employee stress. In this process, the company applied the core elements of Lazarus' theory—cognitive appraisal and coping strategies—to develop skills that enable employees to effectively recognize and manage stress.

Firstly, the company introduced cognitive reappraisal workshops to help employees recognize stress, identify its causes, and explore possible solutions. These workshops taught employees how to proactively manage their stress responses. Particularly, employees were encouraged to view stressful situations from various perspectives and reinterpret them as opportunities for personal growth. For example, the marketing team was encouraged not to view the pressures of product launch deadlines merely as stress factors but as opportunities to enhance their time management and teamwork skills.

Secondly, the company supported each employee in assessing the resources and abilities they have to address their situations. To this end, the HR department provided individual counseling sessions to understand each employee's current level of stress and its causes, and to plan personalized support. Through these sessions, employees learned how to more effectively utilize their internal and external resources.

Thirdly, the company conducted workshops on coping strategies, including both problem-focused and emotion-focused coping. Problem-focused coping workshops dealt with practical skills to change or adapt to specific situations, such as time management and decision-making skills. Emotion-focused coping workshops introduced techniques like emotional management and mindfulness meditation to help employees reduce the emotional burdens they feel at work.

Through these strategies, UVW Company enabled its employees to manage stressful situations more effectively, minimizing the negative impacts while improving work efficiency and individual well-being. This process improved the overall culture of the company and contributed to increased job satisfaction and overall productivity among employees.

This case illustrates how psychological theories can be concretely applied in the workplace, offering ways to enhance employee welfare and organizational productivity. However, psychology is a much broader field, and other psychological theories and approaches can also be very useful in addressing various issues within organizations. Here are some additional psychological theories and resources that can be applied to manage workplace stress and other organizational problems:

1. Social Psychology: This field studies how human behavior is influenced by social interactions. It is useful for understanding various social situations within organizations, such as leadership styles, decision-making processes, and team dynamics. Social psychological principles can be applied when designing leadership development programs or team-building workshops.

2. Cognitive Psychology: This field deals with human thought processes, memory, attention, and perception. Cognitive psychology can help improve employees'

problem-solving abilities and develop learning and training programs. For example, techniques can be trained to help process and remember complex information.

3. Developmental Psychology: This field studies the various developmental stages individuals go through during their life cycle. Organizations can understand the career development stages of their employees and provide support tailored to enhance career satisfaction.

4. Health Psychology: Health psychology studies how psychological factors affect health. This theory can help organizations design employee health promotion programs and develop strategies to enhance well-being in the workplace.

5. Experimental Psychology: This field designs and conducts psychological experiments to understand behavior and thought. This approach can provide data-driven insights for managing organizational change, improving decision-making styles, and more.

These various fields of psychology can be broadly applied to solve various problems within organizations and support the growth and development of employees. Organizations can use these psychological principles and techniques to enhance employee capabilities, improve organizational culture, and boost overall productivity.

9. Leadership Styles and Fiedler's Contingency Theory

Fluid Leadership: Mastering Effective Leadership Changes Through Fiedler's Contingency Theory

Leadership demands more than just giving orders; it requires a complex, multifaceted set of skills. The ability to adapt flexibly to different situations distinguishes a leader, and this flexibility is closely tied to organizational success. Fred Fiedler's Contingency Theory of Leadership scientifically analyzes the optimal match between leaders and their situations, providing a deep understanding of how leaders can harmonize their inherent leadership style with the circumstances they face. This theory explores how leadership styles affect a leader's effectiveness and helps clarify how leaders can achieve optimal performance in various situations.

As globalization progresses, many companies operate across diverse cultures and environments. QRS Corporation, too, faced the challenge of managing cultural differences and diverse work styles during its global expansion. Initially, inconsistencies in leadership styles across regions led to conflicts and problems, particularly where directive leadership was effective in some areas while the same approach provoked resistance in others. This led to reduced work efficiency and hindered the achievement of organizational goals, prompting QRS Corporation to adopt Fiedler's Contingency Theory of Leadership.

This theory asserts that a leader's effectiveness is determined by the degree of match between their preferred leadership style and the situation they face. Leadership styles are classified as either task-oriented or relationship-oriented, and their suitability is assessed based on three critical situational variables: leader-member relations, task structure, and leader position power. QRS's CEO carefully assessed the leaders and situations of each branch based on this theory, applying the most appropriate leadership style to the cultural and work styles of each region.

This approach effectively managed teams across various regions and significantly contributed to the overall performance improvement of the organization.

QRS Corporation established branches in multiple regions during its global expansion. The cultural differences and diversity in work styles in each region presented significant challenges in team management. For example, while directive and authoritative leadership styles were generally effective in Asia, these approaches caused resistance and increased tension among teams in Europe, slowing project progress and reducing overall work efficiency.

In particular, the Brazil branch experienced frequent leadership changes, and new leaders often failed to build effective relationships with local employees, negatively affecting teamwork and productivity. New leaders, typically dispatched from the U.S. headquarters, often had leadership styles that did not align with the Brazilian employees' expectations of mutual respect and teamwork. As a result, employees responded passively to leaders' directives and often performed tasks without clear objectives.

Similar issues arose in the African branch, where leaders preferred a relationship-oriented approach, but this style caused delays in urgent tasks. Employees felt a lack of decisiveness from leaders, leading to frequent failures to meet project deadlines due to delayed decision-making.

The differences in cultural backgrounds and work styles presented numerous challenges to QRS Corporation, with the inability to appropriately adapt to each region's characteristics emerging as a major issue. The mismatch between the leadership styles of each branch and the local employees' work styles not only reduced work efficiency but also decreased job satisfaction and loyalty to the organization. These issues threatened the organization's global expansion strategy and negatively impacted the overall organizational performance.

The mismatches between leadership styles and local employees' work styles in QRS Corporation's global expansion process led to several specific problems that negatively impacted the overall efficiency and job satisfaction within the organization.

The first issue arose when different leadership styles were applied inconsistently across regions. For example, while directive leadership was effective in Asia, the same style caused resistance and conflict in Europe and South America, leading to a lack of cooperation among team members, a lack of clear command structures, and ultimately, delays in projects and failure to achieve objectives.

Secondly, the lack of communication between leaders and employees became a serious issue. Leaders failed to adequately understand the cultural background and work expectations of local employees and did not provide leadership tailored to the characteristics of each branch, causing employees to feel anxious and confused about upper management's decisions. This lowered employees' motivation for work and reduced overall work performance.

Thirdly, a lack of appropriate training and support exacerbated the problem. Leaders did not learn how to adjust their leadership styles to local conditions effectively, significantly reducing the effectiveness of leadership. Additionally, employees struggled to adapt to new work processes or technologies due to insufficient training.

The fourth issue was resistance to change. Changes in leadership, introduction of new work processes, and changes in organizational culture made employees feel insecure and uncertain, increasing distrust and dissatisfaction among employees and fostering tension and division within the organization.

These issues posed threats to QRS Corporation's global expansion strategy and acted as factors hindering the organization's potential for growth. The discrepancies in leadership and employee dissatisfaction became critical issues that needed serious attention for the company to achieve its goals and continue growing.

Fiedler's Contingency Theory of Leadership, developed by Fred Fiedler, argues that a leader's effectiveness is determined by the harmony between their natural leadership style and the situation they face. This theory is one of the first approaches in leadership studies to emphasize the importance of situational leadership. It offers the perspective that leadership style is not absolute but can vary in effectiveness depending on the situation, and it highlights the importance of understanding how a leader's actions are interpreted and accepted within their environment.

Fiedler divides leadership into task-oriented and relationship-oriented styles. Task-oriented leaders prioritize organizational goal achievement and task completion, emphasizing the structure and order necessary to perform tasks effectively. In contrast, relationship-oriented leaders prioritize relationships among team members, focusing on increasing team motivation and satisfaction.

The effectiveness of leadership, according to Fiedler's theory, is greatly influenced by three main situational variables. Firstly, the relationship between the leader and the members determines how close the leader is to the team members and how much they trust and respect the leader. Secondly, the degree of task structure refers to how well-defined tasks are and whether clear guidelines for successful performance are available. Lastly, leader position power indicates how much authority the leader has within the organization and how strong that authority is.

Considering these factors, leaders can adjust their style and situation appropriately to develop strategies to effectively lead their teams. Fiedler's theory emphasizes the need for leaders to flexibly adjust their leadership styles according to the situation, providing a critical foundation for effectively managing team members with diverse cultural backgrounds and work styles. This allows leaders to explore and apply optimal team performance strategies in various situations.

QRS Corporation developed strategies to address leadership issues during its global expansion process based on Fiedler's Contingency Theory of Leadership. When problems arose due to different leadership styles applied in each region, the company focused on analyzing the characteristics of each region and adjusting leadership styles based on this theory.

Firstly, the company conducted detailed diagnostics to assess the leaders' tendencies and situational factors in each branch. Surveys and interviews were conducted to measure the leader-member relationships, task structure, and leader's authority scope to understand each leader's task-oriented or relationship-oriented tendencies and determine the optimal leadership style for each region's cultural and work requirements.

Following the theory, in regions where a task-oriented leadership style was necessary, leaders were encouraged to provide specific goals and clear guidelines for effective task execution. This clarified task priorities and helped team members perform tasks efficiently. In contrast, in regions where a relationship-oriented approach was more effective, leaders focused on strengthening relationships with team members and enhancing communication and teamwork.

Additionally, QRS provided education programs for leaders to adjust their leadership styles flexibly according to the situation. This education provided leaders with opportunities to learn how to adjust their styles in various situations and supported each leader in adopting the most suitable approach for their team and situation.

This approach enabled QRS to effectively manage global teams by developing customized leadership strategies tailored to each region's characteristics, reducing tension between teams and increasing work efficiency. As a result, QRS Corporation improved overall organizational performance through harmonious and effective team operations. This served as a good example of how Fiedler's Contingency Theory of Leadership can be applied to address complex real-world leadership issues.

To further deepen understanding of organizations and leadership, exploring the following theories and related materials might be helpful:

1. Transformational Leadership Theory:
Transformational leadership emphasizes motivation and interaction between leaders and team members. Leaders influence the values and needs of team members, leading to achievements beyond the team's goals. This theory teaches leaders how to promote voluntary participation and innovation among team members.

2. Servant Leadership:
Servant leadership prioritizes meeting the needs of team members and serving them. This leadership style focuses on the growth and well-being of team members,

enhancing overall organizational performance. Leaders support team members in maximizing their potential.

3. The Leadership Pipeline:

This book explores how leaders manage the changing skills and roles required at various levels within organizations. The Leadership Pipeline presents various stages of leader development and helps understand the changes in leadership skills required at each stage.

4. Cultural Intelligence:

Cultural intelligence is essential for leadership in a global environment. Developing cultural intelligence helps leaders communicate effectively and collaborate with team members from diverse backgrounds, turning cultural diversity into an organizational advantage. This includes understanding and respecting different cultural backgrounds and leveraging them for the organization's benefit.

5. The Psychology of Leadership:

This book delves into the psychological aspects of leadership, analyzing how interactions between leaders and team members occur within organizations and how these interactions affect performance. Psychological insights into leadership are crucial for developing effective leadership strategies.

Exploring these materials and theories can help develop leadership skills and understand how to effectively lead in diverse organizational and cultural situations.

10. Employee Retention Strategies and Psychological Contract Theory

Beyond Loyalty: Innovative Employee Retention Strategies Through Psychological Contract Theory

Employee retention is a significant challenge for businesses, extending beyond mere salary increases or bonus offerings to ensuring that employees feel their role within the organization is valuable and that they can make a lasting contribution. This process can be deeply understood through Psychological Contract Theory, which includes unspoken promises and expectations between employees and the organization. When these psychological contracts are well maintained, employee satisfaction and organizational loyalty increase. Conversely, if these contracts break down, it can lead to employee dissatisfaction and increased turnover.

VWX International Trading faced significant challenges in retaining top talent amid rapid market growth. The sales department, in particular, experienced frequent turnover of high-performing employees, which seriously disrupted the company's growth strategy. To address why employees were leaving and how to retain them, the company began a fundamental analysis.

The HR team, through in-depth interviews, discovered that many employees felt their psychological contract with the company had been breached. This contract extends beyond the formal employment agreement to include informal and tacit promises between employees and the organization. Employees felt their efforts and dedication were not sufficiently recognized, and career advancement opportunities were perceived as limited. This perception led to high turnover rates, resulting in significant losses for the organization.

To overcome this problem, VWX adopted a new strategy based on Denise Rousseau's Psychological Contract Theory. This theory centers on mutual expectations and promises between the organization and its employees, explaining that well-maintained psychological contracts enhance employee satisfaction and loyalty, whereas broken contracts increase turnover rates. VWX aimed to rebalance and strengthen its psychological contract with employees to improve retention rates. This initiative involved a deep exploration of how employee expectations and organizational promises can harmonize to foster overall organizational health and growth.

VWX International is recognized for its innovative solutions across various industries and relies heavily on its excellent sales team for its success. However, the high turnover rate, particularly in the sales department, posed serious challenges to project continuity and team collaboration, ultimately impacting the company's overall performance.

For instance, a key salesperson decided to leave the company just before closing a major deal, shocking the team and significantly increasing the workload and stress for the remaining members. This led to project delays and negatively affected relationships with clients, further impacting team motivation and job satisfaction across the company.

To identify the root causes of these issues, the company began collecting data through employee satisfaction surveys and exit interviews. The findings indicated that many employees felt that their psychological contract with the company had been violated. This concept involves more than the terms stated in the formal employment contract, encompassing informal and unspoken promises between employees and the organization.

The employees' perception of their efforts being unrecognized and the lack of career advancement opportunities negatively affected their daily work attitudes and performance, leading to high turnover rates. In response, the company reevaluated its organizational culture and internal communication strategies to better meet the needs and expectations of its employees. Denise Rousseau's Psychological Contract Theory played a crucial role in this process, offering insights into the interplay of actions and attitudes between the organization and its employees. This led to new strategies to strengthen and restore the psychological contract.

VWX International faced major issues with high turnover rates and declining employee satisfaction, particularly pronounced in the sales department. These challenges were directly linked to the company's growth strategy. The HR team's in-depth interviews and surveys revealed that multiple employees felt their psychological contract had been breached, involving more than just the conditions outlined in formal employment agreements.

Employees felt their contributions were not adequately recognized by the organization, particularly regarding rewards for performance and career advancement opportunities. Many employees were unclear about how their work contributed to the company's overall goals, leading to feelings of insignificance. This lack of recognition increased anxiety and dissatisfaction among employees, prompting decisions to leave the company.

Additionally, employees expressed dissatisfaction with the company's communication and leadership styles. A lack of communication from managers, a lack of transparency in decision-making, and insufficient support from senior management were major reasons for considering leaving the company. These elements are crucial for employees to feel engaged and loyal to an organization. Without resolving these issues, employee dissatisfaction and turnover rates will continue, negatively affecting both the company's long-term growth and individual employee development.

These factors collectively exacerbated problems with organizational culture and employee satisfaction at VWX International, requiring comprehensive cultural change and improvement strategies. The HR team introduced the concept of the psychological contract to address the disconnect between employee expectations and organizational promises.

Denise Rousseau's Psychological Contract Theory focuses on analyzing the subtle and implicit promises between employees and organizations, which are not included in formal employment contracts but involve expectations and trust that employees have towards the organization and vice versa. These beliefs, often unspoken, significantly influence employee behavior, attitudes, and overall satisfaction with the organization.

Rousseau, a leading scholar in organizational psychology, emphasizes the importance of psychological contracts in understanding interactions between organizations and employees. Her research provides deep insights into how these interactions form the basis of all interactions within an organization and how the contents of psychological contracts can change over time. For example, changes in organizational policies, management changes, or external economic pressures can alter the nature of psychological contracts.

This theory is particularly important in today's business environment, where organizational changes are frequent. Rousseau's work explains the potential outcomes when psychological contracts are breached, such as loss of trust, lack of motivation, decreased performance, and high turnover rates, and offers direction on how organizations can work to prevent these negative outcomes.

Applying Psychological Contract Theory is crucial for organizations to manage and appropriately adjust employee expectations within changing conditions, minimizing anxiety and dissatisfaction among employees. Additionally, this theory provides valuable tools for assessing how well an organization is meeting employee expectations and how employees perceive organizational promises.

With this theoretical background, VWX International reevaluated its HR policies and communication strategies to strengthen and restore the psychological contract with its employees and improve retention rates. The company focused on regularly surveying employee satisfaction and actively collecting feedback to reduce the gap between employee expectations and what the organization provides. These efforts helped build trust within the organization and maintained high levels of employee loyalty and satisfaction.

VWX International adopted a very specific approach to improving its employee retention strategy by applying Psychological Contract Theory. The company initially conducted in-depth employee interviews and surveys to understand how the psychological contract had been violated. Through this process, employees expressed that their contributions to the organization were not being recognized, leading to dissatisfaction and decisions to leave. Additionally, employees felt that their career development within the company was limited, which negatively impacted their loyalty and satisfaction.

The company developed several strategies to address these issues. Firstly, it introduced regular feedback sessions and open forums to enhance open communication with employees, allowing them to freely share their expectations and concerns, which helped increase understanding between employees and management. Secondly, the company overhauled its reward system to properly recognize and reward employees' efforts and achievements. This system included not only financial rewards but also promotion opportunities, training programs, and public recognition, ensuring employees felt their contributions were valuable and recognized.

Thirdly, the company established personalized career development plans for each employee, regularly reviewed and updated to help employees achieve their long-term career goals. Additionally, the company built open communication channels to effectively manage cultural conflicts within the organization, allowing employees to express their opinions and concerns honestly.

Lastly, the company set up mechanisms to continuously assess and adjust the changes in organizational culture and their effects. This was achieved through regular employee satisfaction surveys, turnover rate analysis, and project performance reviews. These measures allowed VWX to significantly improve organizational culture and employee satisfaction, which led to increased employee retention rates and overall performance improvement. The application of Psychological Contract Theory played a crucial role in enhancing employee motivation and loyalty, and VWX effectively retained top talent through this approach.

Various psychological theories related to employee retention are also worth exploring, including:

1. Herzberg's Motivation-Hygiene Theory: This theory distinguishes between factors that positively affect employee motivation and satisfaction and those that cause dissatisfaction. According to the theory, motivators (e.g., sense of

achievement, recognition, responsibility) and hygiene factors (e.g., working conditions, salary, company policies) affect employee satisfaction differently. Organizations can use this theory to identify specific improvements that focus more on employee satisfaction and retention.

2. McClelland's Theory of Needs: This theory explains how individuals' needs for achievement, power, and affiliation influence their work performance and career choices. Organizations can use this theory to understand the specific needs of each employee and create a work environment that enhances employee retention.

3. Organizational Identity Theory: This theory explores how individuals perceive themselves as part of an organization and how this perception influences their behavior and attitudes towards the organization. When employees deeply resonate with the organization's values and goals and consider their role important, they are more likely to exhibit higher satisfaction and loyalty.

4. Organizational Justice Theory: This theory explains how fairness within an organization affects employee attitudes and behaviors. When employees feel they are treated fairly, they are more likely to contribute positively to the organization and reduce turnover rates.

These theories approach employee motivation and satisfaction in different ways, helping to positively change organizational culture and retain employees. It is important for each organization to select and apply the appropriate theory based on its specific situation and needs.

II. Marketing and Psychology: An Introduction

The Magic of Marketing, The Power of Psychology

Imagine a scenario where an advertisement captures your heart—it's not merely a coincidence. Marketing professionals delve deeply into consumer psychology, crafting messages that tap into our emotions and desires. This process goes beyond selling a product; it's about designing consumer minds and behaviors. If an advertisement has caught your attention and led to a purchase, it certainly isn't by chance. Marketing experts leverage the power of psychology to finely tune our emotional and need-based responses.

This chapter explores how marketing and psychology are powerfully interconnected, and how combining knowledge from both fields can develop more effective marketing strategies. We will deeply explore various psychological theories essential for understanding and predicting consumer behavior, providing a broad range of insights through both theoretical foundations and practical applications.

We start with Freud's psychoanalytic theory, examining how unconscious desires influence consumer behavior. Through Cialdini's principles of persuasion, we analyze how advertisements exert their persuasive power, and using Aaker's dimensions of brand personality, we explore how brands create emotional connections with consumers. Kahneman's prospect theory allows us to review cognitive biases present in consumer decision-making processes, and by applying behavioral economics, we understand that economic decisions are not always rational.

Additionally, we analyze external influences on consumer purchase decisions through social proof and the social influence of information, and delve into the psychological processes that form customer loyalty. Examining Pine & Gilmore's experience economy, we emphasize the importance of providing memorable experiences to consumers, and through Mehrabian's communication rules, we analyze how non-verbal elements significantly impact consumer perception. Lastly, digital marketing and online behavioral psychology will be scrutinized to understand how consumer behavior transforms in digital environments and how these insights can be effectively integrated into marketing strategies.

Through this chapter, marketing professionals will gain powerful tools to deepen their understanding of consumer minds and predict their behavior. The fusion of psychology and marketing offers more than just strategies—it opens pathways to effective communication and deep customer insights, providing the necessary knowledge to design and execute more effective strategies.

1. Understanding Consumer Behavior Through Freud's Psychoanalytic Theory

Marketing's Unconscious Tools: Analyzing Consumer Behavior with Freud's Psychoanalytic Theory

Consider whether all the consumption decisions we make daily are truly conscious choices. In fact, many decisions are driven by desires and cravings rooted deep in our unconscious, beyond our awareness. Freud's psychoanalytic theory reveals the power of the unconscious, providing fundamental reasons why we are drawn to certain products or respond to specific advertisements. Understanding these deep psychological mechanisms is essential for marketers to captivate consumers' minds, requiring the delicacy of an art form.

Imagine this scenario: one morning, as you browse routinely, an advertisement suddenly captures your attention. This ad doesn't just showcase a product; it inexplicably stirs your emotions, igniting a strong desire to own the product. Why is this so? Here lies the intersection of marketing and psychology. Marketing professionals utilize psychological principles to delve into the consumer psyche, employing subtle techniques to guide their behavior. This goes beyond mere advertising to tapping into emotions and desires deeply ingrained in the consumer's psyche, effectively making it a science.

This chapter explores how marketing and psychology merge to influence the consumer's mind. We apply various psychological theories to deeply analyze unconscious desires, the essence of emotions, and their profound impact on decision-making processes. From Freud's psychoanalytic theory to the latest in behavioral economics, we explore how psychological insights can be integrated into marketing strategies, enabling professionals to read, predict, and ultimately influence consumer behavior.

The consumer's mind is a complex and unpredictable maze. Marketers must navigate this labyrinth, and psychology acts as a powerful compass throughout this journey. Each section will explore this maze, using psychological tools and strategies to understand and effectively impact consumer behavior. By doing so, marketers can develop deeper approaches and build strong emotional connections with consumers.

A globally recognized clothing brand, ZetaWear, recently discovered through market research that its main customer base, the younger generation, perceives the brand as "outdated and unappealing." This perception became particularly pronounced after the launch of ZetaWear's latest spring collection. Customers felt that the designs and color choices were not modern and were disconnected from the trends proposed by competing brands.

At this point, ZetaWear decided to thoroughly review its product line and marketing strategy. Within the company, there was a clash of perspectives: some viewed the issue as merely visual and trendy, while others saw it as a deeper problem with the brand's image and identity. The marketing team decided to conduct focus group interviews with different consumer groups to gain deeper insights.

The focus groups revealed that ZetaWear's advertising campaigns were too traditional and lacked a contemporary feel. Particularly, younger consumers felt that the brand did not align with their values and that the "lifestyle" promoted by the brand was disconnected from their everyday lives. This feedback was a shock to ZetaWear, making it clear that the brand needed to reestablish its position in the market and strengthen its connection with consumers.

In response, ZetaWear's executive team began to explore new strategies. They recognized the need to modernize the brand's image and develop marketing strategies that could deeply connect with consumers' psychological needs. This situation exemplifies how marketing and psychology can interlink perfectly. The challenges ZetaWear faced went beyond mere visual enhancements to involve a comprehensive reconfiguration of the brand's overall image and identity, integrating an understanding of consumer psychology into its marketing strategies.

Looking deeper into ZetaWear's situation, the fundamental issue is that the brand has not kept pace with the changing times and evolving consumer expectations. The younger generation does not simply buy products; they significantly value how a brand aligns with their personal beliefs. Their purchasing decisions express their personal identity, which becomes a crucial factor in choosing brands.

Brand image and identity mismatch: ZetaWear's image remained anchored in past successes and did not reflect current market trends or consumer expectations. Consumers felt the lifestyle portrayed by the brand was out of touch with their reality, weakening their emotional connection to the brand.

Failure in communication: ZetaWear's marketing messages did not reflect the current values and desires of consumers. The conservative approach of the advertising campaigns failed to appeal to young, innovative, and creative consumers, indicating that the brand failed to narrow the psychological gap with its audience.

Insensitivity to market trends: It is crucial to sense rapid changes in the market and consumer behavior and adapt accordingly. ZetaWear has remained a follower rather than a leader in trends, attempting to adopt innovative strategies already employed by competitors only belatedly.

These issues indicate that ZetaWear needs to reestablish its market position and strengthen connections with consumers. Overcoming these challenges requires more than just improving the external image; it involves deeply understanding how the brand can appeal to the psychological and emotional aspects of consumers, a process in which psychological approaches play a vital role.

ZetaWear's challenge begins with the mismatch between the brand's image and the contemporary values of consumers. The most appropriate psychological theory to address this issue is Sigmund Freud's psychoanalytic theory. Freud's theory suggests that most individual behaviors are driven by unconscious desires and motives, providing a foundational role in developing marketing strategies that resonate deeply with consumer psychology.

Sigmund Freud, often called the father of psychology, has profoundly influenced not only psychology but also marketing, cultural studies, and the arts. His theory offers insights into how human behaviors, emotions, and thoughts are predominantly driven by unconscious motives and impulses. His approach divides the human mind into three parts:

The conscious includes our aware thoughts and feelings, accessible during our daily interactions. The preconscious contains memories and information not readily accessible but can be brought into the conscious mind when needed. The unconscious is the deepest part of the mind, housing desires, instincts, and memories beyond our conscious access. Freud emphasized that the unconscious significantly impacts human behavior and emotions, arguing that these unconscious elements powerfully drive our decisions and actions.

Freud also introduced three structural elements of personality to explain psychological development: the id, ego, and superego. The id represents instinctual drives and operates on the pleasure principle, seeking immediate gratification. The ego adheres to the reality principle, attempting to balance the desires of the id with the external world. The superego represents morality and ideals, imposing ethical constraints on the ego and enforcing "correct" behavior. The interaction of these elements produces the complexity of individual behaviors and emotions, allowing marketers to understand and utilize these psychological motivations to predict and influence consumer behavior.

Applying Freud's psychoanalytic theory in marketing allows brands to gain a deep understanding of how to resonate and stimulate consumers' unconscious desires. This enables brands to develop powerful advertising messages and design marketing strategies that stimulate consumers' emotions and desires. Such strategies can fulfill previously unrecognized needs or elicit strong desires for specific products, playing a crucial role in brand loyalty and purchasing decisions.

ZetaWear's marketing team deeply understood Freud's theory and based on this understanding, decided to re-create the brand image to be more youthful and contemporary. The process involved several key steps, each applying Freud's theory in detail.

The first step involved the ZetaWear marketing team delving deeply into the consumer unconscious to understand their fundamental needs and motives. According to Freud, consumer purchasing decisions are often significantly influenced by unconscious desires, such as the fundamental human needs for safety, freedom, belonging, and power.

ZetaWear's team researched how the brand could stimulate the desires for freedom and adventure among young consumers. In planning a new advertising campaign, they developed ways to effectively communicate these desires through visual and verbal messages. For instance, the ads depicted young people escaping the hustle of the city to freely adventure in nature, emphasizing that ZetaWear's clothing enables their adventurous and free lifestyle.

In the second step, the brand storytelling was used to build a deeper emotional and psychological connection with consumers. As highlighted in Freud's theory, people are strongly attracted to brands that align with their identity or reflect their ideal selves. ZetaWear restructured its brand story to emphasize youth, innovation, and individuality.

For this purpose, ZetaWear produced advertisements incorporating real consumer stories, conveying the experiences and feelings of freedom and satisfaction gained from using the products. This storytelling approach allowed consumers to identify their experiences and emotions with the brand story, contributing to building trust and loyalty towards the brand.

In the final step, feedback from consumers was actively collected and analyzed to continuously monitor and improve the campaign's effectiveness. Since the unconscious motives and desires understood through Freud's theory can change, ZetaWear closely observed market changes and consumer responses to adjust its strategies accordingly.

This approach allowed ZetaWear to bridge the psychological gap with the younger generation and execute a successful marketing strategy that appealed to their unconscious desires. The deep application of psychological theories played a key role in re-creating the brand and building a strong emotional connection with consumers.

The integration of marketing and psychology is highly effective in understanding and predicting consumer behavior. Besides Freud's psychoanalytic theory, various psychological theories can help design and implement more in-depth and effective marketing strategies. Here are some key areas of psychology that marketing professionals might consider:

Behavioral Psychology: This field studies patterns of human behavior to understand and change behavior. In marketing, behavioral psychology can identify factors influencing consumer purchasing decisions and develop strategies to guide consumer behavior based on these insights. For example, the psychological impacts of product placement, pricing, and promotional activities on consumer purchasing decisions can be analyzed.

Cognitive Psychology: Cognitive psychology studies human cognitive processes, including thinking, perception, memory, and problem-solving. In marketing, cognitive psychology is used to understand how advertising messages capture consumer attention, how information is processed, and how it remains in memory. Additionally, considering how consumers receive and interpret information, the representation and delivery of messages can be optimized.

Social Psychology: Social psychology explores how individual behavior interacts with social situations. This is useful in understanding how advertisements are perceived by consumers and how people make decisions within groups. Additionally, using principles such as social proof and authority can develop strategies to influence consumer purchasing decisions.

Emotional Psychology: This field studies how emotions influence human judgment and behavior. In marketing, understanding the role of emotions can analyze how advertising or brand experiences stimulate consumer emotions and how this can induce changes in consumer behavior. This is particularly important for building brand loyalty or strengthening emotional brand connections.

These diverse psychological theories add depth to marketing strategies, providing a foundation to understand and respond to the complex behaviors and psychological motivations of consumers more precisely. Marketing professionals can creatively use these theories to build stronger connections with consumers and enhance their competitiveness in the market.

2. The Psychology of Advertising and Persuasion: Exploring Cialdini's Principles of Influence

Exploring the Psychology of Advertising That Moves Minds Like Magic: Cialdini's Principles of Persuasion

Marketing transcends the mere act of selling products and services to consumers; it involves a psychological process that delves deep into the consumer's mind and subconscious, steering their decisions. A closer look at everyday advertisements reveals powerful psychological mechanisms at play. Robert Cialdini's Principles of Influence scientifically dissect this aspect of marketing psychology, providing a theoretical foundation that enables marketers to accurately predict and manipulate consumer behavior.

Cialdini's theory outlines six key principles that marketers can use to influence consumer decision-making. These principles—reciprocity, consistency, social proof, authority, liking, and scarcity—cunningly leverage consumer psychology. For instance, the principle of reciprocity exploits the internal compulsion to repay what one has received. Marketers use free samples or gifts to create a sense of indebtedness in consumers, nudging them toward purchasing the product or service.

These principles wield a powerful, subconscious force in consumer choice, allowing marketers to develop more effective advertising and marketing strategies. For example, the principle of consistency takes advantage of the tendency to adhere to initial commitments, guiding consumers towards larger purchases. Moreover, the principle of social proof is particularly effective in uncertain situations, where consumers often emulate the choices of others.

As these principles are applied within marketing campaigns, consumers unknowingly find themselves drawn to the advertisement's message, developing a liking for the product, and ultimately making a purchase through an unconscious process. This demonstrates the potent role of psychology in marketing, akin to the workings of a magician. How marketers harness this power significantly alters the success of advertising and marketing initiatives. This psychological approach is crucial in designing advertising and marketing strategies, forming the core of effective tactics that connect deeply with the deep-seated psychological motivations of consumers.

InnoWear, a globally renowned fashion brand, is currently facing rapid changes in trends and consumer expectations. Although the brand has been pioneering technically innovative products, recent customer perception studies have revealed that consumers find InnoWear's products too technologically focused, lacking in fashion appeal. This perception is particularly strong among younger consumers who seek to express their individuality through fashion.

This has become a critical discussion point in InnoWear's marketing strategy meetings. Recent market research reports have indicated that although InnoWear's sportswear line excels in functionality, it lags behind competing brands in style. For example, while InnoWear's smartwatches offer various fitness tracking features, consumers consider them lacking as fashion accessories. These products, suitable for tech enthusiasts, are not appealing to young consumers who prefer everyday wearability.

Additionally, InnoWear's digital marketing campaigns face similar challenges. Social media analysis shows that InnoWear's advertisements, which focus primarily on technical details, feel too heavy for young consumers who value style and fashion. They have a strong desire to express their identity through fashion, and InnoWear's current messaging fails to meet these needs.

This information suggests that InnoWear needs to reassess its marketing strategies and brand messaging, particularly emphasizing fashion and style to enhance its relationship with the younger generation. The brand needs a more modern and dynamic rebranding strategy to overcome the current market positioning challenges. This situation provides an opportunity for InnoWear to utilize psychological approaches and principles of persuasion actively.

Analyzing the root cause of the challenges faced by InnoWear, it primarily stems from a mismatch between the brand image, market trends, and consumer expectations. InnoWear has been promoting technological innovation as a core value of the brand, emphasizing the unique functional benefits of its products. Although this approach has been effective for a consumer segment interested in science and technology, it has not resonated well with a broader young consumer base that values fashion and style.

This issue is particularly evident in social media and online marketing channels. InnoWear's digital marketing campaigns often focus on the technical details of products, expending significant resources to explain how these features can be beneficial in everyday life. However, this information-centric approach neglects the emotional and aesthetic considerations that consumers take into account when selecting products. Young consumers seek fashion products that reflect their lifestyle and personality, and they are less attracted to brands that solely emphasize functional aspects.

Moreover, consistent patterns have been observed in InnoWear's market research and consumer feedback collection processes. Many consumers have expressed a disconnect between the brand's messaging and their actual lifestyles. They feel that the brand does not sufficiently understand or reflect their social and cultural contexts, leading to decreased brand loyalty and repurchase intentions.

At the core of these issues lies the fact that InnoWear's brand positioning has not kept pace with the changing times and shifting consumer expectations. This indicates that the brand is losing its emotional connection with consumers, underscoring the need to overhaul its brand messaging and communication strategies comprehensively. InnoWear must move beyond its technology-centric approach to actively incorporate consumer emotions and lifestyles, enhancing the visual and emotional appeal of its marketing strategies.

InnoWear can effectively apply Robert Cialdini's Principles of Persuasion to its marketing strategy, which has profoundly impacted advertising and consumer behavior research. Cialdini, a social psychologist, focuses his research on the decision-making process and how individuals are influenced by others. His book, "Influence: The Psychology of Persuasion," outlines six fundamental principles of persuasion used across various fields to understand and predict human behavior.

First, the principle of reciprocity explains the psychological tendency to feel obligated to repay favors or services. In marketing, this principle is leveraged through free samples, discount coupons, and additional service offerings, encouraging consumers to reciprocate by purchasing the product.

Second, the principle of consistency highlights that once individuals publicly commit to something, they are likely to act consistently with that commitment. This principle can be applied in marketing to encourage consumers to make small initial commitments (e.g., signing up for a free membership) and subsequently guide them towards consistent actions (e.g., subscribing to a paid service).

Third, the principle of social proof is particularly potent in uncertain situations, where people tend to emulate the actions of others. In marketing, this principle is utilized through product reviews, user tests, and mentions on social media to influence consumer purchase decisions.

Fourth, the principle of liking suggests that people are more influenced by those they like. This can be enhanced through appearance, similarities, compliments, and cooperation, and is employed in advertising campaigns by using approachable and attractive characters or celebrities to build likeability and instill positive perceptions of the product.

Fifth, the principle of authority increases trust and persuasiveness through endorsements from experts or authoritative figures. In marketing, this is achieved by highlighting product efficacy through expert reviews, scientific research findings, and official certifications to enhance the authority of the product or service.

Lastly, the principle of scarcity suggests that limited access to a resource makes it more valuable. In marketing, expressions like "limited edition," "time-limited discounts," and "last chance" are used to emphasize product scarcity and encourage prompt purchasing decisions.

By strategically applying Cialdini's Principles of Persuasion, InnoWear can refine its marketing strategies, making them more sophisticated and competitive in the market. Each principle plays a crucial role in understanding the psychological factors influencing consumers and building compelling marketing messages based on these insights.

Like InnoWear, marketing strategies can be enhanced and consumer relationships strengthened by applying various psychological theories. Beyond Cialdini's principles, other psychological approaches can also maximize the effectiveness of marketing strategies. These theories significantly impact consumer purchase decisions and brand loyalty formation.

1. Empathy Theory: Based on the ability to understand and empathize with others' feelings, this theory can be utilized in marketing to deeply understand consumer needs and desires, providing customized communication. Effective use of empathy in advertisements can strengthen emotional bonds with consumers and foster positive feelings towards the brand.

2. Anchoring Effect: This explains the tendency to rely on an initial piece of information to judge subsequent information. Particularly useful in pricing strategies, for example, presenting a high price first and then offering a discounted price can influence consumer purchase decisions.

3. Confirmation Bias: This bias indicates that people pay more attention to and place greater importance on information that confirms their existing beliefs or assumptions. In marketing, this bias can be leveraged to reinforce a positive brand image and emphasize positive perceptions already held by consumers to enhance brand loyalty.

4. Framing Effect: This effect demonstrates that the same information can elicit different responses depending on how it is presented. Marketing messages framed positively or that emphasize the benefits of a product can favorably influence consumer purchase decisions.

These psychological approaches not only make marketing strategies more effective but also play a crucial role in deeply understanding consumer behavior. By employing these theories, marketing professionals can optimize the consumer buying experience and develop strategies necessary for building sustained relationships between the brand and its customers.

3. Brand Personality and Aaker's Brand Personality Dimensions

Humanizing Brands:
Captivating Consumer Hearts through Aaker's Brand Personality Framework

Gone are the days when brands were merely seen as collections of products or services. In today's marketing landscape, brands embody unique 'personalities,' which play a crucial role in forging emotional connections with consumers and building brand loyalty. Jennifer Aaker's framework on brand personality dimensions offers marketers a scientific and structured approach to shaping a brand's image.

For instance, if a sportswear brand embodies an 'active and dynamic' image, it reflects the aspirations of consumers who choose the brand to view themselves as active individuals. This emotional connection fosters strong emotional bonds between the brand and its consumers, which can lead to enduring customer loyalty.

Jennifer Aaker categorizes brand personality into five key dimensions: Sincerity, Excitement, Competence, Sophistication, and Ruggedness. These dimensions help marketers clarify a brand's image and forge deep emotional connections with consumers. By integrating Aaker's theory into their marketing strategies, brands can carve out a unique position in the market and strengthen their emotional ties with consumers.

Brand personality goes beyond a simple marketing tool; it is a vital means to establish psychological connections with consumers. It plays a critical role in enhancing brand loyalty and boosting competitiveness in the market. Through brand personality, consumers personalize the brand, deepening their understanding and affection, which in turn, strengthens their emotional bond and significantly influences their purchasing decisions.

Brand personality also clearly defines how a brand should be perceived within the market and integrates the brand into consumers' daily lives and emotions. By applying Jennifer Aaker's theory, marketers can craft unique personalities for each brand, promoting emotional engagement with consumers. This not only fosters strong customer loyalty but also lays the foundation for the brand's long-term success.

The challenges faced by a global fashion brand illustrate the complexities of adapting to market changes. This brand, long celebrated for its elegance and classic appeal, has been popular among a mature customer base. However, recent market research indicates that younger consumers perceive this traditional brand image as outdated, leading to their disengagement. The failure to appeal to newer generations poses significant constraints on the brand's potential for future growth.

This issue is further exacerbated by the use of social media and digital marketing. While competing brands actively engage new consumer segments online, this brand's reliance on traditional advertising methods and limited digital presence fails to meet the dynamics of market changes. In today's digital-centric market environment, this poses a fatal weakness for the brand. Younger consumers, in particular, are drawn to brands that are active online, and their buying decisions are heavily influenced by digital content.

These challenges impose serious concerns for the brand's management. Relying solely on existing brand images and strategies proves insufficient for attracting new customers and retaining existing ones. The management recognizes the need for strategic changes to redefine the brand personality and enhance its market competitiveness. This involves innovating product lines and overhauling brand communication methods to align with the expectations and trends of younger consumers.

Consequently, the brand plans to implement fundamental changes to its brand image and marketing strategies to navigate the current challenges and achieve long-term growth. This will involve more effective outreach to diverse consumer bases and leveraging digital platforms to enhance communication with younger generations. Throughout this process, the brand aims to maintain its traditional strengths while incorporating innovative elements to secure a new position in the market.

The diverse and complex issues faced by the global fashion brand require immediate action to maintain market competitiveness. Although the brand has long championed traditional values and luxury, recent surveys show that its image is viewed as old-fashioned and outdated by younger generations. Modern consumers, especially Millennials and Generation Z, prioritize values such as innovation, individuality, and sustainability, and place significant importance on a brand's digital presence and social media activities. Traditional marketing strategies alone are insufficient to attract this new consumer base.

Moreover, the brand is experiencing significant delays in digital marketing and online communication. While competing brands quickly adapt to the evolving digital marketing landscape and engage directly with consumers, this brand continues to rely on traditional advertising and promotions, which fail to resonate with younger consumers. This results in a lack of online brand recognition and low consumer engagement, ultimately leading to decreased sales and a decline in brand value.

The communication strategy has also been highlighted as a major issue. Often, the brand's messaging is inconsistent and fails to connect deeply with consumers' emotional needs, weakening the emotional bond between the brand and its consumers and potentially leading to decreased brand loyalty. Consumers seek consistency and authenticity in the messages conveyed by brands, using these to justify their choices. Therefore, when messages are unclear or do not align with consumer expectations, this directly impacts trust in the brand.

These issues serve as significant barriers to attracting new customers and retaining existing ones, increasing the risk of weakening the brand's position in a competitive market. To address these challenges, the brand must respond more sensitively to changing market and consumer demands, analyze these issues deeply internally, and develop effective response strategies.

This may involve redefining the brand image, strengthening digital marketing strategies, and developing creative campaigns to enhance consumer engagement.

All measures should focus on restoring market competitiveness and ensuring long-term growth.

Jennifer Aaker's theory of brand personality dimensions views brands as beings with diverse personalities, helping marketers form emotional connections with consumers. This theory enhances marketing effectiveness by allowing for a nuanced analysis and understanding of a brand's personality across various dimensions. Aaker identifies five principal dimensions of brand personality: Sincerity, Excitement, Competence, Sophistication, and Ruggedness, each providing clear guidance on how a brand should be perceived and emotionally connect with consumers.

Sincerity emphasizes a brand's down-to-earth, honest, and welcoming traits, projecting an authentic image that instills trust in consumers. Excitement portrays the brand as contemporary, bold, and active, appealing strongly to younger audiences. Competence shows that the brand is reliable and skilled, particularly advantageous when marketing technologically advanced products or services. Sophistication highlights an elegant and glamorous image, enhancing the allure of luxury brands or high-end products. Ruggedness accentuates a tough and rugged aspect, suitable for products related to adventure or outdoor activities.

By understanding and applying these personality dimensions, marketers can ensure that brands deeply penetrate consumer psychology, form emotional connections, and influence purchasing decisions. Aaker's theory transforms the perception of brands from mere collections of products to entities with distinct personalities, helping marketers approach consumer psychology and emotions with greater finesse. This significantly boosts brand loyalty and strengthens competitiveness in the market.

The company has applied Aaker's theory of brand personality dimensions in-depth, tailoring strategies to refine and specify each brand's personality. In this process, the brand focused on the dimensions of Sincerity and Sophistication, rolling out two major campaigns. To highlight Sincerity, the company planned a campaign that forefronted the authenticity and eco-friendly values of its products. This involved transparently disclosing to consumers where the product materials come from and the processes they undergo, emphasizing environmental responsibility and ethical business practices during this process.

These campaigns were conveyed through social media, blogs, and websites with a variety of storytelling techniques, enabling consumers to recognize that the brand goes beyond mere commercial objectives to assume social and environmental responsibilities. This has helped consumers form a strong sense of trust in the brand. Additionally, this approach has made the brand appear more human and accessible, enhancing emotional bonds with customers.

To emphasize Sophistication, the company conducted advertising campaigns that conveyed luxury and uniqueness. These campaigns highlighted sophisticated imagery and high-end designs, delivering tailored messages aimed at specific target markets. For example, advertisements targeting luxury fashion brands emphasized collaborations with renowned designers or the use of special materials, conveying the unique value of the products and stimulating consumers' desire to own them. These ads were distributed in cinemas, upscale magazines, and online platforms, effectively reaching the targeted customer base.

This redefined brand personality deepened emotional connections with consumers and significantly enhanced brand loyalty. Consumers resonated with the messages delivered by the brand, using the brand to express their identities and values. Through this process, the brand became more than just a provider of products—it became an integral part of consumers' lives, ensuring the brand's sustainable growth in the market.

This strategy also had a positive impact within the company. The marketing team gained a clear understanding of the brand's personality and consistently reflected this in all advertising and promotional activities. This consistency helped consumers more clearly perceive the brand's messages, contributing to strong brand recognition.

Beyond brand personality, there are various psychological theories and approaches that can further improve marketing strategies and strengthen relationships with consumers. In addition to Aaker's brand personality dimensions, several psychological theories can aid effective brand management and understanding of consumer behavior. These theories offer deep insights into consumers' decision-making processes and enhance the emotional connections between brands and consumers.

1. Cognitive Dissonance Theory: This theory explains the psychological tendency of consumers to maintain consistency among their beliefs, attitudes, and behaviors. In marketing, this theory can be used to encourage consumers to maintain a positive perception of the brand, positively influencing their purchasing decisions and brand loyalty.

2. Self-Efficacy Theory: This theory deals with the tendency of individuals to act in the belief that their actions will lead to successful outcomes. Brands that empower consumers or enhance the perception that using the product contributes to personal success can particularly benefit from this theory.

3. Contrast Theory: This theory describes the tendency of people to perceive information in contrast to prior experiences or expectations. In marketing, this can be used to make a brand stand out against competitors and highlight the unique features of a product.

4. Cultural Congruence Theory: This theory deals with how a brand's message aligns with the cultural values of consumers. By providing messages tailored to specific cultural backgrounds, brands can achieve greater empathy and responsiveness from consumer groups.

These psychological approaches help brands understand subtle psychological factors in consumers and effectively integrate them into marketing strategies. Each theory provides insights into how brands can develop more nuanced and differentiated approaches in the market, playing a crucial role in building sustainable relationships with consumers.

4. Consumer Decision-Making and Kahneman's Prospect Theory

Marketing and the Psychology of Consumer Minds: Exploring Kahneman's Prospect Theory

In the world of marketing, understanding the consumer decision-making process is akin to deciphering a form of magic. This complex process may appear as simple decisions at a glance, but in reality, it is deeply influenced by psychological and emotional factors. A pivotal theory in effectively grasping and managing this is Daniel Kahneman's Prospect Theory, which scientifically explains the irrational patterns influencing consumer judgments and actions, providing deep insights for marketers.

The essence of Prospect Theory focuses on how consumers perceive potential losses and gains, and how these perceptions dictate their actions. According to Kahneman, people prioritize avoiding losses over acquiring gains, which has a profound impact on consumer purchasing decisions. This concept, known as 'loss aversion,' implies that people have a stronger emotional response to potential losses, significantly influencing their buying process.

By applying this psychological phenomenon in marketing strategies, businesses can deeply understand consumer psyche and base their marketing tactics accordingly. For instance, rather than increasing prices, strategies could emphasize discounts or price reductions to leverage consumers' loss aversion tendencies. Tactics like "Today only discounts!" or "Limited quantity sale!" trigger urgency and loss aversion, prompting quick purchases.

Additionally, when highlighting product features, marketers can make products more appealing by focusing on reducing potential losses for the consumer. For example, advertising health supplements with messages like "Prevent illness and maintain your health" can tap into consumers' fears of health loss, steering decisions more favorably.

Lastly, it's effective to emphasize the losses consumers might incur by not taking action through promotional messages. Phrases like "Ends when stock runs out" or "You'll regret missing this" instill fear of missing out, fostering purchase actions.

By understanding and implementing Kahneman's Prospect Theory into marketing strategies, marketers can influence the irrational aspects of consumer decision-making. This enables brands to exert a strong influence in the market and build lasting relationships with consumers. Integrating psychological approaches into marketing is a crucial strategy for deeply understanding consumer minds and actively influencing their purchasing decisions.

XYZ Company entered the mid to high-end home furnishing market with a line of luxury products, setting high expectations for market entry. Previously known for its budget-friendly offerings, the company decided to shift towards the luxury market to enhance its brand image and profit margins. The products featured natural materials and premium designs, with marketing strategies emphasizing environmental sustainability to attract consumer interest.

Initially, the products were visually appealing and boasted innovative designs, and the marketing campaigns were extensively rolled out. However, contrary to expectations, sales were disappointing, and initial feedback indicated that consumers were highly sensitive to the pricing. Particularly, the existing customer base expressed dissatisfaction with XYZ's prices being significantly higher compared to its previous products.

Market analysis revealed that while XYZ's target customers recognized the product value, the high pricing made them hesitant to make purchases. Compared to competitors, XYZ's products were priced higher, pushing consumers towards competing brands. Additionally, consumers felt that XYZ had not yet established a reputation as a provider of luxury products, leading to doubts about the brand's credibility.

Realizing the need for further action to resolve these issues, XYZ began considering strategic adjustments to improve consumer perceptions and strengthen its market position. The company needed to lower psychological barriers and more effectively communicate the quality and value of its products.

The challenges XYZ faced in transitioning to the high-end home furnishing market were multifaceted, driven by several factors. The primary issue was a mismatch in consumer perception. XYZ attempted to transition its image to a high-end market, but consumers still held onto its previous budget-friendly image. When the new luxury product line was introduced, consumers struggled to associate the brand's value and quality with the higher price range.

The second issue was a failure in pricing strategy. XYZ's product prices were significantly higher than its previous offerings, negatively impacting target customer purchasing decisions. Consumers did not perceive enough value to justify the high prices, leading directly to purchase resistance. Even in price comparisons with competitors, XYZ's products appeared relatively expensive, making them feel competitively disadvantaged.

The third problem was a lack in marketing strategy. XYZ failed to effectively communicate the luxury attributes of its products to consumers. Sufficient marketing campaigns that highlighted the premium features and benefits were not executed, and consumers failed to recognize the unique value of the products, which justified the high prices.

Lastly, there were issues with internal execution. There was a lack of coordination between product launches and marketing strategies, creating a gap between market demands and the actual value offered by the products. Additionally, the system for collecting and analyzing consumer feedback was not well-established, preventing the company from responding swiftly to initial market reactions.

These issues presented core challenges that XYZ needed to overcome to successfully establish itself in the high-end market, suggesting a need for a fundamental strategic approach and improvement in execution.

XYZ can apply Daniel Kahneman's Prospect Theory, which explains irrational behaviors in consumer decision-making, particularly focusing on concepts of loss aversion and reference point setting. Kahneman found that consumers tend to perceive potential losses more significantly than gains when making economic decisions, a critical consideration when designing marketing strategies.

According to Prospect Theory, people are overly sensitive to losses, creating a strong motivation to minimize them. Applying this in marketing allows XYZ to emphasize the features and benefits of its products to mitigate perceived potential losses (e.g., cost, opportunity loss) and encourage purchases. For example, highlighting a product's unique features or the exclusive value provided by the brand can clarify the benefits consumers would miss if they do not purchase.

Additionally, the theory underscores the importance of reference points, suggesting that consumers make value judgments based on their current state or certain standards. If the reference point is positively adjusted, it can positively affect consumer purchase decisions. XYZ can use this to reset consumer reference points, further emphasizing the uniqueness and necessity of its products. For example, showcasing a particular product's unique design or features and comparing it with market competitors can elevate consumer expectations, utilizing a strategy to highlight how XYZ's products stand out.

By deeply understanding and applying Kahneman's theory, XYZ can comprehend the irrational patterns of consumer behavior and base effective marketing strategies on this understanding. These strategies can actively engage in consumer purchasing processes, using loss aversion and reference point adjustments to influence consumer actions more dynamically. This approach, which analyzes and utilizes consumer psychological patterns in marketing, will maximize product appeal and secure a successful market position for XYZ.

XYZ focused on understanding consumer psychology based on Kahneman's Prospect Theory and integrating it effectively into its marketing strategy. The company specifically targeted consumers' loss aversion tendencies, adjusting its product sales strategies and optimizing advertising campaigns accordingly.

Here is a detailed description of how XYZ implemented these psychological approaches in practice.

Firstly, XYZ adjusted its pricing policy to maximize the fear of loss perceived by consumers. The company conducted time-limited discount events for specific products, emphasizing the message "Discounted only for a limited time." This strategy highlighted the potential for imminent loss, i.e., having to pay a higher price after the discount period, thus spurring purchases. Additionally, the event imparted urgency by suggesting "You might miss out on significant benefits if you don't buy now," prompting consumers to hasten their purchasing decisions.

Secondly, XYZ utilized messages directly stimulating the psychology of loss aversion in its product advertisements. For example, in high-end appliance ads, the message "If you don't buy now, you might miss out on the benefits of the latest technology" emphasized the fear that consumers might fall behind in technological advancements. This approach focused on the potential losses consumers could experience, strongly driving their purchase decisions.

Thirdly, XYZ worked to reset consumer reference points. To this end, the company developed new marketing campaigns that highlighted the unique features and long-term benefits of its products. For example, a campaign for eco-friendly vehicles emphasized the long-term savings on fuel costs and contributions to environmental protection, presenting a new standard for consumers to consider when making car purchases. This introduced a new reference point in the consumer decision-making process and effectively utilized the psychology of loss aversion by highlighting the long-term benefits.

These strategies were focused on maximizing consumer psychological responses by applying Kahneman's Prospect Theory to actual marketing activities. XYZ was able to better understand and predict consumer purchasing patterns through this approach, effectively guiding customer behavior and improving overall sales performance.

Further exploring the intersection of psychology and marketing, here are a few additional theories worth considering:

1. Reactance Theory: This theory explains the tendency for consumers to avoid or rebel against restrictions to regain their sense of freedom. Marketers can use this theory to understand how overly aggressive sales techniques can backfire, developing more subtle and flexible approaches instead.

2. Anchoring Effect: This psychological principle explains how people rely too heavily on the first piece of information (the anchor) presented when making subsequent decisions. In marketing, understanding how the initial price presented shapes consumer price perceptions and expectations can help design more effective pricing strategies and promotions.

3. Cognitive Dissonance Theory: This theory describes the discomfort individuals experience when their behavior contradicts their beliefs or values. In marketing, using this theory can help construct messages and campaigns that assist consumers in justifying their purchasing decisions, thereby enhancing product loyalty and satisfaction.

4. Framing Effect: How information is presented can affect people's responses, even if the information is the same. Understanding and utilizing this principle can help marketers more effectively convey product information, benefits, and risks to consumers.

5. Confirmation Bias: This concept explains the tendency for people to prefer and seek information that supports their existing beliefs. Marketers can use this to create advertising messages that align with or reinforce consumers' existing beliefs, persuading them more effectively.

By studying these theories further and integrating them into marketing strategies, you can deepen your understanding of consumer psychological motives and behaviors, finely tuning your marketing approaches accordingly. This ultimately strengthens your brand and product's position in the market and deepens relationships with consumers.

5. Behavioral Economics and Marketing Strategy

Navigating the Maze of Consumer Psychology: How Behavioral Economics Revolutionizes Marketing Strategies

Behavioral economics is becoming an increasingly significant area in marketing, moving beyond the traditional economic theories that assume perfect rationality, to explore the irrational decision-making processes of humans. The actual purchase decisions of consumers extend beyond simple economic benefits to include personal emotions, social influences, and sometimes even subconscious motivations. Understanding these complex psychological processes provides marketers with a foundation to more accurately predict consumer behavior and develop highly effective marketing strategies.

One of the key concepts in behavioral economics is 'Mental Accounting,' which posits that consumers treat their finances as if they are divided into separate 'accounts,' and perceive spending differently depending on the account involved. For example, people tend to spend gift cards or money earmarked for a specific purpose more freely than regular cash. This perception is crucial for marketers when designing promotional strategies.

Another important concept is the 'Anchoring Effect,' where consumers overly rely on the first piece of information they encounter to make subsequent decisions. For instance, if a consumer sees a high initial price of a product followed by a discounted price, the discounted price appears much more attractive. Marketing strategies leveraging this effect can make consumers feel they are getting a better deal, thus encouraging purchases.

Lastly, 'Loss Aversion' is a concept that highlights humans' extreme aversion to losses, used in marketing to promote messages like "last chance" or "limited quantity." Consumers are highly sensitive to potential losses—the fear of missing out on a good deal or opportunity can powerfully drive their purchasing decisions. Strategies utilizing this are particularly effective.

Thus, behavioral economics offers powerful tools for marketers to deeply engage in the consumer purchase decision process. By predicting and understanding irrational consumer decisions, marketers can design more nuanced and effective marketing campaigns. This approach enriches marketing strategies, forms strong emotional connections with consumers, and helps build long-term customer loyalty.

Bluetech recently launched a new line of smart home devices in the market, but sales have been unexpectedly low. The company has developed products that use smart home technology to simplify users' daily lives. However, the expected market response has not materialized because consumers have not properly recognized the real value and functionality of the products.

Internal company research indicates that consumers are particularly sensitive to the high price of the products, and they do not feel that the benefits justify the cost compared to cheaper alternatives they previously used. Moreover, the features and advantages of the products have not been sufficiently publicized, and customers are struggling to justify the high prices. Particularly, they are not clearly perceiving the actual benefits these innovative features can bring to their everyday lives.

To overcome these issues, Bluetech conducted deeper market research and identified major concerns consumers have about the technology. Consumers particularly expressed anxiety about the complexity and difficulty of using the products and concerns about long-term product support. Based on this feedback, the company realized the need to enhance user-friendliness and build trust regarding product support.

This situation presents Bluetech with an opportunity to more precisely understand consumer psychology and buying motives and to recalibrate product explanations and marketing strategies accordingly. By clearly communicating the value and advantages of the products and addressing potential consumer concerns preemptively, the company can strengthen its position in the market and build long-term customer relationships.

The challenges Bluetech faces in low sales are multi-faceted and occur due to several factors:
Firstly, consumer price perception is closely linked to the problem. Bluetech's smart home devices are priced relatively high in the market, but consumers do not perceive corresponding value, likely because they are not fully aware of the unique features and long-term benefits.

Secondly, the issue is related to the user experience due to the product's complexity. Feedback from customers indicates that many are experiencing difficulties with setting up and using the product on a daily basis. This poses a significant barrier for consumers without technical backgrounds to understand and utilize the product's features.

Thirdly, market uncertainty and intensified competition are factors. Bluetech faces the challenge of showcasing unique products amidst fierce competition from other companies, which offer similar features at lower prices, leading to comparative evaluations among consumers and further weakening the perceived value of Bluetech's products.

Analyzing these issues comprehensively, Bluetech recognizes the need to re-evaluate consumer psychological perceptions and its market position, requiring an overhaul of its pricing strategy, user experience, and marketing approach. This calls for strategic changes to more effectively meet consumer and market demands.

Behavioral economics challenges traditional economic theories by emphasizing that human decisions are not always rational. Key concepts in this field that play a significant role include mental accounting, the anchoring effect, and loss aversion. These theories have been significantly developed in the research of Richard Thaler and Daniel Kahneman.

Mental Accounting, developed by Richard Thaler, describes the psychological process by which people allocate and manage funds for specific purposes like 'travel' or 'education,' affecting their spending decisions. Thaler's concept illustrates the irrationality in economic decisions, providing deep insights into how people make financial choices.

The Anchoring Effect, developed by Daniel Kahneman and Amos Tversky, explains how initial information (the anchor) heavily influences subsequent judgments or decisions. For example, consumers' price perceptions can be 'anchored' by the first price they see, affecting their later price evaluations. This is used in marketing strategies for pricing and discounting to influence consumer purchasing decisions.

Loss Aversion, another concept developed by Kahneman and Tversky, shows that people have a stronger tendency to avoid losses than to seek gains. This principle, a core part of 'Prospect Theory,' highlights consumers' heightened responses to potential losses (e.g., end of a discount, product sell-out), and is used in marketing to stimulate fear of missing out on a product or service, thus driving purchase decisions.

These concepts demonstrate how behavioral economics fundamentally contributes to marketing strategies. Mental accounting helps marketers understand how consumers categorize their spending; the anchoring effect shows how initial information can distort consumer judgment; loss aversion explains the strong consumer drive to avoid losses. Understanding and leveraging these concepts allow marketers to more effectively influence consumer purchasing behavior, shaping marketing campaigns and strategies that utilize consumers' irrational decision patterns.

Bluetech has recently begun actively using the principles of behavioral economics to better understand consumer behavior and aim for increased customer attraction and sales. The company has integrated concepts like mental accounting, the anchoring effect, and loss aversion into its marketing strategies to deeply engage in the consumer purchasing process. This approach has played a critical role in optimizing marketing messages based on actual consumer behavior patterns and has enabled strategic decisions grounded in real consumer actions.

Bluetech applied the principle of Mental Accounting by introducing a points system for product purchases, encouraging customers to perceive each point as actual cash, thereby reducing psychological resistance to using points. Customers felt that using points for additional purchases was easier than spending real money, motivating them to buy more frequently and in larger quantities. This system helped customers perceive their spending as a 'pleasurable experience,' increasing brand loyalty.

Using the Anchoring Effect, Bluetech intentionally set high initial prices for products before applying discounts. This strategy implanted the perception of high product value while making the discounted price seem like a great benefit. For example, a product originally priced at $100 might be marked at $150, then offered at 50% off, effectively making the purchase price $75. This approach made consumers feel they were achieving significant savings, stimulating their desire to purchase.

Through Loss Aversion strategies, Bluetech used messages emphasizing the urgency of product availability to spur consumer purchases. Phrases like "Limited stock available" or "Last chance" triggered fears of missing out, prompting immediate purchase decisions. This method effectively stimulated consumers' fears and loss aversion instincts, hastening their purchasing actions.

These strategies have allowed Bluetech to more effectively understand and control consumer purchasing patterns, significantly contributing to increased sales and customer loyalty. By applying the principles of behavioral economics in real business scenarios, Bluetech was able to reframe marketing messages and strategies with a profound psychological approach, deeply engaging in consumer purchase decisions and designing effective advertising campaigns.

In addition to the marketing strategies based on behavioral economics principles used by Bluetech, here are a few additional psychological theories and approaches that can be applied in marketing:

1. Narrative Advertising Strategy: This approach uses storytelling to deliver advertising content, providing an emotional connection for the consumer. Storytelling helps consumers understand and remember the content more profoundly.

2. Utilizing Confirmation Bias: This strategy leverages the tendency for consumers to prefer information that confirms their beliefs or values. For example, promoting

eco-friendly products to consumers focused on environmental protection can enhance their sense of responsibility toward the environment.

3. Using Frequency Illusion: Products that are frequently exposed are perceived to be more trustworthy and preferable. Consistent brand exposure through advertising can increase consumer awareness and preference.

4. Framing Effect: Changing the way information is presented can alter consumer interpretation and response. For example, presenting "95% success rate" instead of "5% failure rate" can significantly impact consumer perception.

5. Utilizing Expectancy Theory: This approach involves forming and meeting or exceeding consumer expectations to provide a positive brand experience. When a product or service exceeds a consumer's expectations, it can lead to high satisfaction and loyalty.

These approaches help brands build strong psychological connections with a diverse consumer base and develop effective marketing strategies. Understanding and leveraging these various psychological principles, in addition to behavioral economics, enables marketers to gain deeper consumer insights and exert substantial market influence.

6. Social Proof and the Social Influence of Information

The Power of the Majority, Social Proof: Exploring the Influence of Social Proof

Is it really plausible to think that we independently make all the choices we face, given the numerous marketing messages and advertisements we encounter daily?

Modern marketing strategies extend beyond merely communicating the functions or value of a product. They deeply engage with consumer psychology to influence purchasing decisions. In this context, the concept of 'social proof' plays a crucial role. Social proof is a psychological phenomenon where consumers observe the actions, opinions, and experiences of others and incorporate this information into their decision-making processes. This is particularly relevant when product information is scarce or uncertain, as consumers tend to reduce their uncertainty by relying on the choices made by others. This tendency is especially pronounced in online shopping, where product reviews, user ratings, and mentions on social media significantly impact purchase decisions.

The power of social proof manifests in several ways:
First, user reviews and ratings act as indirect indicators of a product's quality and satisfaction level. For instance, products with high ratings and positive reviews on online shopping platforms can engender significant trust among new purchasers.
Second, endorsements by celebrities or experts also represent strong forms of social proof. For example, kitchen gadgets recommended by a famous chef or skincare products endorsed by celebrities can exert considerable persuasive power.
Third, recommendations from friends or family are equally important. A café favored by a friend or a travel destination preferred by a family member carries weight through personal networks, providing a highly trustworthy source of information.

To effectively incorporate social proof into marketing strategies, several approaches can be considered:
First, emphasizing consumer reviews and ratings on product pages or in advertisements is crucial. This can indirectly assure new visitors of product quality and create a positive first impression.
Second, leveraging influencer marketing can enhance the perceived value and trustworthiness of a product. Influencers who use the product and share their experiences can directly influence their followers.
Third, encouraging customers to share their product experiences through social media campaigns can instantly spread positive perceptions of the brand.

Thus, social proof is an indispensable element in marketing strategies. It influences consumer purchase decisions and enhances the credibility and recognition of a brand. Marketers can strategically use this to quickly build trust with consumers and enhance the appeal of their products, providing vital cues in an information-saturated market that help consumers make the right decisions.

Recently, a mid-sized company in the beauty industry, XYZ Beauty, faced challenges in gauging consumer reactions following the launch of a new product line and marketing strategy. Despite the introduction of a premium skincare line, the company recorded lower-than-expected sales in a highly competitive beauty market. XYZ Beauty's products struggled to stand out against established brands.

The company discovered through its market research that consumers primarily consider the experiences and reviews of others when making product choices, especially on online shopping platforms and social media. However, there were few online reviews for XYZ Beauty’s new products, and the initial feedback from consumers generally fell short of expectations.

Moreover, although XYZ Beauty attempted to boost product awareness through famous influencers, this strategy had limited success. This was partly because the influencers might not have genuinely engaged with the product or because their followers doubted the authenticity of the endorsements.

In this situation, XYZ Beauty realized the need for a more strategic approach to address these issues, focusing more on the psychological factors of consumer behavior and the importance of social proof. The company recognized the need to build genuine social proof and actively use reliable consumer feedback to strengthen its market position.

If we analyze the core issues XYZ Beauty faced, several key factors emerge:

First, the failure to differentiate its products was a significant problem. With many skincare products already on the market, XYZ Beauty's new items lacked meaningful distinctions from existing products, causing consumers to hesitate in switching to a new brand.

Second, a lack of consumer trust also contributed to the problem. If a new product has few reviews and the initial feedback is negative or lukewarm, this can negatively impact other potential customers' purchasing decisions. Online consumer reviews and ratings are crucial for the success of new products, and XYZ Beauty's items did not perform well in this area.

Third, the inadequacy of the marketing strategy was also to blame. The limited effectiveness of influencer marketing might have been due to insufficient trust-building between influencers and consumers. If influencers merely promoted the products without genuine endorsements, their recommendations might not have seemed authentic.

Fourth, failing to adequately reflect the rapidly changing market and diverse consumer needs was also a significant issue. Companies that cannot promptly respond to evolving consumer demands may fall behind in competitive markets.

These problems suggest significant hurdles that XYZ Beauty needs to overcome to successfully establish itself in the market. The company needs to develop strategies that address these issues and enhance consumer trust and satisfaction.

The theory of social proof is based on the research of psychologist Robert Cialdini, as outlined in his book "Influence: The Psychology of Persuasion." This principle explains the tendency of people to refer to the actions of others in uncertain situations and consider these actions as the 'right behavior.' Cialdini, a professor at Arizona State University, has conducted significant research in social psychology.

His theory has not only remained relevant in academic research but has also become a crucial tool in understanding and predicting human decisions and behaviors in business environments, particularly in marketing and advertising. The concept of social proof is based on the idea that consumers consider other people's reviews, evaluations, and recommendations when choosing products, which helps them feel more confident and assured in their decisions.

This background knowledge enables marketers to deeply engage in the consumer decision-making process and strategically manipulate it to their advantage. For example, emphasizing consumer reviews and ratings on product pages in online shopping platforms can build trust with new visitors and foster a positive perception of the products. This approach is important for understanding consumer psychological perceptions and adjusting marketing strategies accordingly, thereby enhancing brand credibility and building lasting relationships with consumers.

In the case of Bluetech, the company faced marketing challenges and sought to strategically utilize the principle of social proof to overcome consumer uncertainty and hesitation. Bluetech implemented various marketing strategies to address customers' uncertainties about the authenticity and effectiveness of their products, each having a profound impact on consumer psychological behavior.

As a first strategy, Bluetech launched a major campaign emphasizing product reviews and ratings on online platforms. The company prominently featured real user reviews and high ratings on product pages and online advertisements, indirectly certifying the reliability of their products to new visitors. Since these reviews were based on actual consumer experiences, they were able to instill strong confidence in new customers and significantly contributed to building a positive image of the product.

As a second strategy, Bluetech strengthened its collaboration with influential influencers. The company utilized well-known influencers in the industry to promote its products and shared their product usage on social media, thereby significantly impacting their followers. This strategy ensured that the personal endorsements by influencers acted as trustworthy evidence, enhancing the positive perception of the product.

Thirdly, the company encouraged ordinary consumers to share their product usage experiences through social media campaigns. This campaign enabled consumers to share their honest experiences, and the content generated in this process served as strong evidence of the actual effects and satisfaction levels of the product. Such user-generated content, being voluntary and authentic, played a crucial role in new customers trusting the product and ultimately making a purchase decision.

These strategies, all based on the principle of social proof, played important roles in the consumer decision-making process. They significantly contributed to building trust among consumers and strengthening the positive perception of the product, enabling the company to successfully achieve its marketing goals. This approach effectively reduced consumer uncertainty and quickly built trust in the product.

Based on the strategies used in the Bluetech case, further approaches worth considering include:

1. Case Studies and Success Stories: Develop content that detailedly introduces successful case studies of the product or service. This content can show the effects and value of the product or service with tangible results, enhancing credibility.

2. Utilization of Video Content: Convey consumer experiences vividly through videos showing users interacting with products or services. This can have a significant impact on social media, offering intuitive insights into users' real reactions and satisfaction levels.

3. Community Building: Create online forums or communities where product users can exchange opinions and communicate with each other. In these spaces, users can share their experiences and ask questions, providing feedback on new products.

4. Experience Marketing Events: Operate events or pop-up stores where consumers can directly experience and evaluate products. These direct experiences can strongly influence consumer purchasing decisions.

5. Educational Content Marketing: Provide educational content related to products or services to help consumers better understand and use them. This information

provision emphasizes the necessity and utility of the product, building consumer trust.

6. Use of Digital Certification Marks: Display customer satisfaction, security certifications, and quality assurance marks on product pages or advertisements to indirectly enhance product trustworthiness. These certifications are critical factors that enable consumers to confidently choose a product.

These strategies, utilizing the principle of social proof, can positively influence the consumer purchasing process and contribute to enhancing brand trust and competitiveness in the market.

7. Customer Loyalty and Psychological Biases

Deep Understanding of Loyalty Through the Lens of Psychology: The Psychology Behind Customer Loyalty that Moves Brands

Customer loyalty transcends the mere quality of products or excellence of service. It is a complex phenomenon intertwined with psychological tendencies and emotional connections, crucial for the long-term success of a business. This chapter explores why customers develop deep loyalty towards specific brands and how marketing professionals can understand and enhance this loyalty. We will examine psychological biases and customer behavior patterns to see how they can be integrated into marketing strategies.

Loyalty includes more than just satisfaction—it involves a strong emotional bond. This bond stems from positive feelings, trust, and deep attachment that customers feel towards a brand. Such emotional connections can be clearer through the lens of psychological biases, which deeply influence how customers process information and make decisions. For example, confirmation bias explains the tendency of customers to actively seek positive information about a preferred brand while ignoring negative data. This provides a mechanism that keeps customers loyal to a brand they once favored, continuously harboring positive feelings.

With this psychological understanding, marketers can implement personalized marketing strategies that match each customer's psychological profile. This can include customized emails, targeted ads, and product recommendations based on past purchase data. Such strategies enhance loyalty, foster sustained attachment to the brand, and ultimately lead to long-term customer retention and high satisfaction levels.

Customer loyalty is a critical element for business success. Through a robust understanding of psychological biases and emotional connections, marketers can more effectively move customers' hearts and build lasting relationships with the brand.

In the digital age, the approach to building customer loyalty may differ from traditional methods. Social media and online platforms allow for more frequent and direct interactions between customers and brands, significantly impacting loyalty formation. For instance, forming online communities or providing interactive content can engage customers and build long-term relationships. Immediate feedback and reviews on digital platforms also provide social proof to new visitors, leading to trust and loyalty.

Zeta Electronics, a global company known for its innovative technology and user-friendly designs, has faced increased competition in recent years, making it challenging to maintain customer loyalty. Particularly in the smart device market, emerging competitors have attracted Zeta's customers to other brands.

Analysis shows that Zeta Electronics particularly struggles with retaining younger consumers who tend to prefer competitors perceived as more innovative or offering better value. Although Zeta's products are high-quality, many consumers feel a lack of emotional messaging and connection with the brand.

The challenge of customer loyalty has economically impacted Zeta Electronics, leading to direct sales declines as repeat purchase rates decrease. The marketing team has attempted various strategies to boost loyalty, but beyond short-term promotions and discounts, they struggle to find effective long-term solutions.

Recognizing the need for a deeper understanding of customer behavior and psychological biases, Zeta Electronics plans an in-depth analysis to integrate these insights into its marketing strategies. This will help strengthen brand loyalty and minimize brand switching among younger consumers.

The issues Zeta Electronics faces with customer loyalty largely stem from intense market competition, a disconnect between brand messages and customer emotions, and inconsistency in product experiences. Competitors entering the market quickly with innovative technologies and competitive pricing have an advantage, particularly attracting price-sensitive younger consumers.

Moreover, there's a misalignment between Zeta's brand messaging and consumers' emotional needs. Many feedback that the company's smart devices are complex and not user-friendly, pointing to a lack of consistency in the user experience.

These problems lead directly to decreased customer loyalty, with negative experiences accumulating and increasing distrust in the brand. This dissatisfaction spreads quickly through social media and online reviews, negatively affecting potential customers' buying decisions. Thus, Zeta Electronics needs to enhance product quality, customer experience, and consistency in brand messaging.

Exploring psychological theories applicable to Zeta Electronics' situation, understanding biases like confirmation bias, status quo bias, and groupthink is crucial. These biases significantly affect customer decisions and loyalty.

Confirmation bias leads consumers to prefer information that confirms their existing beliefs and values, ignoring negative information. This bias means that once customers have a positive experience with a brand, they are likely to continue reinforcing their positive impression. To strategically use this bias, Zeta Electronics needs to consistently provide positive brand experiences, actively promote positive feedback through social media and online platforms, and encourage customers to maintain a good impression of the brand.

Status quo bias shows consumers' reluctance to change from products or services they already use, reflecting a tendency to maintain current situations over trying new options. By understanding this, Zeta can update its products while maintaining familiar features, easing customers into new changes without resistance.

Groupthink involves consumers making decisions influenced by the opinions or actions of those around them. Often, people want to ensure their choices are accepted by the majority. To leverage this in marketing strategies, Zeta Electronics can strengthen influencer marketing and customer endorsement campaigns to create positive social proof and enhance brand trust.

These strategies, based on understanding psychological biases, allow Zeta Electronics to increase customer loyalty and build long-term relationships. By focusing on these approaches, the company hopes to strengthen emotional connections with customers and maintain a positive perception of the brand.

To further explore customer loyalty and psychological biases, let's introduce some theories and concepts:
- Endowment Effect: This theory suggests that people value what they already own over what they don't. It's a psychological factor that fosters strong loyalty once a customer purchases a brand.
- Framing Effect: Decision-making can vary based on how information is presented. Marketers can influence customer choices through positive or negative framing, affecting loyalty formation.
- Self-consistency Theory: Individuals tend to maintain consistency with their previous actions. According to this theory, once a consumer chooses a specific brand, they are likely to continue choosing it to justify their initial decision.
- Availability Heuristic: People consider information that is easily recalled as more important. Marketers can use this heuristic to keep their brand top of mind, enhancing loyalty.
- Law of Imitation: People tend to mimic the actions of others. This is related to social proof but particularly focuses on following cultural trends or popular behaviors. If a brand leads these trends, it can further increase customer loyalty.

Through these theories, marketers can more effectively understand customer psychology and develop strategies to enhance loyalty.

8. Experiential Marketing and Pine & Gilmore's Experience Economy

Awakening the Senses: Experiential Marketing

In today's era, consumers value the experience during the purchasing process beyond just acquiring products or services. Understanding and leveraging this shift is crucial for businesses, and Pine & Gilmore's theory of the Experience Economy insightfully explains how companies can achieve a unique market position and competitive advantage by offering meaningful experiences that transcend physical products or services. The goal of the Experience Economy is to provide experiences that leave a deep impression on consumers' emotions and memories, which is vital for deepening the emotional connection between businesses and consumers and building long-term loyalty.

Pine & Gilmore describe an evolution of the economy from a goods-based to a service-based, and now to an experience-based economy, where consumers no longer pay merely for products or services. Instead, they invest in experiences that positively affect their emotions and memories, seeking deeper satisfaction and value. Companies that understand this shift can enhance their brand image and carve out a unique space in the market by offering customized, emotionally engaging experiences.

The strategies of experiential marketing vary, but they are centered around personalization and engagement. Companies provide direct and personal experiences through events, pop-up stores, and user engagement campaigns, which stimulate consumer emotions and leave memorable impressions. These strategies encourage consumers to share their experiences on social media, amplifying the impact and strengthening customer relationships. Additionally, businesses use data analytics to understand consumer preferences and provide tailored experiences that increase satisfaction and enhance brand loyalty.

Successful marketing in the Experience Economy is designed to make every moment special for the consumer, ensuring each experience positively affects their emotions and memories. This approach goes beyond selling products, playing a crucial role in forming strong emotional connections and building long-term relationships, thereby contributing significantly to sustainable business growth.

In the contemporary marketing landscape, experience-centered strategies have become crucial for maintaining consumer interest and loyalty. However, not all companies effectively implement these strategies. For instance, ElectroMax, a major appliance company, recently aimed to enhance consumer experiences through various experiential marketing strategies but faced unexpected challenges.

ElectroMax has been focusing on selling high-end appliances and takes pride in the quality and technological prowess of its products. The company recently enhanced the shopping experience by hosting large-scale pop-up events and offering virtual reality (VR) product experiences. These events were designed to allow customers to directly interact with products, providing a deep understanding of the features and usage.

However, these strategies faced several significant challenges:
Firstly, customer engagement levels were lower than expected. Many customers were not sufficiently aware of the events or VR experiences, and feedback indicated inadequate promotion.
Secondly, some customers encountered technical issues during the VR experience, leading to negative impressions. These problems resulted in ElectroMax failing to provide the positive customer experiences it had hoped for through experiential marketing.

These issues demonstrate that ElectroMax overlooked critical factors in planning and executing experiential marketing:
First, large-scale events and high-tech experiences can lead to negative customer experiences without adequate preparation and testing.
Second, experiential marketing strategies require more than just hosting events; they necessitate careful planning and customer management to truly draw engagement and embed a positive perception of the brand.

Ultimately, for experiential marketing strategies like those of ElectroMax to succeed, clear goal setting, effective customer communication, technical preparedness, and active solicitation and incorporation of customer feedback are crucial. Managing and improving these elements systematically is key to the success of experiential marketing.

A deeper analysis of ElectroMax's experiential marketing strategy issues shows that the problems mainly stemmed from inadequate planning and execution, technical unpreparedness, and poor management of consumer psychological expectations.

The first major issue was lack of customer engagement, with ElectroMax failing to adequately promote its experiential marketing events, especially through digital channels and social media. This resulted in poor event attendance and ineffective marketing messages that did not convey the value of the experiences.

The second issue was the failure in the technical aspects of the experiences, such as VR. Events involving new technologies require substantial technical support and pre-testing.
However, ElectroMax did not adequately prepare for these technical aspects, leading to technical errors that disappointed participants and negatively impacted the overall brand image. These technical issues degraded the quality of the experience and significantly lowered customer satisfaction.

The third major cause was poor management of customer psychological biases and expectations. Customers exhibit confirmation bias, seeking information that confirms their beliefs and ignoring contradictory data.
ElectroMax's initial negative customer experiences reinforced negative brand perceptions due to this bias. Additionally, insufficient information and support during the introduction of new technologies increased customer anxiety and dissatisfaction.

To resolve these issues, ElectroMax must thoroughly review its marketing strategies, seek more effective ways to enhance customer engagement, allocate more resources to technical preparation, and actively manage customer

expectations and psychological biases to ensure the success of its experiential marketing efforts.
These improvements can enhance customer satisfaction and, in the long run, increase brand loyalty.

A deeper understanding of experiential marketing and the Experience Economy theory is provided by Joseph Pine and James Gilmore in their book "The Experience Economy." They emphasize the importance of experiences in the modern economy and offer ways to integrate this into marketing strategies. Their theory explains how the experience itself can become a critical selling point, suggesting that companies should sell experiences beyond products or services.

According to Pine and Gilmore, the economy has evolved to a stage where it provides memorable experiences to consumers, classifying economic development into goods, services, and experiences, with each stage offering deeper emotional value to consumers. In the Experience Economy, consumers perceive the experience as the product and seek emotional satisfaction through it.

This theory plays a vital role in marketing strategies. Companies should design experiences that go beyond simple products or services to engage consumers emotionally. This helps form a strong emotional bond with the brand, leading to brand loyalty and long-term customer relationships.

Experiential marketing involves activities where consumers participate and interact directly, such as attending brand-hosted events or activities, making them feel part of the brand, and leaving a lasting impression in their memories. Moreover, these experiences can influence other consumers through social media sharing, strengthening the brand's market position.

The advancement of digital technology has significantly expanded the scope of experiential marketing. Virtual reality (VR), augmented reality (AR), and interactive platforms offer consumers new experiences that combine real and virtual elements. For example, technology that allows consumers to experience products through VR or place products virtually in their homes using AR maximizes the quality of the experience. These technologies have a strong impact on consumer buying decisions, particularly appealing to younger consumers. A digital experiential marketing example is IKEA's AR app, 'IKEA Place,' which lets users virtually place furniture in their space via a mobile device, allowing them to experience what it would look like before making a purchase.

Pine and Gilmore's Experience Economy theory provides an essential framework for companies to develop and execute experience-centered marketing strategies. By applying this theory, marketers can explore creative and innovative marketing approaches that leave a deep impression on consumers' emotions and memories, serving as a successful differentiation strategy in competitive markets.

Applying the Experience Economy theory to address the challenges faced by ElectroMax is crucial for the company to provide meaningful experiences and gain a competitive edge. Although ElectroMax attempted to engage customers emotionally through pop-up events and VR experiences, multiple execution issues prevented the desired outcomes. The success of experiential marketing relies not just on technical execution but on creating emotional connections and lasting impressions.

Firstly, ElectroMax needs to improve communication with customers to raise awareness of its events and VR experiences. Social media campaigns, targeted email marketing, and online advertising should be employed to promote events, making it easier for customers to access and participate in these experiences. Additionally, adequate market research and customer feedback collection are essential before the event to meet expectations and enhance the experience.

While the role of technology in experiential marketing is important, technology alone is insufficient. When utilizing technologies like VR experiences, thorough testing is necessary to ensure smooth customer experiences, and precautions must be taken to prevent technical issues from impairing the customer experience. It is also vital to monitor customer feedback in real-time at every stage of the event or experience and to have systems in place to respond immediately to any issues.

To strengthen emotional connections, ElectroMax should provide personalized experiences that appeal to customers' emotions. This can be achieved by analyzing customer data to offer content and promotions tailored to individual preferences and behavior patterns. For example, personalized product recommendations or customized promotions can be provided based on the products a customer has shown interest in in the past.

Finally, the success of experiential marketing depends on building ongoing relationships. Beyond creating a one-time impression through events or experiences, it is crucial to continue engaging with customers post-event and actively incorporate their feedback into marketing strategies. This ensures that customers maintain a positive image of the brand and continue their relationship with it.

There are various theories and approaches worth exploring further in experiential marketing. Understanding these concepts can help companies design richer and more effective consumer experiences:

1. Emotional Branding: Developed by Marc Gobé, this theory argues that brands must connect directly with consumers' emotions. Emotional branding focuses on how a product or service meets consumers' psychological and emotional needs.

2. Service Design: This approach applies user-centered thinking to the process of designing services, exploring ways to optimize user experience. Service design aims to ensure that customer experiences are consistent and positive at all touchpoints.

3. Storytelling Marketing: A method of building emotional connections with consumers by effectively conveying a brand's story. Storytelling allows customers to discover personal meaning and value in their relationship with the brand.

4. Multisensory Marketing: A strategy that enhances the brand experience by engaging all of a consumer's senses. It enriches the consumer experience through sight, sound, taste, touch, and smell, strengthening brand memory.

5. Sensory Marketing: Similar to multisensory marketing, sensory marketing creates strong brand connections by stimulating consumers' senses. It is particularly effective in retail environments, for example, by integrating specific scents or sounds to enhance the

shopping experience.

These theories and strategies can assist companies in increasing consumer loyalty and enhancing competitiveness in the market. Each approach focuses on forming deep psychological connections with customers and positively influencing their decision-making processes.

9. Marketing Communication and Mehrabian's 7%-38%-55% Rule

The Magic of the Message: Nonverbal Elements and Mehrabian's Rule

Understanding the psychological aspects of communication is a crucial skill for marketing professionals. Albert Mehrabian's 7%-38%-55% rule is considered a significant theory in this area. This rule illuminates that only 7% of the communication effectiveness in conveying messages is attributed to the choice of words, while 38% is influenced by the tone of voice and 55% by nonverbal elements. This insight suggests that when designing messages, attention should not solely focus on the linguistic content but also on how the message is expressed and delivered.

According to Mehrabian's rule, successful marketing communication plays a vital role in forming emotional connections with consumers. In advertising or brand communications, nonverbal cues that evoke positive emotions can critically impact consumers' perceptions and attitudes. This is particularly important in visual media advertising, where the brand's image and message's reception significantly depend on nonverbal elements. Marketers, therefore, need to effectively manage and utilize these nonverbal elements to maximize the impact of their messages.

Moreover, this rule can be applied in various marketing activities such as social media interactions, video content production, and advertising design. For instance, in video content, the tone of voice or background music can manipulate consumers' emotions, and in social media, real-time feedback and interactions can draw emotional responses from customers.

This approach enables companies to build deep emotional connections with consumers and enhance competitiveness in the market. Ultimately, Mehrabian's rule reminds marketers of the importance of nonverbal elements in influencing consumer emotions and behavior, providing a crucial standard for developing insightful communication strategies. This psychological approach contributes to forming lasting relationships with consumers and enhancing long-term brand loyalty.

Fashion Forward, an apparel brand, has introduced various experiential marketing strategies to attract the attention of a young consumer base. These include online video ads, Instagram live sessions, and interactive website features aimed at projecting a youthful and active brand image. These campaigns are designed to provide direct and personal experiences that deepen consumers' understanding of the products.

However, these strategies have faced issues in being effectively implemented. First, the visual and auditory elements used in online video ads sometimes confused consumers or hindered the transmission of the message. For example, excessively loud background music in advertisements prevented important messages from being heard. Additionally, the expressions of the models in videos sometimes appeared exaggerated or inconsistent with the brand image, undermining consumer trust.

Instagram live events also encountered similar issues. Technical problems frequently interrupted events, significantly reducing participants' enthusiasm and interest. Attempts at real-time interaction with consumers sometimes faltered due to the presenters' lack of preparation or inappropriate responses, leading to doubts about the brand's professionalism.

These scenarios show that despite Fashion Forward's intentions to aggressively adopt experiential marketing, inadequate preparation and inappropriate communication techniques at the execution stage impaired the consumer experience. These efforts ultimately left a negative perception of the brand, revealing significant oversights that Fashion Forward needs to address to strengthen its competitiveness in the market.

The main reasons for the lack of success in Fashion Forward's experiential marketing strategies stem from several complex factors:

First, inadequate market research and consumer analysis at the planning stage were central issues. Fashion Forward failed to accurately grasp the preferences and expectations of young consumers, and there was a mismatch between the experiences consumers actually wanted and what the brand tried to provide.

Second, there were issues in the delivery method of communication. According to Mehrabian's 7%-38%-55% rule, where nonverbal elements play a major part in communication, Fashion Forward's video ads and live events lacked effective use of voice tone, gestures, and facial expressions. Excessive background music and exaggerated acting in ads damaged the authenticity of the message and reduced consumer trust.

Third, there were failures in technical execution. While technology is a critical component of experiential marketing, Fashion Forward did not meet the high technical demands of experiences like VR. Technical glitches severely hindered user experience and left a negative first impression of the brand. These technical issues prevented consumers from fully immersing themselves in the experience, diminishing the overall effectiveness.

Fourth, inadequate promotion of marketing strategies was a contributing issue. Fashion Forward did not conduct sufficient promotion and consumer education for events and VR experiences. This lack of awareness among the target consumer base resulted in low participation rates.

These analyses indicate that the problems Fashion Forward encountered stemmed from a lack of meticulous preparation and systematic approach in planning and executing experiential marketing, providing important lessons for future strategy adjustments and improvements.

Applying Albert Mehrabian's 7%-38%-55% rule, which focuses on the importance of nonverbal elements in communication effectiveness, can guide Fashion Forward in addressing these challenges. This rule, initially focused on face-to-face interactions, is broadly applicable in marketing communication, especially in advertising and brand messaging, emphasizing the need for marketers to consider emotional components when designing communications.

Thus, every advertising campaign Fashion Forward undertakes, particularly in video and social media content creation, should carefully consider the tone of voice and nonverbal elements. For instance, the gestures, facial expressions, and tone of voice of actors in video ads can play a crucial role in reinforcing the brand image and moving consumer emotions.

Moreover, as experiential marketing events involve real-time interactions, training staff in nonverbal communication skills is essential. Event presenters or sales staff who interact positively with customers, using a friendly and warm tone of voice and welcoming gestures, can significantly enhance the customer experience and leave a positive impression of the brand.

The importance of nonverbal elements in digital communication, especially in social media and online advertising, continues to grow. Nonverbal elements in digital media include images, videos, emoticons, and animations, which convey emotional nuances difficult to express in text, attract consumer attention, and elicit strong emotional responses. For example, background music and character expressions in video ads significantly influence how consumers receive the message. Digital age marketers can carefully combine these nonverbal elements to build deep emotional connections with consumers.

Mehrabian's theory aids marketers in understanding consumer psychology and developing methods to effectively appeal to emotions, enabling Fashion Forward to establish more successful communication strategies and enhance emotional connections, thereby increasing consumer loyalty. This approach plays a crucial role in building lasting emotional connections with consumers, ultimately contributing to increased brand preference and loyalty.

By deeply understanding and integrating Mehrabian's 7%-38%-55% rule into its marketing strategies, Fashion Forward can strengthen emotional connections with consumers through video advertising, social media interactions, and personalized marketing messages. This theory highlights the role of nonverbal elements in communication, which significantly influences consumer psychological responses. The challenges Fashion Forward faced were due to low customer engagement and negative experiences resulting from technical issues. To overcome these, the company needs to approach each advertising element with a focus on maximizing emotional impact.

In video advertising, the choice of voice tone and background music should be carefully selected to ensure consumers feel positive emotions. A soft, friendly tone of voice can instill trust, and upbeat, lively background music can effectively convey the energy of the product. Additionally, the gestures and expressions of actors should be natural and approachable, significantly influencing consumer impressions of the product and brand.

In using social media for interaction, real-time events and direct communication are crucial. Introducing products through live streaming and responding promptly to customer inquiries can strengthen real-time connections with customers. Such interactions make customers feel more attached to the brand and contribute to building trust and loyalty.

Personalized marketing analyzes individual customer preferences and behavior to provide tailored communications, creating stronger emotional connections. Targeting based on past purchase data and interactions offers a personalized experience, making consumers respond more positively to the brand.

Through these strategies, Fashion Forward can systematically apply Mehrabian's rule to maximize effectiveness across communication channels. Moving beyond mere information transmission, a communication style that stimulates emotions and drives consumer behavior is crucial for successfully establishing the brand image and securing long-term customer loyalty.

Several theories and concepts can assist in deepening marketing communication and emotional connections, diversifying marketing strategies, and strengthening relationships between brands and consumers:

1. Emotional Contagion Theory: This theory explains that people unconsciously mimic others' emotions, experiencing these emotions through mimicry. In marketing, applying this can convey positive emotions through ads or content to induce emotional responses in consumers.

2. Storytelling Marketing: Powerful stories can touch consumers and evoke emotional responses. Storytelling marketing builds deep emotional connections with consumers through stories surrounding the brand and products.

3. Behavioral Design: This design approach focuses on designing and predicting user behavior. Understanding various psychological factors that influence consumer behavior and incorporating these into product design can guide consumer actions.

4. Multisensory Marketing: This marketing approach stimulates all five senses of the consumer to provide a deeper brand experience. For example, integrating visual elements, sounds, and scents can enhance immersion and create memorable experiences.

5. Research in Consumer Psychology and Behavioral Economics: Continuously exploring and applying the latest research and case studies helps understand changing consumer behavior patterns and develop corresponding strategies.

These approaches can help companies design brand messages and communication strategies more effectively, positively influencing consumer emotions and behavior. Each strategy can play a crucial role in securing a unique market position for the brand and building sustainable relationships with consumers.

10. Digital Marketing and Online Behavioral Psychology

Navigating the Maze of Online Behavior: Psychological Marketing in the Digital Age

Marketing in the digital era starts with understanding consumer behavior and psychology. As technology advances rapidly, online consumer behavior becomes increasingly diverse and unpredictable. Companies face significant challenges in grasping consumer psychology and devising effective marketing strategies tailored to these complexities. Influencing consumers now transcends mere message delivery, requiring deep psychological understanding and sophisticated data analysis.

The behavior of online consumers is rapidly evolving, and understanding their psychological motivations and patterns is central to digital marketing strategies. Online behavioral psychology studies why consumers act in certain ways and what factors motivate their decisions. Concepts like cognitive dissonance, the psychology of rewards, and FOMO (Fear of Missing Out) are applied to explain consumers' decision-making processes online.

Digital marketing strategies build on this psychological understanding to forge deep connections with consumers. For example, personalized advertising crafted through data analysis or content that encourages consumer participation can foster strong community ties. Such strategies increase consumer engagement, promote positive emotions towards the brand, and ultimately lead to purchases.

Digital marketing transcends mere technology use, playing a crucial role in deeply understanding and predicting consumer psychological patterns and behaviors. This is essential for brands to maintain competitiveness and build sustainable relationships with consumers. Such approaches support brands in effectively responding to consumers' evolving needs and expectations, and are critical in determining the success of marketing strategies.

TechForward, a leader in innovative electronic products, recently attempted to enhance its digital marketing strategy. Targeting young consumers, the company rolled out new social media campaigns and advertising strategies, but unexpectedly, consumer engagement and response were low. For instance, campaigns for the latest smartphones emphasized advanced features, yet consumers preferred practical aspects or everyday usability.

Furthermore, TechForward's website and online shopping experience were not user-friendly, often causing inconvenience, especially for mobile users. The complex structure, slow page loading times, and non-intuitive user interfaces led to consumers struggling to find information and frequently abandoning the purchase process, which ultimately decreased overall conversion rates and negatively affected potential customers' experiences.

Additionally, TechForward's advertising and promotional activities failed to consider consumers' emotional responses, focusing instead on technical details and product specifications, which did not sufficiently inspire consumers. The content and format of digital ads did not align with consumers' emotional needs or lifestyles, significantly diminishing the effectiveness of the messages.

To address these issues, TechForward needed to adopt analytical tools and data-driven approaches to more accurately understand and predict consumer online behavior. The company endeavored to thoroughly analyze consumer data to grasp preferences, behavior patterns, and purchasing paths, focusing on developing more effective personalized marketing strategies. During this process, principles of online behavioral psychology were actively integrated to enhance emotional connections with consumers and build trust.

The main reasons for TechForward's digital marketing strategy failures stemmed from several complex factors:
First, the company's marketing communications failed to adequately capture the psychological needs and emotional responses of consumers. While the advertising campaigns highlighted the technical specifications and advanced features of

products, they lacked practical information that could solve everyday problems faced by consumers. This prevented the formation of an emotional connection with the product, leading to lower conversion rates.

Second, TechForward's website and online shopping experience were not user-friendly. The complex structure and slow loading times significantly inconvenienced especially mobile users, leading them to easily drop out of the purchase process and switch to competitors offering faster and simpler services. The non-intuitive user interface also made it difficult for consumers to find and compare products, posing a major issue.

Third, inadequate promotion and information provision in marketing activities caused problems. TechForward's marketing events, such as popup events or VR experiences, proceeded without sufficient prior promotion, leaving many potential customers unaware of the events' existence. This led to low participation rates and minimal effectiveness relative to the marketing resources invested.

Fourth, technical issues related to discomfort negatively impacted customer satisfaction. Especially in VR experiences, technical faults prevented consumers from having a smooth experience, leading to negative perceptions of the brand. The lack of adequate technical preparation and testing was a major factor hindering consumer experience.

These issues suggest that TechForward needs to rethink its experiential marketing strategy and adjust its marketing approach to better meet consumers' psychological needs and technical requirements. Particularly in the digital age, understanding consumer psychological responses and devising appropriate marketing strategies is crucial for enhancing consumer engagement and brand loyalty.

One psychological theory critical in understanding and predicting consumer behavior in digital marketing is 'Cognitive Dissonance Theory,' developed by Leon Festinger. This theory explains the psychological discomfort people experience when there is a lack of consistency among their beliefs, attitudes, and behaviors. To alleviate this discomfort, individuals strive to harmonize these elements. In digital marketing, applying this theory can help reinforce brand loyalty by providing content that helps consumers justify their purchase decisions. For example, continuously providing information on how an environmentally friendly product contributes to environmental protection can reassure consumers that their purchase decision is correct.

Another important theory is 'The Psychology of Rewards,' which originates from behaviorist psychology and discusses how rewards can reinforce behavior. In digital marketing, combining this with gamification elements can drive consumer engagement and build long-term brand loyalty. For example, providing points or discount coupons when consumers write product reviews or promote the brand on social media can strengthen positive emotions towards the brand through positive rewards.

'FOMO (Fear of Missing Out)' is also effectively used in digital marketing. This concept, which involves the fear of missing out on experiences others are having, can be leveraged by marketers to prompt urgent purchases by promoting special discounts or exclusive products available only for a limited time. This strategy is particularly effective in prompting quick purchase decisions online.

These theories are valuable tools for understanding and predicting consumer psychological responses in the digital environment. By basing strategies on this psychological understanding, marketers can more effectively guide online consumer behavior and foster positive interactions with the brand, leading to transformative changes that culminate in purchases and competitive advantage in the digital era.

TechForward successfully integrated these psychological approaches into its revised digital marketing strategy, solving various issues and maximizing consumer engagement. The application of each psychological theory will be examined in detail:

First, TechForward revamped its advertising campaigns to minimize the cognitive dissonance experienced by consumers. Previously, the messages focused on the advanced features of products, which many consumers found difficult to relate to everyday usage. The new strategy included scenarios showing actual consumers using the products, emphasizing the direct benefits consumers could gain from using them. For example, instead of merely listing camera specs in a smartphone ad, real-life examples were shown illustrating how users could easily and beautifully capture significant moments. This approach helped consumers understand how to effectively use the product and enhanced their satisfaction post-purchase.

Second, TechForward designed campaigns that leveraged consumers' 'Fear of Missing Out (FOMO)' to stimulate purchase decisions. The company periodically conducted exclusive discount events or special sales available for a limited time. These events were promoted through social media and email marketing, emphasizing the message that acting immediately was necessary to avoid missing out on substantial benefits. This strategy provided a strong motivation for immediate purchases, leading to an overall increase in sales.

Third, TechForward utilized the power of social proof to influence consumer purchase decisions significantly. The company prominently displayed customer reviews and ratings on product pages and actively showcased positive evaluations of new products. Additionally, videos and case studies sharing real user experiences were shared to substantiate the practical value of the products. This information provided new visitors with a sense of trust and enhanced their affinity for the products.

Finally, TechForward employed advanced data analytics to understand each consumer's behavior patterns and preferences, basing personalized marketing messages on this information. For example, tailored recommendations were provided based on the types of products consumers had shown interest in the past. This personalized approach captivated consumer interest and played a crucial role in enhancing brand loyalty.

By integrating these various psychological strategies, TechForward maximized the effectiveness of its digital marketing and established a foundation for successfully competing in the challenging digital environment. This approach significantly increased consumer engagement, improved conversion rates, and played a decisive role in building strong relationships between the brand and consumers.

If you're interested in digital marketing and online behavioral psychology, you can explore additional psychological theories and approaches not included in the main content. These theories can deepen your marketing strategies and enhance your understanding of consumer behavior:

1. Information Processing Theory: This theory focuses on how consumers collect, process, and store information. Understanding how digital content affects consumers' cognitive processes can help design more effective messages and advertisements.

2. Priming Effect: This psychological effect explains how certain stimuli can condition people's responses or behaviors. Marketers can use priming to shape specific perceptions or expectations that influence consumer purchase decisions.

3. Motivation Theory: This theory studies the internal and external factors that motivate people to engage in specific behaviors. It is useful in designing incentives in digital marketing campaigns to prompt consumer action.

4. Social Learning Theory: Developed by Albert Bandura, this theory emphasizes that people learn by observing and mimicking the behaviors of others. It can be applied to designing influencer marketing strategies on social media.

5. Affect Theory: This theory studies how consumers' emotions affect their behavior and decisions. Understanding and applying emotional messaging in advertising can build stronger customer relationships through emotional connections.

Modern digital marketing strategies leverage the power of AI and big data to more precisely analyze and predict consumer psychology. AI analyzes consumer data to generate personalized marketing messages, while big data identifies patterns in consumer behavior to optimize marketing strategies. For example, AI analyzes a customer's purchase history and online behavior to recommend products they are most likely to be interested in, helping increase customer satisfaction and repeat purchases. Big data-driven marketing strategies quickly identify market trends and adjust marketing campaigns in real-time, effectively reaching consumers.

These psychological theories add depth to the design and execution of digital marketing strategies and help strengthen connections with consumers. Combining each theory with current digital trends to develop new insights and strategies is recommended.

III. Product Development and Psychology

Mastering Psychology in Product Development

Product development is not merely a culmination of technology; it's a creative process deeply connected with consumer psychology. Appropriately integrating psychological principles can stimulate a consumer's psyche, inducing strong emotional reactions and fostering deep loyalty. In the complex and fast-evolving modern market, capturing the consumer's heart has become not just an option but a necessity.

This chapter deeply explores how at the intersection of psychology and product development, one can capture subtle consumer expectations and emotions and reflect them in product design and marketing strategies. We examine the critical role of psychology at each stage, from the initial phases of product design to the execution of marketing strategies, analyzing how products can resonate with consumer needs and emotions in the market.

Product design must center around the user's intuition and experience. Don Norman's design principles emphasize that products must be usable, accessible, and efficient. These principles ensure products are easy to understand and use, creating a positive first impression and ensuring ongoing satisfaction.

Applying Csikszentmihalyi's flow theory in user experience design can greatly enhance user satisfaction by facilitating a state of 'flow' during product use, where the user is so engrossed that they lose track of time. This deeply immersive experience can lead to strong positive perceptions and loyalty towards the product.

Moreover, creativity is crucial in the product development process. Amabile's theory of creativity argues for an environment where team members can freely propose creative ideas that can evolve into actual products. This process requires fostering a culture within the team that motivates and enhances creative problem-solving abilities, enabling the development of innovative products.

Consumer feedback is also a vital resource in product development. Direct feedback from consumers can be used to manage cognitive dissonance about the product and apply it to product improvements and consumer education, thereby enhancing the brand's positive perception. This helps reduce the disparity between consumer expectations and actual experiences, ultimately contributing to increased product and brand loyalty.

The profound insights found at the intersection of product development and psychology enable companies to compete successfully in the market and create products that captivate consumers. Throughout this process, psychology transcends mere theory to become a core element of product design and marketing strategy, decisively influencing the success of a product.

1. Product Design and Don Norman's Design Principles

The First Impression Created by Design: The Impact of Don Norman's Design Principles on Product Success

Product design transcends mere functionality—it shapes user experience, stimulates emotions, and can even alter user behavior. Understanding and leveraging the power of design is crucial, and deeply comprehending Don Norman's design principles is vital. Norman emphasizes usability and human-centered design, advocating that products should offer intuitive and enjoyable experiences to users.

This chapter explores Don Norman's design principles, examining their application in modern product design and their impact on consumer satisfaction and market success. Norman's theories focus on three main elements—usability, understandability, and pleasure—explaining how products designed with these elements deeply integrate into users' daily lives.

Product design should go beyond aesthetic appeal to maximize ease of use and satisfaction for the user. Through Norman's principles, designers can accurately capture user needs and reflect them in products that users can intuitively understand and use comfortably to achieve their goals. In this process, designers must balance technical constraints with market demands while also satisfying emotional needs of users.

Through this chapter, we understand that product design is a critical element that enhances users' lifestyles and explore methods to establish better design strategies based on this understanding. Norman's design principles provide deep insights into how products can seamlessly integrate into consumers' daily lives and enhance their quality of life.

TechDesign, a company recognized for its innovative designs in the smart home device market, has faced several user experience issues with its newly launched smart home product line. While visually appealing, these products have received unexpectedly negative reactions from consumers due to the complexity of the user interfaces.

These products particularly challenged users not familiar with technology. Users found the multifunctional and advanced interfaces unintuitive, and some struggled even with basic operations. This interface issue led to widespread dissatisfaction with the product overall, causing some consumers to completely abandon it.

Additionally, TechDesign's products faced compatibility issues. The company's proposed centralized smart home system was theoretically efficient in integrating various devices, but in practice, it required multiple complex setup and adjustment steps. This led consumers to question the system's efficiency, and the lack of smooth integration between products became a major factor in degrading the consumer experience.

TechDesign's website and online store also encountered issues. These platforms, non-user-friendly and complexly structured, especially frustrated mobile users, complicating the online product exploration and purchasing process and potentially decreasing conversion rates.

These challenges highlighted the need for TechDesign to more deeply understand consumer behavior and psychology in digital environments and develop appropriate approaches. The company realized the necessity to adopt a systematic approach to user behavior analysis and data-driven strategies to enhance user experience. The importance of user-centered design became even more pronounced, becoming a crucial consideration in TechDesign's future product development and marketing strategies.

TechDesign's user experience issues stemmed from multiple fundamental causes. The company's product designs, while modern and sophisticated in appearance, neglected essential human-centered design principles in actual user interface (UI) and user experience (UX) design. This led to a perception of the products as difficult to use, especially among technologically inexperienced users, increasing dissatisfaction.

The first cause was overly complex user interfaces. TechDesign's products offered a variety of functions and settings that allowed high-level control, but this simultaneously made it difficult for users to understand and effectively use the interfaces. More features required users to invest more time and effort to learn how to use them, creating a significant barrier at the initial stages of use.

The second cause was insufficient user education and support. While TechDesign marketed its products by emphasizing advanced features, it failed to provide adequate information and support to enable users to fully utilize these features. User manuals and online resources were often filled with technical jargon, beyond the level of understanding for an average user.

The third cause was an inappropriate target marketing strategy. Although TechDesign aimed its marketing at technology enthusiasts, the actual consumer base was much more diverse. As a result, technologically inexperienced consumers also purchased the company's products, but there was a significant gap between their expectations and actual product use experiences.

The fourth cause involved technical issues and product compatibility problems. Various products from the company did not integrate smoothly, and user problems often directly related to user dissatisfaction, particularly during new updates or system changes. The degraded mobile user experience and lack of user-friendliness on the website were also significant issues. These problems prevented users from finding easy solutions when encountering technical obstacles, leading to overall dissatisfaction and negative perceptions of the product.

These issues indicated that TechDesign had overlooked a user-centered approach in product design and marketing strategies, necessitating fundamental changes to meet the actual needs and expectations of users. The company needed to reestablish its strategy to improve user experience and build closer connections with consumers, based on this realization.

Don Norman's design principles emphasize a user-centered design approach, conveying the concept that products and services should be intuitive and easy to access. Norman particularly advocates for a design that prioritizes user experience, aiming to minimize discomfort during product use. For this, he believes that design should connect not only functionally but also emotionally with the user.

One of the main principles, 'visibility,' ensures that all essential options are clearly visible to the user, allowing them to easily recognize needed information. This helps users understand what functions to use and what actions to take next. Additionally, the 'feedback' principle ensures that every action taken by the user is recognized by the system and provides appropriate responses, confirming for the user that their actions have been successfully reflected. This prevents confusion and enhances user satisfaction.

'Structure' and 'consistency' help users achieve predictable results and perform similar tasks in a consistent manner, reducing the learning curve for users. For example, using buttons located in the same place for similar tasks helps users more quickly understand and effectively use the system.

Error prevention incorporates mechanisms to anticipate and prevent potential errors from the design stage, minimizing the likelihood of user mistakes. For instance, real-time validation of data entry in forms can immediately alert users to errors, providing an opportunity to correct them, enhancing the overall user experience.

Finally, the 'closure' principle emphasizes that the start and end of tasks should be clear to the user, enabling them to recognize when a task is completed and take any necessary subsequent actions. Together, these principles help users more efficiently understand and use a product or service.

In modern digital product design, Don Norman's design principles have become increasingly essential. Digital interfaces and mobile applications must prioritize accessibility, usability, and efficiency to optimize user experience. For example, the user interface (UI) of an application should be intuitive, designed to allow users to easily find and understand necessary functions. Additionally, responsive design ensures a consistent user experience across various devices, providing equal accessibility to all users. These design approaches enhance user satisfaction and strengthen positive perceptions of the product.

Norman's approach emphasizes that design plays a crucial role in user interactions, focusing on optimizing the end-user experience. His theories can be extensively applied not only in product design but also in service and interface design, supporting users to have more satisfying experiences.

TechDesign actively applied Don Norman's user-centered design principles to improve its digital marketing strategy. The company particularly focused on enhancing the user interface (UI) and user experience (UX) of its website and online store.

As a first step, TechDesign analyzed user feedback and website usage data to identify areas where the most problems were reported. This data helped the company understand which pages users visited most and where they typically exited the website. Based on this, the visibility principle was applied to ensure essential information and functions were clearly visible to users. For example, buttons and menus on product detail pages and the checkout process were adjusted to be more prominent and understandable.

Secondly, TechDesign strengthened the website's feedback mechanisms to ensure that every user action triggered an appropriate response. For instance, when users added items to their shopping cart, immediate visually satisfying feedback was provided, confirming that the action had been successfully completed. This immediate feedback increased user satisfaction and enhanced trust in the website.

Thirdly, to enhance structure and consistency, TechDesign simplified the entire navigation structure of the website. A consistent layout and style were used across all pages to make it easier for users to navigate the site. Additionally, consistent interactions were provided for repetitive tasks, allowing users to become more familiar with them more quickly.

Fourthly, error prevention design was applied to minimize the chances of user mistakes. For example, real-time validation features were added to input forms, allowing users to immediately recognize and correct any errors. This provided users with an opportunity to correct mistakes right away, improving the overall user experience.

Lastly, TechDesign applied the closure principle to ensure users clearly recognized when they had completed tasks on the website. A clear confirmation page was provided at the final step of the purchase process, allowing users to know their order had been successfully processed.

These improvements significantly enhanced the satisfaction of website visitors, leading to higher conversion rates. The changes implemented using Don Norman's design principles met user needs while enhancing brand credibility, effectively supporting the company's digital marketing strategy.

Additional psychological theories and related topics to consider include:

1. Motivation Theory: Understanding the various psychological factors that motivate users to take certain actions is crucial for product design. For example, Deci and Ryan's Self-Determination Theory explains that users show higher satisfaction and engagement when they feel in control of their actions. Utilizing this theory in user interface design can increase voluntary user participation and satisfaction.

2. Behavioral Economics: Understanding and predicting consumers' irrational decision patterns, behavioral economics can provide important insights for digital marketing strategies. For instance, the fear of missing out (FOMO) phenomenon can be effectively used to emphasize the urgency of certain products or services.

3. Social Learning Theory: According to Albert Bandura's social learning theory, people learn new behaviors by observing and mimicking others. This can be applied to product design and marketing strategies to change user behaviors or educate them on new product uses.

4. Understanding and Utilizing Emotions: Paul Ekman's emotion theory defines the basic emotions people can experience and how they are expressed. In marketing communications, understanding these emotions can create strong connections with consumers through emotional appeals.

5. Cognitive Load Theory: This theory provides ways to minimize the mental burden users experience while processing information and making decisions. Accordingly, product design and user interfaces should be as simple and intuitive as possible, allowing users to easily digest information and make effective decisions.

By further studying and understanding these theories, companies like TechDesign can develop more effective product designs and marketing strategies, maximizing customer experience and enhancing competitiveness in the market.

2. User Experience and Csikszentmihalyi's Flow Theory

Total Immersion:
Maximizing User Experience with Csikszentmihalyi's Flow Theory

As the digital age continues to evolve, the importance of user experience is increasingly highlighted. Today's users value the experiences provided by products beyond mere usage. This shift significantly impacts technology companies, and firms like InnovateX strive to deliver experiences that deeply immerse users. Csikszentmihalyi's flow theory plays a crucial role in this context, describing a state of 'flow' that users experience when they are fully immersed, achieving maximum satisfaction.

'Flow' is a psychological state that occurs when there is a perfect balance between the user's skill level and the challenge presented, allowing the user to concentrate deeply on the activity without distractions. Users who experience this state exhibit high satisfaction and enhanced brand loyalty. Designing immersive experiences in digital products and user experience (UX) design is crucial for maximizing user satisfaction and securing long-term brand loyalty.

In UX design, immersion goes beyond user satisfaction; it is a psychological technique that makes every moment of the user's experience special. Csikszentmihalyi's flow theory plays a central role, facilitating users' complete absorption in their activities, leading to peak achievement and satisfaction. This immersive state, or 'flow,' makes users lose track of time while using the product, eliciting strong positive responses and ultimately increasing brand loyalty.

This section explores how flow theory can be applied to product design and user interfaces. We will analyze in detail how users can become deeply engaged with specific product features and the role psychological elements play in this process.

Product designers and developers can understand and apply this theory to create products that allow users to immerse deeply, providing richer and more satisfying user experiences.

Additionally, this section introduces various design strategies to optimize immersion, examining how these strategies can be integrated into actual product design. Through this, product developers can design methods that not only meet user needs and expectations but also facilitate deep engagement during the experience. The application of flow theory extends beyond mere design changes, profoundly impacting how users interact with and live with the product, becoming a critical factor in the product's success.

In the digital age, as user experience becomes central, technology company InnovateX faces challenges in improving product design and UX. InnovateX, a developer and seller of advanced consumer electronics, aims to provide fully immersive product experiences to succeed in the market.

The company has recently received feedback that interfaces are too complex and difficult to use, particularly with new smart home devices, leading to increased product returns and declining customer satisfaction. Users have not been able to fully utilize the device features, with dissatisfaction growing especially among those new to the technology.

Moreover, InnovateX's mobile app has also been criticized. Although functionally rich, the user interface was not intuitive, making it difficult for users to find and use various features easily. Additionally, the app's long loading times and slow response hindered the flow state, leaving users dissatisfied with the experience.

InnovateX sought to improve the user experience but found that adding features and making design changes without proper user research only worsened the user experience. The design team failed to adequately analyze and reflect user feedback and behavior data, resulting in product and service improvements that did not meet user expectations and needs.

This situation emphasized the need for InnovateX to accurately understand user expectations and adopt a user-centered design approach, requiring a comprehensive reevaluation of the product and service user experience. The company needed to establish a clear strategy based on psychological principles and user data to improve product design and UX.

Analyzing the root causes of InnovateX's user experience issues reveals several important psychological and design-related factors:

First, the complexity of the user interface made it difficult for users to intuitively understand and use the products, preventing users from overcoming the initial learning curve, especially for those unfamiliar with the technology.

Second, the company's design and development processes did not sufficiently integrate a user-centered approach. InnovateX focused on features and innovation but designed products without adequately considering the actual daily needs and conveniences of users, preventing users from fully utilizing the advanced features and experiencing practical benefits.

Third, technical issues with InnovateX's digital platforms, particularly the mobile app, interfered with users' immersive experiences. The app's poor responsiveness and long loading times failed to provide the immediate feedback necessary for smooth navigation and interaction, reducing user motivation to continue using the app and negatively impacting overall satisfaction and loyalty.

These issues highlight the need for InnovateX to deepen its understanding of customer behavior and psychology and reflect this in product development to improve the user experience. Accurately identifying user needs and expectations and establishing a design strategy based on these insights are crucial. Active use of user research and feedback is essential, integrating the voice of the user into every stage of product development.

Mihaly Csikszentmihalyi's flow theory plays a vital role in user experience design. This theory describes the optimal experience state of 'flow,' where users are fully immersed in an activity without external distractions. Flow occurs when a user's skills perfectly match the level of challenge in the activity, leading to great satisfaction and a sense of achievement. This theory provides essential guidelines for maximizing user immersion in digital product design and development.

Csikszentmihalyi emphasizes that for flow to occur, the activity must match the user's skill level while providing enough challenge, and the user must have clear goals and receive immediate feedback. When these conditions are met, users can fully immerse themselves, enhancing their satisfaction and positive attitudes toward the product. Considering these elements in digital design is crucial for creating products that users want to use frequently.

Actively utilizing flow theory is important for enhancing the quality of experiences provided by digital products and services and maximizing user engagement. For example, in game design, adjusting the difficulty level to match the player's skills provides a continuous experience of challenge and achievement, encouraging longer engagement. Similarly, educational software can promote educational immersion by providing activities that allow users to effectively learn new knowledge while feeling challenged.

Additionally, flow theory helps in designing user experiences that meet users' expectations and needs by providing tailored experiences. When a product or service matches the user's skill level and allows them to see the results of their actions immediately, users are more likely to have a positive experience and develop loyalty. This approach is also crucial for customer-centric marketing strategies, contributing to building long-term relationships with customers through personalized user experiences.

Csikszentmihalyi's flow theory provides a critical theoretical foundation for designing and improving digital products and services, offering valuable insights into the emotional responses and satisfaction users experience while using each product or service. This theory provides essential guidelines for designers and developers to adopt a user-centered approach and optimize user experiences.

Flow theory is used across various industries to enhance user experiences. For example, in video game design, adjustments to storytelling, challenge levels, and graphic design ensure that users can fully immerse themselves in the game. In educational technology, designing content and interactions to maximize learning efficiency promotes educational immersion. In digital media and online content production, optimizing video length, narrative structure, and interactive elements helps users deeply engage with the content. These applications demonstrate how flow theory can maximize consumer experiences and contribute to product success across various industries.

InnovateX recently faced several challenges in strengthening its digital marketing strategy for consumer electronics. The company decided to address these issues by applying Csikszentmihalyi's flow theory, which describes the experience of maximum satisfaction and achievement when an individual is fully immersed in an activity. The immersive experience occurs when an individual's skill level perfectly matches the challenge of the activity, which is crucial for maximizing the depth of personal experience while using technology.

The company began to implement this theory in practice by improving product design and user interfaces. InnovateX simplified and made the interaction with products more intuitive, ensuring that users do not feel technological barriers. This allowed users to perform tasks efficiently without unnecessary stress during product use, improving the overall user experience.

Additionally, InnovateX analyzed user behavior data to provide customized user experiences tailored to each user's preferences and needs. This data was used to identify which features users frequently used and where they encountered problems. Based on this information, the company improved product features and adjusted interfaces to make them more accessible and user-friendly.

To promote user immersion, InnovateX also introduced a feedback system that allows users to check their progress in real-time. This system provided positive feedback each time a task was completed, motivating users and helping them easily track their achievements. This encouraged users to experience immersion more frequently, contributing to higher overall product satisfaction.

This approach played a crucial role in helping InnovateX better understand and meet the changing behaviors and expectations of consumers in the digital environment. The strategic changes based on flow theory built a strong emotional connection with consumers, significantly enhancing customer loyalty and brand value. InnovateX's approach ensured a competitive advantage in the consumer electronics sector and sustained success in the market.

Considering InnovateX's case, the following additional psychological theories could be useful in product development and digital marketing strategies:

1. Behavioral Economics: This field studies how people make decisions in irrational and unpredictable ways, contrary to traditional economic assumptions. Theories in behavioral economics, such as those by Dan Ariely, can help understand the irrational factors that influence consumer purchase decisions.

2. Emotional Design: Donald Norman's emotional design theory explains how products evoke emotional responses in users. This is important for enhancing the pleasure and satisfaction users feel when using products.

3. Social Learning Theory: Albert Bandura's social learning theory explains how people learn new behaviors by observing and mimicking others. This theory can be particularly useful in social media marketing strategies, influencing other consumers' behaviors by sharing positive user experiences online.

4. Psychology of Influence: Robert Cialdini's psychology of influence explains how people's decisions are influenced by the actions of others. This can help develop marketing strategies that provide important social proof when consumers make purchase decisions.

5. Expectancy Theory: Victor Vroom's expectancy theory explains that an individual's

behavior is determined by the relationship between expectations, value, and perceived effort and outcomes. This theory can provide insights into how product features should be linked with consumer expectations.

These theories can help InnovateX overcome the challenges it faces, improve user experiences, and enhance market fit for its products. Each theory offers various perspectives and approaches for product development and marketing strategies, enabling a deeper understanding of consumers and more effective communication.

3. Innovation and Creativity: The Components of Creativity by Amabile

Catalysts of Creativity: Amabile's Theory of Creativity and Innovative Product Development

Innovation and creativity are essential elements for companies to secure a sustainable competitive advantage in today's business environment. Particularly in an era of rapid technological advancement, companies must continually develop innovative ideas and solutions to succeed in the market. Teresa Amabile's componential theory of creativity provides profound insights into understanding and fostering innovative thinking.

Amabile's theory explains that creative performance is determined by the interaction of three basic elements: expertise, creative thinking skills, and motivation. Expertise includes a thorough understanding of knowledge and skills in a specific domain, creative thinking skills refer to the ability to approach problems in novel and unconventional ways, and motivation denotes the energy and passion an individual dedicates to an activity. These three elements are closely linked and play a crucial role in producing creative outcomes.

Companies striving for innovation can maximize their creative potential by enhancing these components. Providing continuous education and training to increase expertise, creating an environment that encourages creative thinking, and supporting employees to be highly intrinsically motivated in their work are critical. This approach can contribute to generating more innovative ideas and enhancing the company's overall capacity for innovation.

This chapter will explore the psychological foundations of innovation and creativity through Amabile's theory of creativity components, and detail how these can be applied in actual business situations. The insights provided by this theory will enable companies to discover methods for creative problem-solving, product development, and differentiation in the market.

In the modern business landscape, creativity has become a crucial competitive factor. For instance, 'SmartTech Innovations,' a company that manufactures innovative smart devices, faces the challenge of continually developing unique products to stand out in the market. This company aims particularly at innovating user experience, thereby providing new devices that can integrate into consumers' daily lives.

Although SmartTech Innovations has received considerable attention for its recently launched series of smart home devices, it encountered several significant issues during the product development process. Technologically advanced, these devices were somewhat disconnected from the actual user experience. Users criticized the complexity of the products, indicating a preference for more intuitive and straightforward devices.

Additionally, it became apparent that the company's internal mechanisms for fostering creativity were not sufficiently effective. The development team often relied excessively on external trends and neglected to seek creative solutions internally. This frequently resulted in products that did not meet market expectations, making it difficult to differentiate based on creative ideas.

The company also failed to adequately utilize the creative potential of its employees. Opportunities for deriving new ideas from the diverse backgrounds and experiences of the staff were insufficiently provided, and the absence of a corporate culture encouraging creative thinking was noted as a problem. This situation significantly hindered SmartTech Innovations' pursuit of product innovation based on creativity.

These issues highlight the need for SmartTech Innovations to seek more effective ways to foster creativity and innovation. To maintain sustainable growth and competitive advantage in the market, it is essential to maximize internal creativity and foster an environment that promotes creative contributions from employees.

A deeper analysis of the issues faced by SmartTech Innovations reveals various obstacles to creativity and innovation at multiple levels:

The first issue lies in the approach to product development. The company focused on technological advancement but tended to develop features that were disconnected from the actual experience of consumers. This approach resulted from starting product design without adequately understanding consumer needs and expectations. A lack of consumer research and market analysis resulted in products that failed to deliver real value to end-users.

The second issue concerns the methods used to foster internal creativity. The corporate culture and organizational structure did not adequately support creative ideas. There was a strong tendency to repeat proven success models rather than encouraging creative thinking, which diminished employees' willingness to try new ideas. Additionally, a lack of collaboration between teams limited the opportunities for integrating different perspectives and ideas.

The third significant cause relates to how technology was applied. While SmartTech Innovations focused on incorporating advanced technology into its products, insufficient consideration was given to how these technologies could integrate into users' daily lives. The failure to make the benefits of technology easily understandable and usable for consumers impeded the user experience and diminished the intuitiveness of the products.

These problems indicate that SmartTech Innovations overlooked crucial psychological and organizational factors when attempting to develop innovative products. It is necessary to find ways to effectively integrate an understanding of user psychology from the initial stages of product design. This requires more systematic consumer research and a cultural shift to utilize the creative potential of employees.

Applying Teresa Amabile's theory of creativity components could be highly beneficial in addressing the issues faced by SmartTech Innovations. Amabile states that creativity is influenced by three main elements: expertise, creative thinking skills, and motivation.

Expertise includes the knowledge and skills accumulated in a particular field, providing the foundation for creative problem-solving. It suggests that the product development team must be well-equipped with adequate background knowledge and technical skills to generate creative solutions. SmartTech can create innovative products by leveraging the various technical expertise in product design and development.

Creative thinking skills involve the ability to approach problems in new and non-standard ways. This includes flexibility, originality, and the ability to define and solve problems. SmartTech should encourage this kind of thinking within its team, actively seeking new ideas by fostering collaboration across different departments and forming interdisciplinary teams.

Motivation indicates how passionately an individual engages in creative activities. According to Amabile, intrinsic motivation—where the activity is rewarding and enjoyable in itself—is the strongest driver of creativity. Through this, SmartTech should create an environment where employees are deeply engaged in their work, aligning their personal satisfaction with the company's goals. Providing autonomy and real opportunities to implement their ideas can enhance their intrinsic motivation.

By integrating these three components into the product development process and team management, SmartTech Innovations can develop concrete strategies for substantial creativity enhancement and innovation promotion. Amabile's theory not only focuses on generating creative ideas but also on creating an environment where these ideas can be accepted and implemented by various stakeholders within and outside the team.

SmartTech Innovations has begun to overhaul and improve its innovation processes by applying Teresa Amabile's theory of creativity components. The company has implemented several strategies to ensure that creativity deeply permeates the corporate culture and structure, going beyond merely generating excellent ideas.

The first step involved expanding internal training programs for the product development team, allowing employees to deepen their understanding of the latest technological trends and user experience design principles, and applying these in their actual work. These training sessions particularly emphasized creative thinking and problem-solving skills, enabling employees to acquire various techniques and methodologies essential for realizing user-centered design.

Secondly, the company established innovation teams composed of employees from diverse backgrounds to facilitate multidisciplinary collaboration. These teams had opportunities for regular brainstorming sessions and workshops, allowing them to exchange knowledge from different fields and experimentally test new ideas. These activities helped team members creatively address customer problems using each other's expertise.

Thirdly, SmartTech worked to create an organizational culture where employees could freely propose and experiment with ideas. The company emphasized a tolerant environment for failures, allowing employees to suggest and try new ideas without fear. This reduced the burden associated with taking creative risks and played a crucial role in encouraging innovative thinking.

Fourthly, the company made customer feedback a core element of the product development process, establishing systems to collect and incorporate feedback in real time. This allowed for immediate adjustments to ensure that products in development aligned well with market demands. Directly incorporating customer voices into product development was crucial for enhancing user satisfaction.

These strategies enabled SmartTech Innovations to ensure that creativity became a key driver of the company's continuous growth and innovation. Integrating Amabile's theory of creativity components into this approach not only led to positive changes in product development but also improved overall company operations, enhancing competitiveness in the market. All these efforts focused on creating an environment where employees could express their creativity and produce innovative products.

Contemporary examples include startups and technology-focused companies utilizing Amabile's creativity theory. For instance, startups in Silicon Valley often require creative solutions in a rapidly changing technological landscape. These companies adopt frameworks based on Amabile's theory, creating a culture where employees can freely propose and experiment with new ideas. This approach facilitates rapid innovation and strengthens competitive positioning in the market. Such cases demonstrate how effectively Amabile's theory can be applied in challenging contemporary business environments.

Additional psychological theories and related topics worth exploring to enhance SmartTech Innovations' approach to boosting creativity include:

1. Flow Theory: Already mentioned as the theory of immersion, Csikszentmihalyi's Flow Theory describes a state where an individual is completely engaged in their work, experiencing maximum satisfaction and performance. Studying this theory in depth can help devise ways to create a work environment where employees can experience 'flow' in their tasks.

2. Multiple Intelligences Theory: Howard Gardner's theory describes the various types of intelligence individuals possess, enabling a comprehensive understanding and utilization of personal potential. Applying this theory can help recognize the talents of employees with diverse intelligences and incorporate this into team and project configurations, maximizing creative outcomes.

3. Design Thinking: This provides a repetitive and user-centered approach to problem-solving. Through the design thinking process, teams can deeply understand user needs and develop innovative solutions based on this insight.

4. Creative Self-Efficacy: This psychological concept describes the extent to which individuals believe they can perform creative tasks. Organizations can develop strategies to enhance employees' creative confidence through this concept.

5. Emotional Intelligence: Emotional intelligence represents an individual's ability to recognize and manage their own and others' emotions. This plays a crucial role in improving communication and collaboration within teams, fostering a creative work environment.

6. Positive Psychology: This field emphasizes the positive aspects and assets of individuals, focusing on enhancing employee well-being and motivation. Research has shown that happier and more satisfied employees are more likely to be creative.

Exploring and applying these theories further can support SmartTech Innovations in developing a richer and more layered approach to continuous innovation and creativity.

4. Consumer Feedback and Cognitive Dissonance Theory

Understanding the Consumer Mind: The Power of Feedback and Cognitive Dissonance Theory

Capturing the consumer's mind is an art that goes beyond simple product sales. At the heart of this art is consumer feedback. The cognitive dissonance experienced by consumers forms the foundation of product development and marketing strategies. This chapter delves deeply into cognitive dissonance theory, analyzing how consumer feedback crucially influences the strategic direction of brands and product improvements.

Cognitive dissonance theory explains the psychological discomfort consumers feel when their expectations do not match their actual product experiences. This discomfort can lead consumers to change their perception of the product or feel the need to change the product itself. This theory provides crucial insights for marketers and product developers to use consumer feedback more strategically and seek ways to enhance brand loyalty.

This chapter demonstrates how cognitive dissonance theory can be applied in the field through case studies. For instance, it analyzes in detail how a company modified and improved a product following feedback from a new product launch that failed to meet customer expectations. It also provides insights into how the company turned customer disappointment into an opportunity for improvement.

Finally, through theoretical background and practical applications, the chapter offers a deep analysis of how cognitive dissonance theory can redefine digital age marketing strategies. It helps readers gain a clear understanding of how a deep psychological understanding of consumer feedback plays a vital role in modern marketing. This chapter provides essential tools and insights for marketers and product developers to make strategic decisions based on consumer feedback and suggests ways to strengthen emotional connections with consumers.

In the face of digital transformation, the mid-sized company 'SmartTech' faced challenges requiring swift action to maintain competitiveness in the market. As a mid-sized player in the consumer electronics sector, SmartTech has offered a range of high-performance products. However, increasing customer dissatisfaction led to the spread of negative feedback online. Customers particularly pointed out issues encountered during product use and the disparity between their actual usability expectations and the product's performance.

SmartTech's management team took these issues seriously. Especially after poor initial responses to new product launches, they realized that the cognitive dissonance surrounding these launches was damaging the brand image. Consumers expected convenience and innovation from using SmartTech products, but the actual experiences often failed to meet these expectations. This led customers to reconsider their purchase decisions, and some began to express their dissatisfaction publicly.

The company decided that it needed to systematically collect and analyze customer feedback to overcome these issues. They began an intensive investigation of customer complaints and issues using data collected from social media, customer service call centers, and product review sites. This data formed the basis for product improvements and played a crucial role in bridging the gap between customer expectations and the company's products.

Additionally, the company introduced usability tests and focus groups to improve the actual user experience. This approach focused on minimizing cognitive dissonance from the early stages of product design by incorporating consumer feedback. Through this process, SmartTech was able to enhance product usability and more accurately reflect the real needs and expectations of customers.

SmartTech's efforts gradually began to bear fruit. The newly improved products received positive responses in the market, and customer satisfaction surveys scored higher than before. These changes were an important first step in regaining customer trust and laid the foundation for increasing long-term brand loyalty.

The problems SmartTech faced stemmed from two main causes related to product design and customer feedback mechanisms.

The first issue originated from the complexity of the user interface and lack of usability. Although SmartTech's products were launched with technologically advanced features, actual users found it difficult to utilize these features routinely. The complexity of the user interfaces made it hard for average consumers to access and understand, which led to underutilization of advanced features and decreased product satisfaction.

The second cause was the absence of an effective customer feedback system. SmartTech had not established a systematic method to collect and reflect customer feedback in product improvements. Feedback collected from customers was not properly analyzed and managed, leading to the continual occurrence of recurring issues. This increased customer dissatisfaction, ultimately affecting brand trust and decreasing repurchase rates.

This situation indicated the need for SmartTech to adopt a new approach that would improve product usability while effectively collecting and reflecting customer opinions. To actively address the issues faced by customers, it was first necessary to simplify the user interface to make it more intuitive. Additionally, improving customer service processes to swiftly collect feedback and use it for product improvements was essential.

To achieve this, SmartTech could introduce a digital platform to collect and analyze customer feedback in real-time and strengthen internal processes for smooth communication between customer service and product development teams. Analyzing customer usage patterns to deeply understand how they use the products and re-establishing a product design philosophy centered on user experience could also be beneficial. These measures would significantly enhance product usability and customer satisfaction, contributing to long-term customer loyalty and brand value enhancement.

This case revolves around the application of cognitive dissonance theory, a psychological concept developed in the 1950s by Leon Festinger. The theory explains the psychological tendency of individuals to maintain consistency among their attitudes, beliefs, and behaviors. According to cognitive dissonance theory, individuals experience discomfort when they encounter information or behavior that contradicts their belief systems, and this discomfort motivates them to change their attitudes or behaviors to reduce the dissonance.

Cognitive dissonance is closely related to consumer behavior. For example, if a consumer purchases an expensive product and then finds that the product's performance does not meet expectations, they may resolve the resulting psychological discomfort by emphasizing the product's positive aspects or ignoring negative information. This phenomenon provides important implications for managing customer feedback and user experiences in marketing.

When applying this theory to resolve the issues faced by SmartTech, the company can minimize consumer cognitive dissonance and enhance positive user experiences, thereby increasing product satisfaction. For instance, by transparently communicating about potential issues during product use and collecting feedback in real-time to take immediate corrective actions, the company can resolve customer complaints and strengthen positive brand perceptions.

This approach should focus on reducing the gap between consumer expectations and actual product performance from the early stages of product development. Additionally, marketing communications should realistically set consumer expectations and accurately convey the true value and benefits of the product. By doing so, SmartTech can rebuild consumer trust and secure long-term customer loyalty.

SmartTech applied the cognitive dissonance theory to analyze consumer dissatisfaction and its causes to resolve the issues. The company noted that consumers continued to use its products and feel dissatisfied even after having negative experiences with the product's functionality, a phenomenon related to the psychological discomfort caused by the inconsistency between behavior and attitude as described in cognitive dissonance theory.

First, SmartTech conducted extensive surveys and feedback sessions to identify specific discomforts consumers experienced during product use. Through this, they gathered critical data indicating that the user interface (UI) was not intuitive and that the product's functions did not align well with users' everyday needs.

Based on this feedback, SmartTech decided to completely overhaul the UI design to make it more user-friendly. They also adjusted the product's functions to better connect with users' daily lives, enhancing practicality. For example, they added an energy-saving mode to smart home appliances and developed solutions to minimize user inconvenience through automatic update features.

Furthermore, SmartTech enhanced communication with consumers by opening new channels of communication. Using social media and online forums, they enabled consumers to provide real-time feedback, allowing the company to respond promptly. This reduced psychological discomfort among consumers and increased brand trust and satisfaction.

These measures allowed SmartTech to reduce consumer cognitive dissonance, enhance product satisfaction, and improve long-term brand loyalty. The company plans to continue improving its products and services based on the lessons learned from this process and to further strengthen its consumer-centered approach. This strategic approach has been recognized as an excellent example of effectively applying psychological theory to solve practical business problems.

When interpreting consumer feedback, cognitive dissonance theory may operate differently across various consumer segments. Factors such as cultural background, age, and gender may affect how consumers resolve the dissonance between their expectations and experiences. For example, younger consumers might have higher expectations for technology-based products and are more likely to provide stronger negative feedback if those expectations are not met. On the other hand, consumers from different age groups or cultural backgrounds may be more sensitive to other factors. Understanding and appropriately responding to these differences is important for finely tuning product development and customer service strategies.

Additional psychological theories worth exploring in relation to SmartTech's case include:

1. Social Proof Theory: This theory explains the tendency of individuals to imitate the actions of others. By utilizing user reviews, ratings, and mentions on social media, SmartTech can enhance positive perceptions of new products or improved features.

2. Expectancy Theory: This theory describes the rewards individuals anticipate when they engage in certain behaviors. Using this theory, SmartTech can plan product improvements in a direction that manages and meets consumer expectations.

3. Emotional Contagion Theory: This concept suggests that emotions can be transferred from one person to another. By conveying positive emotions through advertising or marketing campaigns, the company can induce positive emotions about the product among consumers.

4. Behavioral Economics: Challenging the predictable rationality of traditional economics, this field focuses on how people actually make decisions. Insights from this area can help understand and predict irrational or emotionally based consumer decisions.

5. Group Dynamics: This theory describes how individual behavior is influenced within a group and how group decisions and actions are formed. Through this theory, SmartTech can develop strategies to enhance product perceptions and preferences within consumer groups.

All these theories can help SmartTech deepen its understanding of consumer behavior and psychology, providing a basis for more effective marketing strategies.

5. Product Positioning and Perceptual Mapping

Where Should You Place Your Product in the Market?: The Role of Product Positioning and Perceptual Mapping

Success in the market goes beyond just creating a superior product; it hinges on how the product is positioned and perceived by consumers. Product positioning and perceptual mapping play vital roles in tackling these challenges. These tools are essential for marketers to accurately analyze a product's position within the market, visually represent its relationship with competing products, and measure and understand consumer perceptions.

This chapter will deeply cover the importance of product positioning and how perceptual mapping integrates into marketing strategies to optimize a product's market position. We will explore the basic principles of perceptual mapping and how it can capture and understand subtle differences in consumer perception.

Additionally, we will analyze how consumers make choices among numerous products in a competitive market and how certain products meet consumer expectations and needs. By mapping the characteristics of the product, consumer needs, and the relationship with competing products, marketers can develop clearer market positioning strategies.

Developing strategies through product positioning and perceptual mapping adds depth to advertising, promotion, product development, and customer service strategies. This approach is crucial for introducing products to the market and building lasting relationships with consumers. Especially through perceptual mapping, marketers can understand how they appear in consumers' eyes and create emotional connections, optimizing brand messaging based on this.

The process provides critical insights beyond simple mapping, establishing strategies for maintaining a sustainable competitive advantage in the market and building deep emotional connections with consumers. This chapter will examine strategic approaches to achieving market success and establishing a place in consumers' minds through product positioning and perceptual mapping.

VisionTech, an innovative consumer electronics company and a leader in market innovation, has deeply realized the strategic importance of product positioning and perceptual mapping. The company has built its reputation on developing high-end smart home products using cutting-edge technology but faces new challenges in meeting changing market and consumer expectations.

VisionTech's portfolio includes a variety of products, each targeting specific consumer segments. However, the company has experienced issues with recent products not achieving as much recognition in the market as anticipated and failing to stand out against competitors. In particular, a newly launched line of smart home devices has not elicited the market response expected.

Through consumer research and internal analysis, VisionTech discovered that its products were not sufficiently differentiated from competitors and were perceived similarly. Additionally, despite the products' functional and quality excellence, the problem was analyzed as a lack of emotional connection. Consumers recognized the technical excellence of VisionTech's products but had relatively low awareness of how these products integrated into their daily lives or provided emotional value.

Based on this problem recognition, VisionTech decided to reestablish its product positioning and perceptual mapping strategies. The company needed to clearly define each product's position in the market and modify its product strategies to meet both the emotional and technical needs of consumers. To this end, it began mapping consumers' perceptions and expectations more accurately, refining each product's positioning based on this data.

During this process, VisionTech utilized market research and consumer feedback as critical resources to gain insights into how each product could naturally integrate into consumers' daily lives. This effort aimed to reflect consumer opinions from the early stages of product development, effectively integrating real users' experiences and expectations into product design and functionality.

The fundamental causes of the problems faced by VisionTech stemmed from several key factors:

First, the lack of product differentiation in the market was a major issue. Although the company's products offered technically superior performance, many consumers did not feel these features were applicable in real life. The existing marketing strategy focused on conveying the technical superiority of the products to consumers, an approach disconnected from the emotional elements and personal values consumers consider when making purchases.

Second, the problem was the ambiguity in the market positioning of VisionTech's products. Compared to competing products, VisionTech's offerings did not provide a clear differentiation, and consumers did not clearly perceive how VisionTech's products could meet their needs or desires. This resulted in consumers not forming strong connections or loyalty to the brand, assessing the products only on functional aspects.

Third, VisionTech's online marketing channels and social media strategies were not effectively managed. Digital marketing plays a crucial role in modern business, but VisionTech failed to maximize interaction with consumers and drive engagement through these channels. In particular, the execution of social media campaigns was not engaging enough to elicit consumer participation and response, negatively affecting overall brand perception.

Finally, VisionTech's website and online shopping experience were not user-friendly. The site's navigation structure was complex, and inadequate mobile optimization made it difficult for users to find product information or proceed smoothly with the purchasing process. This was particularly inconvenient for mobile device users and directly led to a decline in online sales conversion rates.

These various issues emphasize the need for VisionTech to approach product development and marketing strategies through a psychological understanding and analysis of consumer behavior patterns. The company must recognize these problems and seek solutions appropriate to each cause to strengthen brand positioning and improve relationships with consumers.

When discussing product positioning, perceptual mapping is an extremely important tool for visually analyzing and understanding a product's position within the market. This technique allows companies to grasp how consumers perceive their products and clearly define the differences and positioning of their products compared to competitors. In this process, the important psychological concept of 'positioning' signifies the unique place a product occupies in consumers' minds, playing a critical role in establishing marketing strategies.

Perceptual mapping uses Multidimensional Scaling (MDS) to graphically represent the similarities and differences between products based on consumer perception data. This method captures unconscious perceptions and explicit preferences of consumers, providing insights into how a product or brand should be positioned in the market. For example, if consumers value high quality and reliability, drawing conclusions that emphasize these aspects in brand positioning is crucial.

This analysis provides a strong foundation for making critical decisions in marketing strategies and product development. By considering the characteristics of the product, consumer expectations, and competitive conditions comprehensively, companies can adjust their products to fit the market. Additionally, perceptual mapping helps companies establish effective strategies when expanding their product lines or targeting new market segments.

The key in this process depends on how well a company understands consumer perceptions and psychology. Understanding consumer psychology requires more than just statistical data; it involves comprehensively grasping their lifestyles, values, and the psychological factors that influence their purchasing decisions. This enables companies to design and market products that meet or exceed consumer expectations.

Ultimately, product positioning and perceptual mapping apply psychological principles at the intersection of product development and marketing, paving the way for more detailed and effective strategies. This approach is essential for companies to captivate consumers' minds and secure a sustainable competitive advantage in the market.

Tech company 'InnovateX' faced the complex task of resolving the discrepancy between consumer perceptions and product positioning using perceptual mapping. This company manufactures high-performance computing devices, but market research showed that consumers perceived InnovateX's products as expensive and complex to use. This perception negatively impacted sales, and there was a need to reestablish product positioning.

InnovateX first used multidimensional scaling to visualize its products' perception positioning in the current market. This data clearly showed how consumers perceived InnovateX products and the differences compared to competing products. The analysis revealed that while InnovateX products were technically superior, they lagged in accessibility and ease of use.

To address this, InnovateX improved product designs to introduce more user-friendly interfaces. At the same time, it realigned its marketing communication strategy to not only highlight the advanced features of the products but also emphasize the ease of use in everyday scenarios. These changes focused on reconstructing consumer perceptions, with insights gained from perceptual mapping forming the foundation.

Additionally, InnovateX actively collected and analyzed consumer feedback to reflect consumer opinions in the product development process. This allowed the company to quickly identify problems experienced by users during product use and apply improvements to new products. This increased customer satisfaction and promoted a positive perception of the products.

Lastly, InnovateX strengthened its online marketing and social media strategies to expand customer touchpoints through digital channels. These efforts focused on enhancing the products' online visibility and strengthening relationships with consumers through real-time communication. Content marketing and targeted advertising played important roles in this process, with all activities planned and executed based on data obtained through perceptual mapping.

By integrating perceptual mapping and psychological theories, InnovateX successfully improved its product positioning in the market. This demonstrates the importance of a systematic and scientific approach across various business areas, from product development to marketing strategies.

In the digital age, data analysis and consumer behavior analysis tools are revolutionizing Perceptual Mapping. Utilizing the latest technologies, marketers can analyze large volumes of consumer data in real time, allowing them to map the market position of products more accurately and dynamically. For example, analyzing consumer reactions and behavior patterns on social media enables real-time adjustments to product positioning and agile adaptation of marketing strategies. This approach allows for more precise and effective market analysis, helping companies maintain competitiveness and respond quickly to market changes.

The following psychological theories provide deeper insights into InnovateX's case and can be considered further:

1. Organizational Behavior and Culture Change Models: These explain how behavior and culture change within an organization. The theories clarify the factors that drive organizational changes and can help manage the attitudes and behaviors of employees during the process of reestablishing product positioning strategies.

2. Motivation Theories: Theories like Deci and Ryan's Self-Determination Theory explain intrinsic and extrinsic motivations of individuals. These can be applied to design incentive systems that stimulate creativity and innovation among employees.

3. Technology Acceptance Model (TAM): This model explains how users accept and use new technologies. It is useful in emphasizing the importance of user interface (UI) and user experience (UX) in the process of improving product designs.

4. Law of Attraction: This theory argues that positive thoughts attract positive outcomes. When a brand aims to build positive emotional connections with consumers, this theory can be used to enhance positive perceptions among consumers.

5. Behavioral Economics: This field emphasizes that economic decisions are not always rational. Applying behavioral economic principles when developing discount, reward, and pricing strategies can influence consumers' purchasing decisions.

These theories can help InnovateX gain a deeper understanding of consumer behavior and psychology, and based on this, establish more effective marketing strategies. Each theory is applicable to various business scenarios, particularly in digital marketing and product development, where they can have a significant impact.

6. Functional Design and Gibson's Ecological Psychology Theory

Design Encompassing the Environment: Exploring the Aesthetics of Functional Design Through Gibson's Ecological Psychology Theory

The products we use every day go beyond mere functionality; they play a crucial role in how we interact with our environment and engage our senses. James J. Gibson's theory of ecological psychology investigates the essence of these interactions and has a profound impact on product design and user experience (UX). This theory explains how products integrate naturally into the user's environment and influence their behaviors, thus aiding designers in creating more intuitive and seamless user experiences.

Gibson's theory of ecological psychology describes how human perception evolves through continuous interaction with the environment. Central to this theory is the concept of 'affordance,' which refers to the action possibilities that an object provides. For example, a chair offers the possibility to sit, which is naturally understood from its form and structure. From this perspective, product design must transcend aesthetics to consider the user's lifestyle and behavioral patterns.

Modern designers apply this theory to create designs that enable users to use products more easily and effectively. This approach plays a significant role, especially in the design of mobile devices, smart home devices, and user-friendly web interfaces. Gibson's theory helps in understanding how products can meet the physical and cognitive needs of users, contributing to the development of more efficient and intuitive product solutions.

This approach is increasingly important as technology advances rapidly and the complexity of digital environments grows. Gibson's ecological psychology provides invaluable insights for modern companies aiming to optimize user experience and maximize the real value of their products and services. Thus, this theory influences not only product design but also strategic business decisions, playing a crucial role in enabling companies to maintain a competitive edge and achieve sustainable growth.

Focusing on functional design, the hypothetical tech company 'SmartDesign Technologies' is committed to developing user-friendly smart home devices. The company has experienced rapid growth over recent years, creating products that integrate seamlessly into daily life. However, a major challenge they faced was an overly tech-centric approach in the early stages of product development. Prioritizing technical performance often led to a neglect of actual user needs and experiences.

For instance, SmartDesign's recently launched smart lighting system, while technologically advanced, was perceived as complex and difficult to use by typical users. The system offered various lighting modes and color adjustments, but the interface was not intuitive, rendering many features unused.

Additionally, the company struggled to balance the aesthetic and functional aspects of product design. While the products boasted modern and sleek designs, some users felt these designs compromised ease of use. For example, a slim-designed remote control was hard to hold and had small buttons that made actual use cumbersome.

In response to this feedback, SmartDesign recognized the need to reassess its product development strategy and considered a shift towards a design approach focused on user experience. The company aimed for a more balanced approach between usability and functionality, enhancing research on how products can more naturally integrate into users' everyday lives. In this process, the insights provided by Gibson's ecological psychology were instrumental, guiding the company towards designing products that better fit the needs and environments of users.

SmartDesign Technologies faced several underlying issues in its development process:

Firstly, the company's development process was heavily focused on a tech-centric approach, leading to results that were somewhat detached from intuitive user experiences. This approach enhanced the functional features of the products but created interfaces that were complex and difficult for average users to understand and access, reducing user satisfaction.

Secondly, there was a failure to balance the aesthetic and functional aspects of product design. SmartDesign's products attracted visual attention with their modern and stylish appearance, yet the convenience and ease of use required for daily operation were overlooked. For instance, the slim and sleek design of the remote control was uncomfortable to hold and difficult to operate, which did not align with the actual user experience.

Thirdly, SmartDesign's marketing and promotional strategies were not sufficiently effective. Although campaigns emphasized the advanced features and design of the products, they lacked specific examples or explanations of how these features could be utilized in daily life. This led to a lack of understanding among consumers about the practical value and necessity of the products, making it difficult for them to form an emotional connection or loyalty to the brand.

These issues ultimately emphasized the need for SmartDesign to shift towards a user-centered design approach. The company recognized the need to invest more in user-friendly interface design and consider how products could be integrated into the lives of users from the earliest stages of product development. Actively collecting and incorporating feedback to align the products with the real needs and expectations of users became a crucial strategic direction.

James J. Gibson (1904-1979) was an American psychologist, whose main field of study was the psychology of visual perception. His theory of ecological psychology significantly contributed to understanding the interaction between humans and their environment. During an era dominated by behaviorist psychology, Gibson sought to explain human perception not merely as a stimulus-response connection but as an active perception formed within the environment. His theory presented the viewpoint that the perceived world is a world of meaning, emphasizing that our perception is not just a collection of sensory data but includes meanings and functions that guide our actions.

One of Gibson's key concepts was 'affordance,' which refers to the action possibilities provided by objects or environments in specific contexts. For example, a chair provides the action possibility of sitting, directly related to its physical form. This concept also helps users recognize the latent functions of objects. This is a critical element in user experience design (UX), facilitating products or services to approach users in a natural and intuitive manner.

Gibson's theory of ecological psychology has had a profound impact on the advancement of design and technology. It has particularly influenced designers to consider not only the visual appeal and functionality of products but also how products are perceived and used within the user's environment. This consideration enhances the practical use value of products and services, thereby maximizing user satisfaction.

Thus, Gibson's theory provides guidelines for modern companies not only in terms of technical performance but also in designing user experiences. By applying this theory, companies can create products that integrate into users' lives from the initial stages of product development, enhancing their competitive edge in the market.

By understanding and applying Gibson's theory, we can gain deeper insights into how products and services are perceived by users and how their usability can be maximized. In this regard, Gibson's ecological psychology is not merely a theoretical framework but a practical guide for real-world design and product development, enabling companies like SmartDesign Technologies to develop products that achieve high user satisfaction by focusing on enhancing usability based on profound psychological insights.

Modern smart home technology can naturally integrate with Gibson's ecological psychology theory. For example, a smart home system that learns the user's daily activities and automatically adjusts the environment accordingly ensures that the user's natural living patterns are perfectly harmonized with their surroundings. Adjustments in lighting, temperature, and even music selection are optimized to match the user's current activities and mood, enabling a more comfortable and productive environment. This technological application demonstrates how Gibson's theory can be meaningfully applied to contemporary living space design.

Further psychological theories that could be applied to SmartDesign Technologies' smart lighting system to deepen our understanding of product improvement and user experience include:

1. Cognitive Load Theory:
This theory explains how cognitive resources are utilized during the learning process. Applied to product design, it could help simplify the smart lighting system's interface to reduce cognitive load, making it easier for users to understand and use by transforming complex functions into simple, intuitive commands.

2. Usability Testing:
While not a direct psychological theory, usability testing is a methodology in user experience (UX) research that systematically analyzes users' experiences with a product to provide insights. SmartDesign can use usability testing to understand how users perceive and interact with the smart lighting system's interface, using this data to make better design decisions.

3. Social Learning Theory:
Albert Bandura's social learning theory emphasizes learning through observation. By applying this theory to product use, features that allow users to observe and learn from others' usage patterns could be added to facilitate product use. For example, incorporating functions that enable users to share or recommend their lighting settings allows users to learn from each other.

4. Kansei Engineering:
Kansei engineering is a design approach that considers how products connect with user emotions. For the smart lighting system, features that automatically adjust lighting color or brightness based on the user's emotional state or time of day could be developed, modifying the user's mood accordingly.

Applying these various psychological theories and methodologies to the improvement of SmartDesign's smart lighting system could enhance both the functionality and user satisfaction of the product. A more in-depth analysis may be necessary to understand how each theory can be applied in practical scenarios.

7. User Testing and Piaget's Cognitive Development Theory

Designing with an Understanding of Developmental Stages:
User Testing and Piaget's Cognitive Development Theory

Understanding how psychology can innovate product design and user experience is an intriguing journey for anyone. Jean Piaget's cognitive development theory provides a powerful tool for deeply understanding users' perception methods and product usage experiences. Starting from the perspective of "seeing the world through the user's eyes," let's explore how Piaget's theory can be applied to product development and the positive changes it can bring to user experience.

Piaget's cognitive development theory is divided into four stages: sensorimotor, preoperational, concrete operational, and formal operational. Each of these stages provides essential insights into how users perceive and process the world. Considering these stage-specific characteristics when designing and conducting user tests allows a clearer understanding of how products truly meet users' needs.

For example, when developing digital learning tools for children, it's crucial to consider that children in the preoperational stage have not yet fully developed logical and systematic thinking. For these users, visual elements and simple interaction designs that aid symbolic thinking and intuitive understanding are necessary. In contrast, users in the formal operational stage, who possess abstract thinking and systematic problem-solving abilities, would benefit from complex functions and advanced user settings.

This psychological approach transforms user testing from a simple error detection process to understanding and fulfilling deep psychological needs and expectations.

By integrating psychological principles into product design and user experience, we can offer users more familiar and satisfying products, ultimately leading to market success. This chapter will explore specific methods for applying Piaget's theory to user testing and the results through case studies. This understanding will help product developers and designers handle users' complex cognitive processes more effectively.

SmartDesign Technologies recently faced significant challenges through user feedback and market research. As technology rapidly advanced, products became increasingly complex, causing confusion and dissatisfaction, particularly among middle-aged and older users. Many users struggled with learning to operate smart devices, resulting in decreased satisfaction with the products. This posed a severe threat to the company's long-term growth and brand credibility.

To address this issue, the company decided to rethink its product development approach. The goal was to enhance user-friendly design and develop products that all age groups could easily use. At the core of this new strategy was the application of psychological theories to product design.

The R&D department began extensively researching Jean Piaget's cognitive development theory. Piaget's theory explains that human cognitive development progresses through distinct stages: sensorimotor, preoperational, concrete operational, and formal operational. Each stage is associated with specific ages, and cognitive abilities at each stage significantly impact product design and usability.

Based on this theoretical background, the company conducted user research to gain a deeper understanding of how various age groups perceive and interact with products. Special consideration was given to middle-aged and older users, who might resist technology more and take longer to adapt to new technology. The research team found that this age group was more accustomed to physical controls like switches and buttons and began exploring how to seamlessly integrate these with digital interfaces.

In the project's early stages, the research team created several prototypes and tested them through small focus groups. They visited actual users' homes to observe how they used the smart lighting system and gathered their reactions and feedback.

During this process, they discovered that middle-aged and older users preferred physical controls over digital ones. This insight significantly altered the direction of product development.

SmartDesign Technologies is thus exploring ways to develop products that satisfy all users by considering users' cognitive development stages and psychological characteristics. This process goes beyond solving technical problems to creating products that meet deep psychological needs and expectations.

Analyzing user feedback on SmartDesign Technologies' smart home lighting system, the development team identified several key issues. These problems were mainly raised by middle-aged and older users, highlighting accessibility and usability concerns.

The first major issue was technical complexity. Many middle-aged users struggled with handling technically complex products. The smart home lighting system was primarily operated through a mobile app, which could be intuitive for younger generations but posed a significant barrier for older users feeling alienated by rapid technological changes. These users were more familiar with traditional wall switches and found navigating various menus and options within an app burdensome.

The second issue was the lack of intuitive interface. The smart home lighting interface aimed to offer multifunctionality, cramming numerous features into a single screen. This complexity made the interface convoluted, requiring users to navigate multiple steps to access essential functions like adjusting brightness or changing colors. This complexity led to significant inconvenience for users.

The third issue was inadequate user education and information provision. Without sufficient explanations or tutorials, users had to explore and understand the product's functions independently. Many middle-aged users needed additional support in acquiring new technology, and the lack of such support resulted in negative perceptions of the product.

By comprehensively analyzing these issues, SmartDesign Technologies' development team learned several crucial lessons. They recognized the importance of making technology products, especially smart home systems, accessible and easy for all age groups to use. They also realized that user interfaces must be as simple and intuitive as possible and that user education and support play a critical role in the successful adoption and use of products. Based on these insights, the team began exploring new strategies to enhance user experience.

When aiming to develop user-friendly smart home lighting systems, SmartDesign Technologies decided to apply Jean Piaget's cognitive development theory. Piaget, a Swiss psychologist, deeply studied the cognitive development process in children, explaining how humans perceive and understand the world through distinct stages. Applying this theory to product design offers an opportunity to create products that meet users' needs across all age groups.

According to Piaget, human cognitive development progresses through several important stages, each associated with specific ages. Initially, in the sensorimotor stage, infants learn to interact with the world using their senses and motor skills, understanding that their actions cause effects. The preoperational stage follows, where children can think symbolically using language but not yet logically. In this stage, children exhibit egocentric thinking and struggle to understand different perspectives. In the concrete operational stage, children can think logically about physical objects, and in the final formal operational stage, they can think abstractly and hypothetically.

Understanding these stages provides SmartDesign Technologies' product development team with crucial insights. Specifically, in the formal operational stage, which includes middle-aged and older users, there is an enhanced ability to understand abstract concepts but potentially lower accessibility and usability of new technology. Based on this understanding, SmartDesign Technologies can simplify user interfaces and strengthen intuitive design elements to help this age group more easily accept new technology.

Furthermore, applying Piaget's stage theory in user testing allows for a clearer understanding of how each age group uses the product and the difficulties they face. This enables optimization of the product interface and functions by age group and the collection of essential feedback for developing products that satisfy all users.

Through this psychological approach, SmartDesign Technologies plans to introduce a smart home lighting system that maximizes usability and appeals to users of various ages. By integrating Piaget's cognitive development theory into product design and user experience, the company aims to pursue user-friendly innovation and enhance its market competitiveness.

SmartDesign Technologies' systematic approach to applying Piaget's cognitive development theory to the usability issues of their smart home lighting system led to significant improvements. The company recognized the accessibility and ease-of-use challenges faced by older users and adopted a multi-step approach to address these issues.

First, the company identified the difficulties users faced with the current interface and interaction methods through user testing. Based on these results, the design team referred to Piaget's cognitive development stage theory to develop an interface suited to the users' age and cognitive development level.

In the second phase, the focus was on simplifying product design and making it intuitive. For example, sliders for adjusting lighting brightness were made larger, visually clearer, and easier to manipulate. Color-changing functions were redesigned to be accessible with just one or two taps, significantly reducing the complexity of use. Immediate feedback for each function was provided, making it easy for users to understand the outcomes of their actions.

Thirdly, SmartDesign Technologies enhanced user education to help users understand and use the product's features effectively. Intuitive tutorial videos and user guides explaining each function were provided, supporting users, particularly those unfamiliar with technology, in easily using the product. These materials played a critical role in ensuring that users could conveniently use the product from the start.

Finally, new prototypes incorporating all these changes were reintroduced into user testing. This testing evaluated how the improved interface and functions enhanced the user experience. As a result, users found the new design much more intuitive and easier to use, with especially high satisfaction among older users.

By adopting a user-centric approach based on Piaget's cognitive development theory, SmartDesign Technologies successfully resolved the usability issues of the smart home lighting system. This process greatly contributed to aligning the product's design and functions with the actual needs and expectations of the users.

SmartDesign Technologies can consider applying other psychological theories to further improve the smart home lighting system and deepen the understanding of user experience:

1. User-Centered Design
 - User-centered design focuses on prioritizing user needs and experiences throughout the product development process. This approach involves analyzing and incorporating user feedback from the initial design stages through to final product testing. For instance, SmartDesign Technologies can conduct user interviews and observations to deeply understand how users interact with the lighting system, using these insights to refine the interface.

2. Behavioral Economics
 - Behavioral economics studies how psychological, social, and emotional factors influence economic decisions. In the context of the smart home lighting system, features can be implemented to encourage energy-saving behaviors. For example, the system could provide tips on conserving energy or automatically turn off lights after a certain period, prompting users to adopt more cost-effective habits.

3. Experience Design
 - Experience design involves creating products that offer a holistic and emotionally satisfying user experience. This approach goes beyond functionality to include the user's emotional response and overall satisfaction. SmartDesign Technologies can incorporate features that personalize lighting settings based on user preferences or change lighting according to the user's mood, enhancing the emotional experience of using the product.

4. Cultural Fit
 - Cultural fit means designing products that are suitable for the specific cultural context in which they will be used. Different cultures have varying preferences and

usage patterns, so it's important to consider these differences in product design. SmartDesign Technologies could adapt lighting colors or control methods to align with cultural preferences in different regions.

5. Gamification
- Gamification applies game-like elements to non-game contexts to increase user engagement and motivation. For the smart home lighting system, gamification can make the process of adjusting settings or saving energy more enjoyable. Features like setting energy-saving goals and rewarding users for achieving them can encourage more interactive and engaging user experiences.

Applying these diverse psychological theories and approaches to the development of SmartDesign Technologies' smart home lighting system can significantly enhance product usability and user satisfaction. Each theory's practical application requires a detailed analysis to understand how it can be effectively integrated into real-world scenarios.

8. Pre-Market Launch Strategies and Rogers' Diffusion of Innovations Theory

Navigating the Waves of Innovation: The Art of Launching in the Market

Introducing a new idea or product into the world resembles navigating uncharted waters. To sail these waters successfully, it's insufficient to merely have a good ship and an excellent crew. One must understand and leverage natural elements like winds, waves, and currents. Similarly, in the realm of market launch strategies, employing insights from Rogers' Diffusion of Innovations Theory provides a crucial key to navigating market currents and setting sail for success. In the world of innovation, innovators are the sowers of new ideas. They boldly conduct experiments at the forefront of technology, often embracing high risks to explore new possibilities. Early adopters follow these innovators' paths, adopting new ideas with caution yet passion. These individuals with high social influence play a pivotal role in shaping new trends and using their credibility and influence to spread innovations more broadly.

When crafting market launch strategies, it is essential to have a clear plan for how to approach and engage innovators and early adopters. For instance, with cutting-edge technology products, these individuals possess the capacity to deeply understand the technology's performance and its innovative features. Therefore, marketing messages must emphasize the technical details and the significant changes the product brings. Conversely, products aimed at a broader audience should highlight ease of use, accessibility, and everyday practicality to attract early and late majorities. A successful market launch of a product or service requires thorough market research and precise targeting strategies. It's crucial to clearly understand the product's features, benefits, and its position in the market, focusing on meeting the unique needs and expectations of each customer segment. One recent example is a high-performance smartwatch introduced to the market, which quickly gained popularity among health-conscious young professionals thanks to its innovative features focused on health and fitness. The product development team meticulously analyzed the lifestyle and needs of this target group, positioning the smartwatch not just as a timepiece but as a partner in health management. Additionally, marketing campaigns that highlighted the tangible benefits early adopters would gain from using this product helped leverage their social influence to spread positive word of mouth. This strategy fortified the product's market launch and facilitated its expansion to a broader customer base.

Technovibetex has garnered attention in the tech industry by successfully developing advanced portable health monitoring devices. The company's product, which tracks users' health status in real-time and provides customized health management advice based on the data, was positioned at the forefront of technological innovation. It received high praise for its innovation and practicality, generating significant anticipation within and outside the industry before its launch.

However, as the launch approached, Technovibetex faced several unexpected challenges. First, the company began experiencing difficulties in sourcing key components due to global supply chain issues. Delays in component supply hindered the final assembly of the products, significantly disrupting the overall launch schedule. Supply chain issues not only caused delays but also led to additional costs, placing a considerable burden on the startup.

Another challenge was the target market's reaction. Although Technovibetex developed its product with a tech-savvy young demographic in mind, it found itself needing to appeal to users across various ages and technical skills. Initial user feedback indicated that the product's user interface was overly complex, particularly among older users who found it difficult to learn how to use the device. This feedback limited the product's mass appeal and reduced its potential success in the market.

Additionally, formulating an effective marketing strategy to launch a unique product in the competitive tech industry became a crucial task. Technovibetex needed to devise creative and effective marketing campaigns to emphasize the product's unique features and secure a differentiated position in the market. However, limited budget and resources made it challenging to launch a large-scale campaign, necessitating a more strategic and focused approach to communicating with potential customers.

In this context, Technovibetex's management needed to find solutions to successfully launch the product and stabilize the company's growth trajectory. The product's technical excellence and competitive positioning in the market were both crucial tests the company faced.

The problems encountered by Technovibetex had various causes, and analyzing and understanding these provided the company with significant insights. The first major issue, supply chain problems, was analyzed more deeply and found to be part of a more complex chain reaction in the global economy. Technovibetex relied heavily on a few suppliers in Asia for certain key components, but natural disasters in the region, combined with a global pandemic, disrupted production and shipping schedules. This led to several postponements of the scheduled product launch, diminishing investors' and the market's expectations.

The second issue, the complexity of the user interface, stemmed from Technovibetex's internal design approach. While the company focused on incorporating technical excellence and innovative features into the product, it designed it without adequate consideration of the actual user experience. Initial market research targeted tech enthusiasts and young consumers, but the product had to appeal to a broader range of consumers, especially older adults who were less familiar with technology. The complex features of the product turned out to be a burden rather than a benefit for these users, who found navigating between various functions difficult and felt the product lacked intuitiveness for everyday use.

There were also issues with the marketing strategy. Technovibetex made significant efforts to publicize the product's unique features, but limited budget prevented a large-scale campaign, leading to insufficient market awareness at launch. This resulted in poor initial sales performance, and the product's complexity and high pricing also hindered its initial market penetration. The company needed to focus more on targeted marketing and consumer education to address these issues.

From these challenges, Technovibetex's management learned crucial lessons about product development and launch strategies, including the need for diversifying supply chains, optimizing user experience, and implementing effective marketing strategies. Based on these analyses, the company developed long-term improvement plans to regain market trust and strive for product success. These plans involved significant internal changes and a transformation in how the company communicated with the market, providing a foundation for overcoming new challenges and fostering growth.

One psychological theory that could be applied to address these issues is Everett Rogers' Diffusion of Innovations theory, first introduced in his 1962 book, "Diffusion of Innovations". Rogers' theory explains how new ideas or technologies spread within a society, offering deep insights into how innovations are adopted and diffused among individuals and social groups. This provides very useful guidelines for companies introducing new products or services into the market.

Rogers' theory of innovation adoption describes the successful diffusion of innovations through five key elements: relative advantage, compatibility, complexity, trialability, and observability. Among these, relative advantage includes the perception that the innovation offers better benefits than existing alternatives. Compatibility refers to how well the innovation fits with the potential adopters' existing values, experiences, and needs. Complexity indicates the degree of difficulty involved in understanding and using the innovation, with lower complexity facilitating adoption. Trialability means the opportunity for potential adopters to experiment with the innovation before making a purchase, and observability is how easily others can see the results of the innovation.

In Technovibetex's case, the company could apply strategies to reduce complexity and improve the user interface. Additionally, enhancing the product's compatibility by considering users' existing habits and cultural backgrounds is essential. Clarifying the relative advantages by clearly communicating to consumers the specific benefits the product offers over existing alternatives is also crucial.

For practical application of the theory, Technovibetex can conduct initial market research to understand the expectations and needs of target customers. This data can guide product development and allow early adopters to test the product, providing trialability. If the product demonstrates successful outcomes, these can be used in marketing materials to enhance observability, helping to generate positive word of mouth among consumers.

These strategies will greatly assist Technovibetex in facilitating success in the market and securing long-term customer loyalty. Rogers' theory not only applies to the introduction of new technologies or products but also provides fundamental principles necessary for managing change and successfully driving innovation. This will play a crucial role in enabling Technovibetex to respond to various challenges and pursue sustainable growth in the future.

Technovibetex decided to actively apply Everett Rogers' Diffusion of Innovations theory to solve several problems encountered in the market launch of its innovative portable health monitoring device. The company undertook a complete overhaul of the user interface, simplifying technical jargon and complex menu structures. It rearranged the interface with large buttons and simple icons, minimizing screen transitions to make it easier for older users and those unfamiliar with technology to navigate. Additionally, to increase trialability, Technovibetex set up free trial booths at community centers, senior citizen centers, and health fairs, allowing users to wear the product and test its functions. The company introduced a program to lend the product free of charge for a certain period, enabling users to try it in their daily lives and apply their experiences realistically.

The company also developed a marketing strategy to make the product's positive effects easily observable, creating video content featuring real users' experiences and sharing it on social media and the company's website. These videos highlighted the convenience of using the product and the process of improving health, allowing potential customers to see the benefits firsthand. This approach began to receive positive feedback from consumers unfamiliar with technology as the user interface improved, and the experience programs helped users understand and appreciate the product's value more deeply. As a result of enhanced observability, the market response gradually improved, and the product began to overcome initial challenges and achieve increasing sales.

This strategic approach by Technovibetex, deeply rooted in Everett Rogers' Diffusion of Innovations theory, provided a strong framework for successful market launch. By applying each element of the theory to product development and marketing strategies, the company overcame existing challenges and laid the groundwork for sustainable success in the market. This process also provided important learning opportunities within the company, reaffirming fundamental principles needed to respond to various challenges and pursue sustainable growth in the future.

The digital age has added a new dimension to the Diffusion of Innovations theory. The influence of social media, the role of online communities, and viral marketing techniques have fundamentally changed how products are introduced and spread in the market. For example, marketing campaigns through social media platforms can quickly raise product awareness and provide immediate access to a broad consumer base, spreading the product faster than traditional marketing methods. These strategies reflect the core principles of Rogers' theory while being adjusted for the modern technological and media landscape.

The experience of applying Everett Rogers' Diffusion of Innovations theory in real situations, as demonstrated by Technovibetex, has provided valuable lessons. Based on this experience, I propose exploring the following related topics and concepts, which can enhance understanding of innovation and technology adoption, and explore their applicability in various scenarios:

1. Technology Acceptance Model (TAM):
 - This theory explains how users accept and use new technology. It is useful for predicting user behavior intentions, especially where ease of use and perceived usefulness are significant factors.

2. Behavioral Economics:
 - Behavioral economics studies how psychological, cognitive, and emotional factors affect economic decisions. It explores consumer behavior, pricing strategies, and how to integrate psychological elements into marketing strategies.

3. Change Management:
 - Researches strategies and approaches to effectively manage and implement change within organizations. It explores how companies like Technovibetex manage market changes or internal innovations.

4. Cross-Functional Teams:
  - Explores the benefits and challenges of team compositions that include experts from different departments such as product development, marketing, and supply chain management. It investigates how collaboration can lead to innovative solutions and optimize communication within organizations.

5. Sustainable Innovation:
  - Examines the process of designing and developing products or services considering environmental, social, and economic sustainability. This approach helps companies achieve long-term success and make a positive social impact.

6. Market Segmentation:
  - Investigates effective market segmentation strategies to provide tailored products or services to specific consumer groups. This improves target marketing strategies and more accurately identifies consumer needs and preferences.

By deeply researching and applying these topics, companies like Technovibetex can strengthen their competitive edge in the market and pursue sustainable growth. Each topic can significantly influence strategic decision-making and innovation management, helping companies more effectively respond to market changes and create new opportunities.

9. Product Lifecycle and Psychological Factors

The Product Lifecycle: The Role of Psychological Factors

Modern society is rapidly changing, and these changes are influencing our everyday health care practices. 'VitaGreen,' an innovative nutritional supplement developed to meet the demands of modern life, allows busy individuals to easily consume essential nutrients. This product is specifically designed for modern people concerned about nutritional deficiencies, aiming to support daily health in an efficient and balanced manner. However, not all innovative products seamlessly settle into the market from the outset. VitaGreen has also encountered various challenges and opportunities throughout its lifecycle after its introduction.

The product lifecycle, much like a human life, progresses through several stages, with consumers' psychological responses critically influencing the success of the product at each stage. Understanding these psychological factors and appropriately incorporating them into the product strategy is essential for sustained success in the market. Through the journey of VitaGreen, we will deeply explore how the product's introduction, growth, maturity, and eventual decline phases are influenced by psychological changes in consumers and how these changes are reflected in marketing strategies.

Each stage of VitaGreen's market presence offers unique psychological challenges and opportunities. During the introduction phase, consumers experience curiosity and uncertainty; during the growth phase, trust in the product and the importance of social proof increase; the maturity phase sees intensified competition and higher consumer expectations; and in the decline phase, interest wanes as alternatives are sought. We will examine how VitaGreen has captivated consumers' hearts and overcome market challenges at each stage, and which strategies were effective.

HealthGlow held high expectations when launching the 'VitaGreen' dietary supplement into the market. VitaGreen was designed to support the health of modern people, enabling those with busy lifestyles to conveniently consume essential nutrients. This product went through various market reactions from its initial release through growth and maturity stages, ultimately reaching the decline phase.

When VitaGreen was first introduced to the market, consumers displayed great anticipation but also significant skepticism. Initial market entry was more challenging than anticipated, with low product awareness among consumers and some disbelief in its actual efficacy. Under these circumstances, VitaGreen struggled to meet its initial sales targets.

As VitaGreen moved into the growth phase, it gradually began to establish its position in the market. Marketing efforts and positive word-of-mouth began to take effect, leading to an increase in sales. During this period, VitaGreen established a unique positioning, differentiating itself from competitors and expanding its market share through various channels.

However, as the product reached maturity, competition within the market intensified, and VitaGreen faced an increasing number of competing products. At this stage, consumers had more choices, and VitaGreen needed further innovation and an enhancement of marketing strategies to maintain consumer interest. Maintaining a unique position in the market became increasingly challenging.

Ultimately, VitaGreen entered the decline phase. The continuous introduction of new technologies and products began to diminish VitaGreen's appeal. At this stage, HealthGlow faced critical moments of deciding whether to reinvent VitaGreen or seek new strategies for repositioning it in the market. The company now needed to make strategic decisions on how to overcome these challenges and reposition the product in the market.

A thorough analysis of the challenges faced by VitaGreen reveals several key issues. Initially, VitaGreen struggled with low awareness and credibility among consumers due to complex ingredient descriptions and excessive health benefit claims causing confusion. Additionally, VitaGreen's high pricing acted as a significant barrier for consumers willing to try new products. These factors increased consumer hesitation at the initial market entry, resulting in lower-than-expected initial sales.

As VitaGreen entered the growth phase, it gradually began to build market recognition, but problems continued. Competing products started offering similar benefits at lower prices, posing difficulties in expanding VitaGreen's market share. The marketing strategies of this period were not effective enough to accelerate sales growth.

During the maturity phase, market competition became fiercer, and VitaGreen began to lose its competitive edge due to a lack of continuous innovation. Consumers started exploring new options, and even existing customers of VitaGreen began considering switching to other brands. Additionally, a lack of product differentiation failed to maintain ongoing interest among consumers.

As it entered the decline phase, VitaGreen failed to adapt to market changes properly, and delays in developing new products accelerated the brand's decline. New health supplements and competing technologies continued to be introduced to the market, and VitaGreen was unable to present new innovations in response. This led to a gradual weakening of its market position, ushering in the decline stage of its lifecycle. Through this analysis, HealthGlow recognized the need to understand the root causes of the problems VitaGreen faced in the market and to develop strategies to address them. In this process, HealthGlow conducted various market research to gather consumer opinions and secure specific data needed for product improvement.

One psychological theory applicable to addressing the challenges related to VitaGreen's market entry is Robert Cialdini's psychology of persuasion. Cialdini's theory explains how people are persuaded and led to certain behaviors. This theory revolves around six key principles: liking, reciprocity, social proof, consistency, authority, and scarcity. These principles can significantly impact consumers' buying decisions and can be effectively used in VitaGreen's marketing strategy.

Consumers are more influenced by the opinions of people they like or respect. HealthGlow can collaborate with respected experts or influential influencers to promote VitaGreen, enhancing the product's credibility and building consumer liking. Additionally, by offering free samples or trial opportunities based on the principle of reciprocity, positive reactions to the product can be elicited.

The principle of social proof utilizes the tendency of consumers to mimic the actions of others. HealthGlow should widely share positive user testimonials and success stories of VitaGreen, reassuring new consumers when they try the product. It's also important to encourage consistent use of the product by emphasizing consistent messages and values associated with VitaGreen's purchase and use.

By incorporating the principle of authority, HealthGlow can build trust in the product by including endorsements from medical professionals or nutritionists. Finally, using the principle of scarcity to highlight the unique features of the product or special offers available for a limited time can stimulate consumers' desire to purchase.

By integratively using these psychological principles, HealthGlow can overcome the market challenges faced by VitaGreen, capturing consumers' hearts with a robust marketing strategy. This strategy will help VitaGreen successfully establish itself among consumers and play a crucial role in building long-term brand loyalty.

HealthGlow has restructured VitaGreen's marketing strategy based on Cialdini's theory of persuasion to address the problems encountered during market entry and growth stages. The company initially simplified and clarified campaign messages to effectively convey VitaGreen's unique value to consumers. In this process, the main benefits of the product were highlighted, and cases demonstrating how these benefits can help in consumers' everyday lives were prominently featured.

HealthGlow utilized the principle of reciprocity by offering free samples to consumers, allowing them to directly experience the quality and effectiveness of the product, building trust and encouraging positive word-of-mouth. Additionally, by integrating satisfied customers' reviews and recommendations into marketing materials using the principle of social proof, new consumers' purchasing decisions were influenced.

To apply the principle of consistency, HealthGlow developed various programs to encourage consumers to continue using VitaGreen once they started. This took the form of a subscription service, ensuring that consumers regularly receive the product, maintaining consistency of use. By applying the principle of authority, HealthGlow emphasized medical validation and expert recommendations for the product, implemented through product packaging and advertising that highlighted endorsements from doctors and nutritionists.

Lastly, by using the principle of scarcity, HealthGlow attracted market attention through special promotions and limited-edition product releases. This strategy perceived the product as a unique purchasing opportunity and hastened consumer purchases. All these strategies played a vital role in overcoming the initial challenges faced by VitaGreen and successfully establishing its position in the market. This approach effectively repositioned VitaGreen's marketing strategy, established consumer trust, and ultimately contributed to sustainable success throughout the product lifecycle.

Additionally, these strategies remained significant as VitaGreen navigated through the growth and maturity stages amidst fierce market competition, maintaining differentiation from other brands. By deeply understanding consumer behavior patterns and psychological motives, HealthGlow could execute customized marketing strategies, significantly enhancing brand loyalty and building long-term customer relationships.

After applying these psychological strategies, HealthGlow experienced significant changes in VitaGreen's marketing approach. The applied strategies greatly improved VitaGreen's market positioning and consumer perception, leading to increased sales. As the product's efficacy and value became clear, consumers grew more trusting of VitaGreen, and the consumer base gradually expanded. After overcoming the initial challenges, VitaGreen was able to establish a strong position in the market as it moved from the growth phase to maturity.

During the maturity phase, HealthGlow focused on continuous product innovation and consumer relationship management. Expanding the product line to meet diverse consumer needs and conducting regular consumer surveys to collect and reflect feedback allowed for ongoing product improvement and sensitive response to changing consumer needs. Additionally, HealthGlow strengthened consumer loyalty programs to maintain long-term customer relationships and enhance brand loyalty.

As it entered the decline phase, VitaGreen faced the emergence of new competing products and technologies. As market changes and consumer expectations evolved, HealthGlow recognized the need for repositioning and innovating VitaGreen. Consequently, the company updated the product to reflect the latest health and nutrition trends and developed new marketing campaigns to maintain competitiveness in the market. These strategies provided a foundation for VitaGreen to continue its growth trajectory even during the decline phase.

Overall, HealthGlow's strategic approach based on psychological principles enabled VitaGreen to successfully compete at each stage of the product lifecycle and effectively respond to market changes. This was a crucial factor in achieving sustainable success and long-term survival in the market.

Additional topics that can be learned from the experiences of HealthGlow and VitaGreen include:

1. Product Adaptation Cycle and Consumer Education: In the case of VitaGreen, insufficient product education at the initial market entry caused significant consumer uncertainty. To overcome this, HealthGlow could enhance educational materials and activities to increase product understanding. Consumer education programs can clearly convey the characteristics and benefits of the product, teach proper usage, and reduce initial market resistance, facilitating product acceptance.

2. Digital Marketing and Consumer Engagement: In the digital age, marketing through online platforms is crucial. VitaGreen can enhance interactions with consumers and increase engagement through social media, content marketing, and online advertising. These strategies are particularly effective for young consumers, contributing to brand awareness and consumer loyalty.

3. Competitive Analysis and Market Positioning: Products like VitaGreen operate in a highly competitive market environment. HealthGlow should conduct regular competitive analyses to reassess its position in the market and develop strategies to

secure a competitive edge. This is important for clarifying product differentiation factors and establishing strategies to gain an advantage over competing products.

4. Systematic Collection and Analysis of Customer Feedback: Consumer opinions and feedback are the foundation for product improvement and innovation. HealthGlow can build a systematic feedback collection mechanism to reflect consumer voices in product development and marketing strategies. This process accurately identifies consumer needs and complaints, forming the basis for continuous product improvement.

5. Sustainability and Corporate Social Responsibility (CSR): Consumers increasingly prefer products from companies that emphasize environmental and social responsibility. Products like VitaGreen can highlight sustainable sourcing and manufacturing processes and actively participate in corporate social responsibility activities to build consumer trust and establish a positive market image.

By exploring these additional topics, HealthGlow can effectively manage VitaGreen's product lifecycle and develop strategies to proactively respond to market trends. These strategies are not only applicable to VitaGreen but also to other product lines, contributing to the overall competitive strength of the company.

10. The Psychology of Customized Products and Personalization

Customization Magic:
The Psychology of Customized Products and Personalization

This chapter explores how consumers react more strongly to personalized products and how businesses can leverage psychological factors by offering customized products. Customization and personalization have become vital elements in modern marketing strategies, aiming to meet consumers' desires and expectations more precisely.

Personalization involves tailoring a product or service based on the consumer's characteristics, preferences, and behaviors. This strategy can evoke a deeper emotional connection and loyalty to a brand. For instance, many online shopping platforms analyze customers' purchasing history and browsing patterns to recommend personalized products. This approach provides a more relevant and appealing shopping experience, leading to higher satisfaction and repeat purchases.

From a psychological perspective, personalization deeply connects with consumers' needs for self-expression. People have a strong desire to express their individuality and identity, which they often wish to reflect through their choice and use of products. Personalized products allow users to showcase their tastes and personality to the outside world, also offering a sense of 'specialness' that delivers powerful emotional gratification.

However, to implement personalization strategies effectively, it is crucial to accurately understand the psychological profiles of consumers and reflect this in product design and marketing strategies. Data analysis, consumer behavior studies, and the application of psychological theories play significant roles in this process. For example, using color psychology can align product colors with consumer tendencies, helping businesses capture their audience's attention and stand out in a competitive market.

This chapter will delve deeper into these concepts and examine how real-world corporate examples have successfully implemented personalization strategies. Personalization goes beyond mere marketing tactics; it establishes an ongoing relationship with consumers and enhances brand value.

To understand the impact of personalization and customized products on consumer psychology, it's essential to examine several key psychological concepts:

Firstly, personalization is deeply involved in consumers' self-identification processes. When consumers' choices align with their personality, they experience greater satisfaction, enhancing positive feelings towards a product or brand. This phenomenon can be explained by the self-congruity theory, which suggests that consumers choose products that reinforce their identity.

Secondly, personalization increases consumers' sense of control. When users can select or adjust specific product features, they feel more effectively in meeting their needs and desires. This is related to the psychological concept of the illusion of control, where consumers perceive that their decisions have a direct impact on the final product, leading to greater satisfaction and brand loyalty.

Thirdly, personalization increases the consistency between consumers' expectations and experiences. When a product or service is tailored to individual specific needs, consumers can use the product as they wish, making the experience more closely match their expectations. This consistency enhances consumer satisfaction and positive evaluations of the product.

Fourthly, personalization increases consumer engagement. When a personalized experience is offered, consumers are more deeply involved in the selection process, enhancing their understanding and attachment to the product. This involvement ultimately contributes to a closer consumer-brand relationship.

By leveraging these psychological advantages, businesses can more effectively execute personalization strategies, enhancing consumer relationships and building brand loyalty. Next, we will explore real corporate examples to see how these personalization strategies have been successfully implemented, revealing how businesses can apply these strategies to their products or services for more detailed insights.

This chapter aims to highlight the importance of understanding the psychology behind customized products and personalization strategies in the modern business environment. By providing personalized experiences, businesses can create a profound emotional connection with consumers, leading to brand loyalty and long-term business success. Additionally, these personalization strategies offer businesses a means to effectively respond to the constantly changing needs and expectations of consumers.

As technology advances, personalization is expected to evolve further. Technologies like big data, artificial intelligence, and machine learning are becoming more sophisticated, allowing businesses to understand and predict consumer behavior, preferences, and even emotions in real-time. This capability will enable the provision of more accurate and personalized products and services, maximizing consumer experience and creating new business opportunities.

Moreover, personalization strategies play a crucial role in the global market. Due to the diverse needs and expectations of consumers in different cultures and regions, global businesses must adopt tailored approaches that consider local characteristics. This emphasizes the importance of personalization in international marketing strategies and shows that culturally sensitive customized marketing is a key element of corporate success.

In conclusion, customized products and personalization strategies provide significant competitive advantages across all business sectors. How businesses utilize and implement these strategies will be crucial in determining their innovation, customer-centricity, and sustainable success in the market. Through this chapter, readers are encouraged to understand the importance of personalization strategies and explore ways to apply them in their businesses to build deeper relationships with consumers.

IV. Investment Attraction and Psychology

The Art of Capital Raising: A Strategic Approach to Investor Psychology

The process of capital raising transcends a mere business proposition, representing a complex set of psychological strategies aimed at captivating investors' minds and gaining their deep trust. This involves a precise understanding of investor psychology and identifying the subtle psychological factors that influence their decision-making. In the chapter "Fundraising and Psychology," we explore these intricate psychological interactions and deeply analyze the psychological factors at play when investors decide where to allocate their capital.

Investor psychology plays a crucial role in managing uncertainty and shaping expectations. Often, investors evaluate risks and rewards irrationally, guided by Kahneman and Tversky's Prospect Theory. By understanding this theory, entrepreneurs and startups can design more attractive investment proposals and effectively present a balance of risk and reward. Moreover, understanding the psychological contract with investors allows for the development of strategies to build strong trust relationships.

This chapter also details investors' psychological motivations and the cognitive and emotional processes they undergo when making investment decisions. These psychological insights significantly influence how investors commit capital, and incorporating this understanding into investment attraction strategies is essential. For instance, by understanding and strategically managing the psychology of 'loss aversion' experienced by investors, the appeal of investment proposals can be enhanced.

Through this chapter, readers will deeply comprehend the psychological elements in the capital raising process and learn how to effectively integrate them into their own fundraising strategies. By grasping and responding to investor psychology, the likelihood of successful capital raising can be significantly increased. This chapter provides valuable insights to entrepreneurs by offering practical case studies and strategies based on understanding investor psychology.

1. Investor Psychology and Kahneman and Tversky's Prospect Theory

The Psychology of Investment Decisions: Unraveling Investor Irrationality through Prospect Theory

In the modern business world, attracting investment goes beyond just showcasing financial metrics and business plan merits—it's a complex process that involves emotions, psychology, and the innate nature of investors' decision-making mechanisms. The chapter "Investor Psychology and Kahneman and Tversky's Prospect Theory" explores how these psychological elements impact investment decisions.

This chapter will analyze the internal conflicts and psychological motivations investors face when deciding on capital allocation, looking for ways to effectively manage and leverage these aspects. Daniel Kahneman and Amos Tversky's Prospect Theory provides an essential framework for this analysis. This theory explains how investors perceive and react differently to losses and gains, particularly highlighting how the fear of loss dominates investor behavior.

We will explore how to optimize investment attraction strategies based on these psychological insights, aiming to understand the psychology of investors and earn their trust. This will provide business leaders with valuable knowledge to comprehend the subtle psychological aspects of raising capital and integrate them into their strategies. Let's delve into the practical situations investors face, analyzing their psychological motivations and decision-making processes in depth.

Startup ABS is a company developing innovative healthcare technology. Their latest project involves a system that monitors and analyzes patient health data in real-time, providing valuable insights to physicians. Although this technology holds great potential in the market, the company has struggled with product development and market entry due to insufficient capital. During the initial phases, the CEO of Startup ABS met with several investors, but they were hesitant to invest due to concerns about the project's potential risks.

This situation showcases the complexity of investors' psychological concerns and economic decisions. Startup ABS faced difficulties in securing the necessary funds due to investors' loss aversion tendencies and sensitivity to risk. Moreover, investors were uncertain about the market success of Startup ABS's technology. They were significantly worried about the possibility of their investment failing and looked for other investment opportunities with lower risks.

Startup ABS's example illustrates the typical psychological obstacles and practical barriers that startups may encounter during the investment attraction process. The psychological unease of investors can limit the opportunities for innovative ideas to be implemented in the market, directly affecting the growth potential of startups. This situation suggests that Startup ABS needs to rethink its strategy for attracting investments and manage investors' psychology more effectively.

The investment challenges faced by Startup ABS stem from complex causes. While the company is developing innovative healthcare technology, the technical complexity and market uncertainty have heightened investors' anxieties. Investors assessed the potential risks highly amidst this uncertainty, feeling unsure about how the technology would perform in the market. The fact that the technology was still in the early stages of development, making it difficult to fully prove its performance and stability, was also a major factor complicating fundraising efforts.

Additionally, economic instability and the competitive environment in the healthcare technology market forced investors to make more cautious investment decisions. The presence of numerous competitors in the market means that a new player must secure a significant competitive advantage to establish itself. This competitive landscape made investors perceive greater risks, resulting in a tendency to seek other investment opportunities with lower risks.

Particularly, investors' loss aversion tendencies had a significant impact on these investment decisions. Considering that the psychological pain of losses is much greater than the pleasure derived from equivalent gains, investors are reluctant to invest due to potential losses. This is consistent with Kahneman and Tversky's Prospect Theory, which explains that people tend to place more weight on potential losses than on potential gains. In the case of Startup ABS, investors hesitated to invest due to fears of failure.

Moreover, a significant issue was that Startup ABS's investment proposal did not provide sufficient trust and reassurance to investors. The failure to adequately highlight the technology's advantages and market potential in the investment proposal, and not presenting a clear risk management strategy, were key reasons for the unsuccessful fundraising. This prevented investors from fully understanding and empathizing with Startup ABS's vision and long-term value.

All these factors collectively resulted in Startup ABS facing difficulties in attracting investment. Next, we will look in detail at psychological theories and the scholars who proposed them to overcome these problems. This will explore ways for Startup ABS to readjust its investment attraction strategy and more effectively manage investor psychology.

The core psychological theory that could help resolve Startup ABS's investment challenges is the Prospect Theory developed by Daniel Kahneman and Amos Tversky. This theory, which evolved at the intersection of economics and psychology, plays a crucial role in explaining the irrational behaviors of humans in decision-making processes.

Prospect Theory offers insights into how investors perceive and react differently to losses and gains. The theory emphasizes that human reactions to losses are significantly stronger than reactions to gains, a phenomenon known as 'loss aversion.' People tend to avoid taking excessive risks to avert potential losses.

Daniel Kahneman and Amos Tversky through their theory, have elucidated various irrational behaviors of humans that traditional economic theories could not explain. Their research provides a deep understanding of how emotions and cognitive biases influence economic decisions. Specifically, they introduced the concept of 'cognitive framing,' which demonstrates how the same choice scenario can lead to different decisions depending on how it is presented.

This theory is of great significance to business leaders and investors. When preparing an investment proposal, utilizing this theory can help develop strategies that consider investors' loss aversion tendencies to alleviate their anxieties and encourage investment. For example, the investment proposal can honestly describe potential risks while highlighting clear plans to mitigate these risks along with emphasizing potential gains to increase investors' psychological comfort.

Startup ABS can use these psychological insights to influence the decision-making process of investors and expect significant improvements in their investment attraction activities.

Firstly, it is necessary to restructure the investment proposal. For this, it is crucial for Startup ABS to transparently disclose the potential risks of the technology while setting up specific plans to manage and mitigate these risks. For example, including initial test results as a risk management strategy and specifying situations that have already been reviewed and prepared for can reduce investors' psychological anxiety. Additionally, emphasizing how technical risks are minimized through various partnerships or cooperative relationships as a risk diversification strategy can alleviate the anxieties felt by investors.

Next, it is important to present the potential benefits more concretely and persuasively in the investment proposal. Providing a competitive analysis of the healthcare market based on market research results and detailing how Startup ABS's technology holds a competitive edge over its competitors is essential. Additionally, showing the market acceptance potential of the product through initial customer feedback and emphasizing how the product meets market needs can help investors more clearly recognize the potential for profit.

Alongside this, strategies should also be developed to provide psychological reassurance to investors. Proposing various safeguards that can reduce investment risks will make investors feel more secure about their investments. For example, clearly presenting a profit-sharing plan based on performance or considering measures that give investors priority in additional funding can help reduce the fears investors feel about potential losses and enhance their trust and willingness to invest in Startup ABS.

Through this strategic approach, Startup ABS can manage investors' loss aversion tendencies and psychological anxieties while increasing the chances of successful capital raising. Next, we will look in more detail at the additional opportunities and potential effects of this approach that Startup ABS may experience after applying these strategies. These specific application cases will show how psychological theories can be effectively used in real business situations.
Startup ABS will then examine how they implemented this approach and observed the results after restructuring their investment attraction strategy using Prospect Theory. The application of psychological understanding and strategic approaches in the investment raising process was a crucial turning point for Startup ABS.

Startup ABS first restructured the messages across their investment proposal and presentation materials to consider investors' loss aversion tendencies. They clearly presented specific measures that could minimize investment risks and emphasized how these risk management strategies could lead to substantial potential profits from the technology. For example, Startup ABS provided investors with clinical data and market research results that demonstrated the potential of their technology to innovatively improve early disease diagnosis. This data played an important role in proving the practical market applicability and profit-generating capability of the product.

Furthermore, Startup ABS proposed higher profit distribution and priority in additional investment opportunities to early investors to reduce the psychological anxiety they felt during the investment process. This assured investors that their investments were secure and that they could achieve greater profits if Startup ABS was successful, positively impacting the investment attraction.

This strategic approach successfully managed investors' psychological anxieties and enhanced their trust in Startup ABS's investment proposal. Consequently, Startup ABS was able to secure the necessary funds and strengthen relationships with investors. This case demonstrates that the application of psychological theories in the investment raising process can lead to practical business outcomes beyond theoretical approaches.

Recent investment trends, such as investments in digital assets, can also be analyzed through Prospect Theory. For instance, investments in cryptocurrencies like Bitcoin involve high uncertainty and volatility, clearly revealing areas where investors' risk biases and loss aversion behaviors can be distinctly observed. The excessive optimism or fear displayed by investors when investing in these digital assets are behavioral patterns explained by Prospect Theory. Analyzing investors' reactions to the rapid value fluctuations of digital assets through Prospect Theory can help clearly understand how investors can make irrational decisions.

Next, we will explore in more depth the additional opportunities this approach by Startup ABS could create in the broader business environment and the inspiration it could provide to other startups or companies.

Another important psychological theory that could be applied to solve the investment attraction problems faced by Startup ABS is the optimism bias theory by Richard Thaler and Cass Sunstein and the satisficing theory by Herbert Simon. These theories can be useful in understanding the psychological factors that influence investors' decision-making processes and strategically utilizing them.

Optimism Bias Theory

Optimism bias explains the tendency of people to overestimate the probability of positive events happening to them and underestimate the probability of negative events. Richard Thaler and Cass Sunstein have studied how this bias impacts individual behavior and decisions. By utilizing this theory, Startup ABS can emphasize the probability of their product's success in the market in their investment proposal, encouraging investors to focus more on these positive possibilities. This can leverage investors' natural optimism, raising expectations for positive outcomes in investment attraction.

Satisficing Theory

Herbert Simon's satisficing theory deals with the concept that humans lack the capability to process all the information necessary to make perfect decisions, often settling for decisions that are 'good enough.' This theory explains how investors might act when they need to make decisions with limited information and time. By using this theory, Startup ABS can design their investment proposal to provide information concisely and clearly, helping investors make decisions quickly.

Additionally, by utilizing this theory, investors' expectations can be clearly defined, providing them with the satisfaction needed to decide to invest in Startup ABS.

These theories, along with Prospect Theory, can help Startup ABS diversify and enrich their investment attraction strategy. Each theory provides a different perspective on investors' psychological motivations and decision-making processes, allowing Startup ABS to develop more effective strategies to persuade investors and secure the necessary capital.

2. Risk-Taking and Investment Decisions: Prospect Theory

Beyond Risk:
The Psychology of Investment Decisions through Prospect Theory

Through Prospect Theory, we delve deeply into investors' risk-taking behaviors in the decision-making process of investments. This theory provides crucial insights into how investors handle risk and uncertainty and why they often make irrational decisions. Notably, investors perceive and react differently to potential losses and gains, showing unusually high sensitivity to losses.

During the investment decision-making process, investors tend to place greater emphasis on subjective values and anticipated losses rather than objective probabilities and expected returns. This is driven by a powerful motivator known as loss aversion. Loss aversion means that investors may forgo opportunities for substantial gains to avoid relatively small losses, leading to choices that are unexpected when only economic rationality is considered. This behavior increases the psychological stress and difficulty of decision-making for the investor.

This chapter analyzes various investment scenarios based on Prospect Theory, exploring how investors avoid losses and seek maximum returns with minimal risk. Additionally, it details various psychological factors that influence investors' decision-making processes—such as overconfidence, confirmation bias, and availability heuristic—and analyzes how these cognitive biases impact actual investment outcomes.

The aim of this chapter is for investors to recognize the pitfalls that can occur in their decision-making processes and learn how to manage them effectively. By doing so, investors can make more rational and efficient investment decisions and, over the long term, optimize the performance of their investment portfolios. A deep understanding of Prospect Theory is essential for investors to navigate market uncertainties effectively.

Consider the case of SmartWell, a startup developing a portable health monitoring device aimed at revolutionizing the market. This device is designed to track and analyze users' health data in real-time, offering an innovative approach to disease prevention and health management. SmartWell was confident that this technology could potentially revolutionize the management of chronic diseases.

The founding team of SmartWell was deeply passionate about their project and had a clear vision of how their technology could transform the current healthcare market. In the early development stages, they conducted several key clinical trials to demonstrate the effectiveness and stability of the device. The data and results were quite impressive and successfully proved the validity of the technology.

However, during the fundraising process, SmartWell faced a variety of responses and psychological barriers from multiple investors. Despite the startup's technology being innovative and having a bright outlook, many investors hesitated due to the high risk and uncertainty associated with this new technology. Particularly in the medical technology sector, the complexity of regulations and high market entry barriers added to the burden of investment decisions.

This situation suggested that SmartWell needed to understand the psychology of their investors and find ways to manage their concerns and expectations. The diverse reactions from investors emphasized the need for the SmartWell team to adjust their proposals more effectively and develop strategies that could meet the psychological needs and expectations of investors.

The challenges SmartWell faced in raising investments were primarily related to the psychological reactions of investors. These challenges can be analyzed into three main causes:

The first cause is investors' aversion to uncertainty. Most investors tend to minimize risks as much as possible when allocating capital. Although SmartWell's innovative medical technology could offer high potential returns, it also inherently carried significant risks of failure. Investors generally prefer more stable investments, especially in the strictly regulated medical field where new technology investments come with greater uncertainties.

The second cause is the investors' loss aversion psychology. According to Kahneman and Tversky's Prospect Theory, people feel losses more acutely than they do equivalent gains. This means that investors tend to focus more on potential losses than on potential gains when making decisions. In SmartWell's case, the possibility of device development failure or market entry failure negatively impacted investment decisions.

The third cause involves groupthink and information asymmetry among investors. In the investment decision process, investors often reference the opinions and actions of other investors, which can lead to similar decisions within a group. If some investors hold negative views about certain technologies or markets, this can influence other investors and lead to adverse outcomes for fundraising overall. Additionally, if there is an imbalance between the information held by the startup and that held by investors, investors often make conservative decisions based on incomplete information.

These causes represented major obstacles that SmartWell needed to overcome through strategic approaches in their investment-raising process.

Analyzing SmartWell's investment-raising challenges, the psychological theory particularly useful to apply is the Prospect Theory developed by Daniel Kahneman and Amos Tversky. This theory, which has evolved at the intersection of economics and psychology, is particularly effective in explaining the irrational behaviors exhibited by investors during decision-making.

Prospect Theory, introduced by Kahneman and Tversky in 1979, was developed to explain the psychological processes humans undergo when making economic decisions. The essence of the theory is that people react differently when they experience potential losses and gains. In particular, the fear of loss is emphasized to be stronger than the satisfaction of an equivalent gain, a concept known as 'loss aversion.' This theory explains why most people are inclined to take greater risks to avoid losses.

Daniel Kahneman, a psychologist, worked with Amos Tversky to make significant contributions to the field of behavioral economics. Kahneman was awarded the Nobel Prize in Economics in 2002 for this research. Their work has influenced not only economics but also marketing, policy-making, and psychological therapy, among other fields. Prospect Theory provides a crucial theoretical foundation especially in areas like financial decisions, investments, and insurance, playing a vital role in understanding individual economic decisions.

In SmartWell's case, applying Prospect Theory could allow them to understand and overcome investors' loss aversion tendencies. For example, SmartWell needs to emphasize in their investment proposals how their technology can manage and minimize potential risks. Additionally, providing case studies or data that highlight the reliability and market readiness of their technology can increase investors' psychological comfort by reducing the uncertainties they feel.

SmartWell can analyze investors' psychological profiles and establish a communication strategy tailored to them using Prospect Theory. This allows them to manage investors' irrational fears during the fundraising process and seek ways to positively influence their investment decisions.

The approach taken by SmartWell to address the challenges faced in their fundraising process was deeply integrated with psychological insights. Initially, the company analyzed investors' loss aversion tendencies and responded by explicitly emphasizing elements in their investment proposal that minimize potential risks. This focus included detailing the technical safety of the product, the success of clinical trials, and the regulatory approval process, all aimed at alleviating investors' anxieties.

Furthermore, SmartWell provided regular progress updates to investors and highlighted key successes at each development stage, offering psychological reassurance. In this process, the company emphasized the successful achievement of each milestone, instilling confidence in investors that the risks they were taking were being adequately managed.

Through direct interactions with each investor, SmartWell was able to understand the individual concerns and expectations of investors and conducted tailored communications accordingly. This played a crucial role in building trust by analyzing the detailed psychological profiles of investors and responding to each investor's specific needs.

In addition, SmartWell added emotional appeal elements to their investment proposal to elicit positive responses from investors. The company emphasized how their product could create social value and improve the quality of life for users, thereby enhancing investors' pride and satisfaction. This strategy was successful in effectively managing investors' irrational fears and biases, positively influencing their investment decisions.

The psychologically enriched approach to SmartWell's investment strategy provides deep insights into the decision-making process of investors. This approach can be further expanded and developed through various psychological theories and techniques. Readers interested in further exploration are encouraged to explore additional psychological topics and theories. These theories can provide valuable tools for deeper understanding of investor behavior and psychology, aiding in the design and execution of effective fundraising strategies.

1. Behavioral Finance: This field focuses on understanding irrational decisions and behavioral patterns of investors, including various concepts such as mental accounting, confirmation bias, and heuristics beyond Prospect Theory. It provides insights into how investors are influenced by emotions and biases and how these can be managed.

2. Cognitive Psychology: Cognitive psychology studies how individuals process, remember, and use information. It is useful for understanding how information is processed during the investment decision-making process and how this can be improved.

3. Social Psychology: This field studies how individuals behave in social situations. It can help analyze group dynamics and the impact of groupthink among investors, developing strategies to effectively manage these influences.

4. Emotional Psychology: This field explores the role of emotions in investment decisions and provides ways to control or positively utilize them. It assesses the impact of emotions such as fear, greed, and happiness on investment behavior.

5. Neuroeconomics: A combination of neuroscience and economics, this field analyzes investors' brain activity to understand decision-making mechanisms. It provides insights into the psychological patterns and brain responses of investors, helping them make more effective decisions.

These psychological theories and research provide essential tools for a deeper understanding of investor behavior and psychology, greatly assisting in the design and execution of investment-raising strategies. Readers are encouraged to further explore and learn these theories, enhancing the psychological skills and knowledge necessary to increase the success rate of investment attraction.

3. Psychological Contracts and Investor Relationships

Building Trust with Investors: The Role of Psychological Contracts

In the chapter "Psychological Contracts and Investor Relationships," we explore how psychological contracts between investors and companies are formed and how these contracts influence investment relationships. A psychological contract extends beyond the content written in formal contracts, encompassing the implicit expectations and promises between both parties. These implicit contracts significantly affect the trust, loyalty, and interaction style between investors and companies.

To analyze various situations that can occur in the relationship between investors and companies, we will use the investment firm Dela as an example. Dela invests in numerous startups and plays a role in maintaining relationships with these companies and supporting their growth. However, recent issues in some of these relationships have highlighted the importance of psychological contracts.

The primary issue between investment firm Dela and the startups stems from a mismatch in psychological contracts. For instance, Dela expects the startups it invests in to achieve certain milestones, whereas the startups have different expectations regarding the scope and nature of the support they anticipate from the investment firm. This discrepancy leads to ineffective communication, and when each party's expectations are not met, feelings of disappointment and distrust begin to emerge.

A deeper analysis of these problems shows that they arise because the implicit expectations between investors and companies are not clearly communicated. During the initial investment negotiations between Dela and the startups, there was a lack of clear definition of roles and responsibilities, leading to misunderstandings and conflicts in subsequent interactions.

The psychological contract theory by Chris Argyris can be applied to address these issues. Argyris researched how implicit contracts between organizations and individuals influence employee behavior and organizational performance. Psychological contract theory explains that strong trust and commitment are formed when the expectations of both parties are met. Conversely, distrust and a decline in performance can occur when these expectations are not fulfilled.

Investment firm Dela can use this theory to ensure that expectations are clearly defined and communicated to all parties at the outset of their negotiations with startups. Additionally, regular communication and feedback can help manage and adjust these expectations continuously.

This approach will help Dela improve its relationships with startups and maintain more robust investment relationships over the long term. By effectively applying psychological contract theory to real-world investment relationship management, investment firms and startups can build mutually trusting and successful collaborative relationships.

In the case of investment firm Dela, applying Chris Argyris's psychological contract theory can address issues stemming from psychological contract mismatches. This theory deals with the impact of implicit expectations and promises on behavior, explaining problems that arise when these implicit contracts are violated. The conflict between Dela and the startups primarily resulted from discrepancies in implicit expectations, with each party entering the investment relationship under different assumptions. While investors expected startups to achieve certain levels of performance, startups had different expectations about the extent and nature of support from the investment firm. This led to increased disappointment when actual performance did not meet expectations, which in turn negatively impacted the investment relationship.

Dela can use Argyris's theory to align expectations clearly at the initial stages of investment and maintain and verify these expectations through ongoing processes. This highlights the importance of clear communication of intentions and expectations throughout the investment process and the need for regular communication to check whether these expectations remain unchanged or need adjustment due to new circumstances. Additionally, establishing clear mechanisms for resolving conflicts can quickly and effectively address issues arising from violations of psychological contracts.

This approach can significantly contribute to minimizing the psychological discomfort and misunderstandings that may occur during the investment process. A strategy based on psychological contract theory is crucial for stabilizing investment relationships and laying the groundwork for long-term success. By doing so, Dela can build a more robust investment portfolio and develop trust-based partnerships with startups. Such relationship building benefits both parties and is a key factor in increasing the success rate of investments.

Applying psychological contract theory, Dela can take specific measures to improve relationships with startups, focusing on reducing uncertainties and distrust that may arise during the investment process and strengthening trust and cooperation between the parties.

First, it is crucial for Dela to clarify implicit expectations and promises during the initial negotiation process of investments. This involves not only including explicit conditions in the investment contract but also understanding the essential roles and responsibilities necessary for the success of the investment relationship. The investment firm should ensure that these implicit expectations are repeatedly discussed and confirmed in all meetings with startups, ensuring that both parties share the same goals and expectations.

Second, establishing a regular communication and feedback mechanism is essential. Dela should set up regular meetings with startups to provide mutual feedback on progress, issues, and performance. This approach provides opportunities to identify and resolve any discrepancies or issues early, ensuring that the psychological contract is continuously maintained and updated.

Third, a clear conflict resolution mechanism must be established. Dela needs to set up clear and fair procedures for resolving conflicts that may arise in relationships with startups. For example, mediation or arbitration through a neutral third party can help minimize unnecessary misunderstandings and conflicts, and facilitate quick resolution.

Fourth, providing education and workshops related to psychological contracts is also important. Dela should conduct training for startups on the importance of psychological contracts, how to manage mutual expectations in investment relationships, etc., laying the foundation for more effective cooperation between the parties.

These measures will help Dela strengthen the psychological contracts with startups and build a robust investment relationship that fosters long-term success and mutual benefits. This process contributes to minimizing psychological discomfort and distrust that may occur during the investment process.

The measures taken to strengthen the relationship between Dela and the startups have led to positive changes in several aspects of the investment process.

First, clear expectation setting and regular communication between Dela and the startups significantly improved trust between the parties. The expectations and roles defined during the initial negotiation stage enhanced the quality of interactions during the investment period, making each party feel more accountable to the other. This increase in trust contributed to both parties raising and resolving issues in a more open and transparent manner.

Second, the establishment of regular meetings and feedback mechanisms provided a foundation for quickly resolving issues faced by startups and continuously assessing progress. This approach allowed Dela to participate more actively in the growth process of the startups, enabling the startups to use resources more effectively to achieve growth goals.

Third, the establishment of clear conflict resolution mechanisms was very helpful in quickly resolving any discrepancies or misunderstandings that occasionally arose. Mediation or arbitration procedures through a neutral third party allowed both parties to find objective and fair solutions in situations that could become emotionally charged.

Fourth, education and workshops on the importance of investment relationships and psychological contracts enabled the management of startups to better understand the psychological aspects of the investment process and effectively integrate them into their business strategies. This training played a crucial role in teaching startups how to maintain and strengthen relationships with the investment company from a long-term perspective.

These changes made the relationship between Dela and the startups more robust and played a decisive role in enhancing the success rate of investments. The strategic approach based on psychological contract theory enhanced trust and cooperation between the parties and laid a solid foundation for long-term business success.

These opportunities are potential benefits that the investment company and startups can gain by effectively managing and maintaining psychological contracts.

The strengthened investment relationship allowed Dela to become more deeply involved in the growth of the startups. This involvement put the investment company in a position to provide advice on business strategies and operations, which could accelerate market entry for the startups and enhance their competitiveness. Additionally, the clarity and reliability of psychological contracts strengthened the willingness of startups to cooperate with the investment company from a long-term perspective, helping to foster a corporate culture that pursues sustainable growth and innovation.

Furthermore, the trust-based relationship between Dela and the startups also sent positive signals to other potential investors. A well-managed investment relationship that upholds psychological contracts enhances the reputation of both the investment company and the startups in the market, creating favorable conditions for attracting additional capital. In such an environment, startups can more easily secure the necessary capital and resources, directly contributing to the acceleration of corporate growth.

The relationship built around psychological contracts between Dela and the startups also provides a robust support network in various crisis situations that the startups may face. The support of a trustworthy investor during crises enables startups to overcome uncertainties and proactively respond to market changes, improving the survival rate of startups and enabling successful long-term business operations.

This relationship-building based on psychological contracts plays a crucial role in allowing Dela to share in the long-term success of the startups and optimize the overall performance of its investment portfolio. Through this, the investment company can maximize the investment value as the startups grow and strengthen its competitiveness in the investment market.

Strengthening the relationship based on psychological contracts between Dela and the startups enhances the success rate of investments and provides long-term benefits to both parties. However, maintaining and developing this relationship requires continuous effort and management. This chapter will explore additional strategies for maintaining and strengthening the relationship between Dela and the startups.

Continuous Education and Development:

One of the key factors in strengthening the relationship between Dela and the startups is continuous education and development. The investment company should provide regular training sessions and workshops to the management and staff of startups, helping them deeply understand the importance of psychological contracts and their impact on both sides of the investment relationship. These educational programs are crucial for startups to recognize the psychological factors that can occur during the investment process and learn how to effectively manage them.

Strengthening Feedback Mechanisms:

Additionally, Dela should enhance feedback mechanisms to effectively maintain communication with startups. Regular mutual feedback ensures that both parties clearly understand each other's expectations and performance, and can make necessary adjustments promptly. As part of the psychological contract, this mutual feedback contributes to achieving results that are satisfactory to both parties.

Flexible Conflict Resolution Strategies:

Since conflicts can occur in any investment relationship, Dela needs to have flexible strategies for resolving conflicts. Mediation, regular problem-solving meetings, etc., using a neutral third party can effectively manage conflicts and minimize damage to psychological contracts.

Continuous Renewal of Psychological Contracts:

Lastly, Dela should continuously renew and update the psychological contracts with startups. As business environments and market conditions change, the expectations and promises set initially may no longer be appropriate over time. Regular reviews and adjustments enable the investment company and startups to effectively respond to changing conditions and continuously develop the relationship.

These strategies are crucial for Dela to maintain a long-term and stable relationship with startups, laying a solid foundation for mutual success. The enhanced psychological contracts increase trust between the parties and serve as a key element for long-term business success.

4. The Psychological Design of Investment Proposals

Moving Minds: The Psychological Design of Investment Proposals

In the chapter on "The Psychological Design of Investment Proposals," we explore how investment proposals can psychologically influence investors' decision-making processes, and examine psychological strategies for crafting effective investment proposals. This chapter demonstrates that investment proposals can function as more than just tools for conveying financial details—they can actively engage and persuade investors by tapping into their psychology.

A key element in designing investment proposals is to capture the investor's attention, build trust, and facilitate decision-making through the way information is presented. Proposals should be structured considering the cognitive and emotional responses of investors. This approach ensures that proposals do more than just introduce a business plan; they should also satisfy the psychological needs and expectations of investors.

The first consideration when designing an investment proposal is understanding the psychological profile of investors. Each investor may have different perceptions of risk, expectations from investments, and decision-making styles. For example, some investors might prefer high risks with high returns, while others might favor more stable returns. Investment proposals should identify these psychological traits and provide customized information to meet the specific needs and desires of each investor.

When constructing the content of an investment proposal, principles of persuasion psychology can be utilized. For instance, applying the principle of social proof by providing information that other investors have already invested in the opportunity can encourage a more positive reaction from potential investors. Additionally, employing the principle of scarcity by highlighting the uniqueness and limited availability of the investment opportunity can prompt investors to make quicker decisions.

While it is crucial for investment proposals to provide logical and objective data, considering the emotional needs of investors is equally important. It is vital to demonstrate how an investment can fulfill emotional needs, such as the desire for stability, achievement, or belonging. These emotional factors can enhance the persuasiveness of a proposal and motivate investors to act.

Finally, the visual elements and clarity of presentation in an investment proposal are important. Information should be clearly and easily understandable, and using visual aids like charts or graphs to emphasize key data can be effective. Clear and intuitive proposals help investors quickly absorb the information and understand the value of the proposal.

By effectively integrating these psychological elements, investment proposals can transcend mere information delivery to actively stimulate investors' psychology and persuade them effectively. This plays a crucial role in enabling investment firms to attract investors and secure the necessary capital.

Startup SJ, a company developing innovative healthcare technology, exemplifies this. Their latest product has the potential to significantly enhance the efficiency and accuracy of patient monitoring systems. Despite this innovation, Startup SJ has faced challenges in attracting sufficient investment.

A primary issue for Startup SJ has been that investors struggle to understand the technical complexity and practical applicability in the market. Many investors are not fully acquainted with the specifics of the healthcare sector and the advanced technical content, making it difficult to accurately assess the innovation's potential success in the market. Moreover, investors are hesitant due to the high risks and long development cycles associated with product development.

To address this, Startup SJ improved the psychological design of their investment proposal, adopting an approach that considers the psychological reactions of investors.

Firstly, Startup SJ minimized technical complexity in their proposal by providing concise and clear information. Using simple language and visual tools to explain the product's functions and market applicability helped investors easily grasp the value of the proposal.

Secondly, Startup SJ integrated principles of social proof and scarcity into their proposal. They highlighted early partnerships with major healthcare companies and emphasized the unique position the product could occupy in the market as a positive social signal to investors. They also specified that the investment opportunity was available only for a limited time, encouraging quicker decision-making.

Thirdly, Startup SJ effectively incorporated emotional elements, appealing to investors' psychological needs. They emphasized the positive impact the product could have on patients' lives and its innovative role in the healthcare market, thereby stimulating investors' emotional empathy and motivation.

Through these approaches, Startup SJ significantly enhanced the persuasiveness of their investment proposal and successfully secured the necessary capital.

After successfully attracting investment with a psychologically designed proposal, let's analyze the positive changes in the investment relationship that emerged. These changes were evident in several aspects, including building trust with investors, maintaining and strengthening ongoing relationships, and enhancing the startup's market position.

Firstly, the psychologically enhanced investment proposal significantly boosted trust among investors in Startup SJ. A clear and comprehensible proposal allowed investors to better understand the startup's vision and strategy, reducing uncertainty in the investment decision process. Investors recognized that the startup's product and market strategies were well-formulated, fostering belief in them.

Secondly, positive outcomes in maintaining and strengthening relationships with investors were observed. After attracting investment, Startup SJ continued regular updates and feedback sessions with investors, keeping them well-informed about the startup's progress. This maintained satisfaction with the investment decision and helped build long-term relationships. Additionally, the startup's proactive communication and problem-solving approach when issues arose further solidified investors' trust.

Thirdly, Startup SJ's market position was strengthened due to the psychological design of the investment proposal. The emphasis in the proposal on the product's innovation and uniqueness resonated well with investors, playing a crucial role in securing a competitive advantage in the market. With investors' support, Startup SJ could accelerate product development and strategize market entry more effectively.

These positive changes demonstrate that Startup SJ effectively designed its investment proposal with psychological considerations and maintained and strengthened investor relationships post-investment. This approach was not only crucial for investment success but also supported the startup's growth and competitive presence in the market continuously.

The successful investment attraction and relationship enhancement experienced by Startup SJ through the psychological design of their investment proposal provide insights for other startups. This highlights the importance and effectiveness of incorporating psychological elements in investment proposal design, offering a broader understanding of its impact.

Startup SJ's case provides lessons for startups in various sectors. The design of investment proposals, considering psychological elements, is not limited to just the healthcare technology field but can be beneficially applied across various industries. For instance, startups developing innovative products or services in fields like technology, education, and environment can make their proposals more persuasive through this approach. The key is to understand the psychological profiles of investors and build appropriate persuasion strategies.

The relationship strengthening between Startup SJ and its investors played a vital role in investment success. This emphasizes the importance of long-term business relationships, suggesting that startups should view relationships with investors not just as a means of raising funds but as partnerships for mutual growth. Continuous communication and trust-building with investors create value for both parties and lay the foundation for effectively responding to changes in the business environment.

Moreover, Startup SJ's case has educational significance. Entrepreneurial education programs or business schools can use this case to teach the principles of psychological design and explore how they can be applied in real business scenarios. Students and entrepreneurs can learn how psychological elements can impact the design of investment proposals and how to integrate them into their projects.

Through the successful investment attraction case of Startup SJ, we can confirm that the design of investment proposals, considering psychological elements, can play a decisive role in business success. This approach is crucial for startups to persuade investors and build long-term business relationships.

The success achieved by Startup SJ through the psychological design of their investment proposal not only facilitated investment attraction but also had a positive impact on building and maintaining relationships with investors. We will now examine several strategies and related theories that could further maximize the effectiveness of this approach.

When designing an investment proposal, understanding and strategically using human psychological biases is crucial. For example, 'confirmation bias' describes the tendency of investors to pay more attention to information that confirms their beliefs. By considering such biases in the proposal and providing data and cases that reinforce the positive thoughts already held by investors, persuasiveness can be enhanced.

Storytelling is a powerful tool that can make investment proposals more impressive and memorable. Unraveling the technical and complex content of a proposal into a story helps investors easily understand and emotionally connect with it. Clearly conveying in the narrative how a product or service differentiates in the market, what problems it solves, and why investment is necessary can effectively attract investors' attention and prompt action.

As investors become more diverse, their needs and expectations vary as well. Emphasizing diversity and inclusivity in investment proposals can provide broader appeal to investors. For example, presenting cases that investors from various cultural backgrounds can empathize with or incorporating elements that investors of different genders, ages, and regions can understand and relate to is beneficial.

Reflecting the latest market and technology trends is also important when designing an investment proposal. Investors consistently monitor new technologies and market changes, and proposals that show how current and future trends will be utilized are more likely to capture their interest. Therefore, it is essential for proposals to clearly outline how they plan to leverage these latest trends to gain a competitive edge.

Effectively designing investment proposals for the global market requires considering the psychological needs and anticipated responses of investors from diverse cultural backgrounds. For example, investors from Asia and Europe may have different perceptions of risk and psychological reactions during the investment decision process. Asian investors often are more influenced by family members or social networks, while European investors might focus more on personal financial goals and long-term investment value.
Considering these cultural differences, investment proposals should be customized to reflect the cultural values and expectations of the specific region. For example, when targeting Asian investors, the proposal can emphasize the values of family and community, while for European investors, focusing on sustainability and long-term growth potential can be an effective approach.

Through these strategies and approaches, the psychological design of investment proposals can be more effectively utilized, not only facilitating investment attraction but also significantly aiding in building and maintaining long-term investor relationships.

5. Investment Attraction Strategies Using Psychology

Psychology That Moves Investors: Strategic Mind Games

In the chapter "Investment Attraction Strategies Using Psychology," we delve deeply into how psychological principles and techniques can be applied during the investment attraction process to favorably influence investors' behaviors and decisions. This chapter acknowledges that investors are not merely rational actors who seek economic benefits, but complex entities influenced by various psychological factors, and explores how to strategically utilize this understanding. Comprehending these psychological elements and effectively leveraging them is a critical competitive advantage for companies seeking to attract capital.

Attracting investment goes beyond a simple numbers game; it requires understanding the psychology of investors and employing a tailored approach based on this knowledge. It is crucial to understand the psychological states of preferences, fears, and expectations of individual investors, and based on this information, design investment proposals that stimulate their psychological motivations. For example, investors often have a tendency to excessively fear potential losses, known as "loss aversion." By considering this in investment proposals, emphasizing risk minimization and stability can capture the interest and build trust with investors.

Additionally, utilizing the principle of "social proof" during the investment proposal process can be beneficial. Investors tend to react more positively to proposals that others have already invested in or endorsed. Therefore, including successful case studies or endorsements from industry leaders in proposals can heighten investors' psychological comfort and expedite their decision-making.

The role of emotions is also vital in attracting investments. Emotional connections help investors engage more deeply with a proposal and motivate them to maintain long-term relationships. Employing storytelling techniques can embed moving and memorable stories into a proposal, making investors feel a personal connection and emotionally inclined to invest.

The psychological approaches presented in this chapter can play a significant role in increasing the success rate of attracting investments. By precisely analyzing the psychological profiles of investors and designing strategic investment proposals based on these analyses, companies can more effectively secure the necessary funds in the capital market. This strategic approach transcends mere capital attraction and extends to building strong, enduring relationships with investors.

Startup Robotics, a company developing cutting-edge robotic technology, possesses innovative technologies that have the potential to revolutionize the medical and industrial automation sectors. Their technology, particularly aimed at applications in surgical robots and factory automation systems, could significantly enhance surgical precision and maximize production efficiency. Startup Robotics' technology has already shown high success rates in initial tests and has garnered considerable interest from experts in the field.

Despite its technological potential, Startup Robotics faces difficulties in securing the necessary funding from the capital market. The company's management needs to attract sufficient investment to maximize the commercial potential of their technology, but the process of persuading investors has proven to be more complex and challenging than anticipated. This is primarily due to investors feeling uncertain about understanding the technical complexity and long-term market applicability of the startup's innovations.

A major challenge for Startup Robotics is that investors do not fully comprehend the technology's complexity, leading to a lack of confidence in its long-term value and competitive edge in the market. This uncertainty causes many investors to hesitate to take on high risks by investing in early-stage tech companies. Moreover, the substantial time and money required for technology development, coupled with a long and uncertain return on investment period, make it difficult for Startup Robotics to attract funding.

In this situation, Startup Robotics is exploring ways to capture the interest of investors and positively influence their investment decisions. The startup is considering developing an investment proposal strategy that leverages psychological elements. This strategy would manage investors' perceptions of uncertainty and risk and effectively convey the advantages and uniqueness of the technology in the market, potentially increasing the success rate of investment attraction. In this process, Startup Robotics is meticulously analyzing the psychological motives and responses of investors and seeking ways to reflect these appropriately in their investment proposals to positively influence investors' decisions.

A deep analysis of the problems faced by Startup Robotics reveals that the main issue lies in investors' inadequate understanding of the technology's complexity and market applicability. Investors' vague fears about the complexity and doubts about the startup's ability to realize its long-term vision significantly hinder the investment decision process, causing hesitation to undertake high risks.

Moreover, Startup Robotics' focus on technical descriptions in their proposals may miss elements that could emotionally resonate or connect with investors. While numbers and data are important, investors also seek to feel a personal connection or emotional motivation with the companies they invest in. When an investment proposal lacks these human elements, it becomes difficult for investors to feel a personal interest or passion for the proposal.

Additionally, the failure of Startup Robotics to clearly communicate the value and benefits it offers to the market and investors also complicates the fundraising process. Investors want to clearly understand the specific benefits they will gain from their investment and the potential for the company's growth. If the startup cannot effectively convey this, investors are unable to see the direct benefits of their investment and find it difficult to make a decision.

To overcome these challenges, Startup Robotics needs to more actively utilize psychological elements in the investment proposal process to attract investors' interest and manage their uncertainties and fears. By doing this, the startup can lower investors' psychological barriers, simplify the complexity of the technology in an easy-to-understand manner, and enable investors to feel an emotional connection with the company.

Potential psychological theories that can be applied to address Startup Robotics' challenges include "Cognitive Dissonance Theory" and "Framing Theory." These theories can provide deep insights into investors' decision-making processes and help the startup optimize its investment proposals.

Developed by Leon Festinger, the Cognitive Dissonance Theory explains the tendency of individuals to change their attitudes or beliefs to alleviate discomfort caused by conflicting beliefs, information, or actions. Startup Robotics can use this theory to find ways to alleviate the anxiety and doubts investors feel due to the complexity of the technology. For example, Startup Robotics could simplify the explanation of the technology's complexity and present real-world success stories or test results to reduce investors' cognitive dissonance and encourage positive decisions.

Framing Theory, developed by Daniel Kahneman and Amos Tversky, deals with the concept that the way information is presented can influence people's interpretations and decisions. According to this theory, the same information can elicit different responses depending on how it is framed. Startup Robotics can apply this theory to adjust the communication style of their investment proposals. For instance, instead of emphasizing potential risks, they could frame the same information from a perspective of positive outcomes, focusing investors' attention on the value of the opportunity.

By effectively applying these psychological theories, Startup Robotics can manage investors' uncertainties and fears and create a compelling proposal that persuades them to invest in the startup. An important aspect of this process is accurately understanding the psychology of investors and optimizing the investment proposal based on this understanding. Through these measures, Startup Robotics can increase its success rate in attracting investments.

The positive changes experienced by Startup Robotics in the investment proposal process by applying Cognitive Dissonance Theory and Framing Theory represent significant advancements in strategic approaches to fundraising. These changes, through a customized approach that considers the psychology of investors, have had a decisive impact on strengthening relationships with investors and securing capital.

Firstly, Startup Robotics restructured information in its proposals and presentations to simplify the complexity of the technology while ensuring that investors could clearly understand the intrinsic value of the technology. In this process, they reduced technical jargon and complex explanations, switching to intuitive and easy-to-understand language, minimizing the cognitive load on investors. Additionally, Startup Robotics presented practical use cases to highlight the product's practicality and market applicability. These practical examples helped investors intuitively grasp the product's potential and form a belief in the technology.

Secondly, Startup Robotics shifted the framing of its investment proposal to emphasize the positive aspects, guiding investors' attention. They restructured the content of the proposal to minimize risk elements and instead focus on the potential benefits and growth opportunities in the market that the investment could bring. This positive framing made investors think optimistically about the proposal and provided emotional motivation for making investment decisions. By painting a picture of successful scenarios that investors could expect, they implanted a positive image in the investors' minds.

Thirdly, Startup Robotics strengthened its continuous communication with investors through regular meetings and updates. This allowed investors to stay well-informed about the startup's progress and provide feedback on the investment. Startup Robotics actively accepted investors' feedback and responded promptly to any issues, laying an important foundation for maintaining trust and long-term relationships with investors.

This strategic approach played a crucial role in enabling Startup Robotics to strengthen its relationships with investors and secure the necessary capital. As a result, Startup Robotics not only increased its success rate in attracting investments but also successfully built long-term partnerships with investors. This experience demonstrates the extensive influence that an investment proposal strategy considering psychological elements can have, extending beyond mere capital attraction to building strong, ongoing relationships with investors.

The case of Startup Robotics provides important lessons for continuous improvement in investment attraction strategies. Utilizing psychological theories to understand and cater to the psychology of investors is crucial not only for the success of fundraising but also for managing relationships post-investment. This has greatly assisted Startup Robotics in developing its relationship with investors from a mere capital raising effort to a strategic partnership for long-term growth and success.

This case has established itself as a significant example for other startups and companies, showing how important a psychological approach can be in investment attraction and relationship management. Strategically using psychological elements is essential for increasing the success rate of fundraising and through this, companies can strengthen their competitiveness in the capital market.

Now, let's explore additional psychological strategies and theories that Startup Robotics could investigate further following the successful improvement of their investment proposal and fundraising. These additional approaches can help Startup Robotics further develop its relationship with investors and ensure success in future funding rounds.

Beyond Emotional Appeal: Psychological Strategies

While Startup Robotics has effectively used emotional elements in its investment proposals, it could consider strategies that go beyond 'emotional connection.' For example, applying the theory of 'emotional adaptation' could develop strategies for investors to continuously maintain and strengthen the positive emotions they feel in their relationship with the startup. This can make investors perceive their relationship with the startup as more valuable and satisfying, encouraging long-term investment and support.

Applying Behavioral Economics

To provide deeper insights into investors' decision-making processes, principles of behavioral economics can be applied. For instance, using the 'anchoring effect' theory could help understand the tendency of investors to make decisions based on their first impressions or initial information about the startup, and actively use this in the investment proposal process. By strongly implanting a positive impression in the initial proposal, continuous interest and positive evaluations from investors can be elicited.

Expanding Social Proof

The principle of 'social proof' already utilized in investment proposals could be further expanded to strengthen the network effect among investors. Startup Robotics could develop strategies to attract new investors by actively using the positive experiences and evaluations of existing investors. This would encourage investors to reference each other's investment decisions and create a positive feedback loop.

Continuous Communication for Building Trust

Continuing and transparent communication strategies are essential for deepening and maintaining trust with investors. Startup Robotics can strengthen its relationship with investors through regular updates, open feedback sessions, and investor events. These efforts ensure that investors are continuously well-informed about the startup's progress and performance, and provide a foundation for responding quickly and effectively when issues arise.

These strategies will play a crucial role in enhancing Startup Robotics' competitiveness in future fundraising activities and further developing its relationships with investors. Through these measures, Startup Robotics can establish itself as a continuously growing and successful company.

6. Building Trust with Investors

The Psychology of Trust: How to Forge Trust with Investors

Building trust with investors is an essential process for startups and growing companies. Trust serves as the foundation for strong relationships between investors and companies, enhancing the potential for long-term capital financing and business expansion. Successfully building and maintaining trust requires a precise understanding of investors' expectations and concerns, responding to their psychological needs. During this process, investors need assurance that their investments are being managed securely and that the company possesses the capability to realize its long-term vision.

The process of building trust with investors can be approached in various ways. First, transparent communication is a key element of building trust. Companies must regularly provide investors with information about business progress, financial status, key issues, and opportunities. This information helps investors clearly understand the company's current status and future outlook, ensuring transparency in investment decisions.

Moreover, companies must demonstrate the ability to effectively manage crises that could arise in their relationship with investors. The ability to respond quickly and effectively to various crises, such as market volatility, competitive pressures, or internal issues, provides significant reassurance to investors. Preparing a crisis management plan in advance and sharing it with investors is an important factor in enhancing trust.

The trust built through these efforts plays a crucial role in enabling companies to attract additional capital and strengthen their competitiveness in the market. Trust transcends mere financial resources, serving as a foundation for drawing in strategic advice, network access, and other resources. This chapter will deeply explore how companies can effectively manage their relationships with investors and secure their ongoing support, seeking strategies for long-term success.

Now, let's examine a specific company facing challenges. Tech startup GYS has a vision to develop innovative artificial intelligence solutions applicable across various industries. This startup, particularly in the finance and healthcare sectors, holds technologies with significant potential. However, startup GYS faces a series of challenges in its relationship with investors. Despite demonstrating high technical potential in the initial stages of investment attraction, it has struggled to secure long-term capital without having yet proven actual market performance.

Investors recognize the potential value of GYS's technology, but they are skeptical about its potential success in the market. This skepticism stems from a disparity between the growth projections initially presented by GYS and its current performance. Additionally, GYS's management has been criticized in self-assessments for lacking transparency and consistency in communication with investors. This has led to a lack of trust among investors, making it even more difficult to raise additional funds.

The issues arising from GYS's failure to manage investor relationships are negatively impacting the company's long-term growth strategy. As investors lose confidence in the management's vision and market strategy, it becomes a significant obstacle to securing the necessary capital and support. This situation presents a major challenge for GYS in securing the essential resources to achieve rapid innovation and growth demanded by the market.

Analyzing the reasons behind GYS's trust issues with investors reveals several key factors:

Firstly, the management's overly optimistic forecasts and exaggerated reports of market potential inflated investors' expectations, and subsequent underperformance in the market damaged trust.

Secondly, GYS's communication with investors lacked consistency and transparency. The company failed to provide investors with regular and accurate updates, leading to doubts about the management's reliability.

These issues have caused investors to reconsider their long-term investments in GYS. Investors began to doubt the accuracy of the information provided by the management, negatively affecting discussions for additional capital financing. Moreover, the lack of communication among investors prevented GYS from receiving necessary support during crises.

In this context, various psychological approaches can be applied to GYS's situation. Specifically, theories such as "Trust Restoration Theory" and "Crisis Communication Theory" from psychology could offer suitable solutions. Trust Restoration Theory provides strategies on how organizations can recover trust after it has been damaged, and Crisis Communication Theory focuses on finding effective communication methods in crisis situations. These theories can help GYS develop strategies to restore trust with investors and rebuild long-term relationships.

Crisis Communication Theory, developed through the research of Tim Coombs, advances methods for organizations to effectively communicate with the public in crisis situations. Its core principle involves the organization being honest and transparent about the crisis, actively working to resolve the issue. This helps maintain or quickly recover trust during crises. Coombs emphasizes the importance of speed, accuracy, and consistency in crisis communication, which helps minimize uncertainty and anxiety during crises and fosters positive evaluations of the organization's response by investors.

Trust Restoration Theory, derived from the research of psychologist William Benoit, explores how organizations can effectively regain public trust after damaging incidents. Benoit argues that it is crucial for organizations to acknowledge responsibility and take specific actions to minimize damage for trust restoration. According to this theory, the trust restoration process should include clear communication, sincere apologies, and proactive improvement efforts. Throughout this process, organizations need to demonstrate authenticity to their investors and present ways to rebuild trust from a long-term perspective.

These two theories provide invaluable insights into managing organizational crises and building trust, essential strategies for maintaining and strengthening long-term investor relationships. By applying these theoretical approaches, startups and businesses can transform crises into opportunities and reestablish close partnerships with investors.

Startup GYS has actively utilized Crisis Communication Theory and Trust Restoration Theory to address its trust issues with investors and develop strategies for rebuilding relationships. The cornerstone of this strategy is to communicate swiftly and transparently with investors during crises, acknowledge responsibility, and present concrete solutions.

Firstly, GYS strengthened its regular communication channels with investors, ensuring that all important updates and the company's progress are relayed in real-time to investors, and any issues are immediately shared. This approach has helped investors better understand the situation at GYS and reduced anxiety by preemptively informing them of potential issues.

Additionally, GYS acknowledged its past overly optimistic growth forecasts and officially apologized for the inconvenience and anxiety caused to investors due to these exaggerated projections. This act reflects the importance of acknowledging responsibility, as emphasized in Trust Restoration Theory, and was a crucial step in showing authenticity to investors. GYS also introduced specific measures to prevent similar mistakes and shared these with investors, committing to enhanced transparency in future business operations.

The company also improved its communication strategy during crises. GYS provided investors with immediate information during crises, clearly communicated the situation's analysis, expected outcomes, and plans for resolution. Throughout this process, GYS strictly adhered to the principles of speed, accuracy, and consistency as outlined in Tim Coombs' Crisis Communication Theory. This helped investors better understand the crises and trust GYS's response methods, aiding in managing uncertainty and anxiety.

Through these strategic approaches, GYS is gradually restoring trust with investors and laying the foundation for maintaining and strengthening long-term relationships. This strategy, based on psychological theories, contributes to enhancing not only investor relationship management but also the organization's overall crisis management capabilities. This will play a crucial role in effectively addressing various challenges that GYS may face in the future, ensuring sustainable growth.

After successfully implementing its crisis communication and trust restoration strategies, this approach has brought about significant changes in the relationship with investors. In fact, investors have highly valued GYS's improved transparency and communication efforts, contributing to restoring and strengthening trust between the company and its investors.

During this process, GYS shared updates on business progress and key achievements with investors through regular meetings, while also discussing potential risks and their mitigation strategies. These open discussions positively influenced investors' belief in GYS's long-term success potential, encouraging further financial support.

Moreover, GYS provided investors with newsletters containing industry trends, technology development updates, and competitive analysis, ensuring that investors have a deep understanding of the market environment and confidence in GYS's business model. This information played a crucial role in enabling investors to properly assess GYS's strategies and performance, continuing to provide necessary support.

As a result of these efforts to strengthen investor relationships, GYS achieved more successful outcomes in funding rounds and experienced a continuous increase in corporate value. Furthermore, this trust relationship has enabled GYS to effectively manage crises and maintain stable growth even in uncertain market conditions.

This case provides important lessons to other companies. Building and maintaining trust with investors is a critical factor not just for capital raising but for securing long-term success and competitiveness in the market. Managing investors' expectations through transparent and consistent communication and continuously strengthening trust with them is a strategic priority at all stages of business growth.

Following the successful implementation of GYS's investor trust-building and crisis management strategies, this approach has brought positive outcomes across all aspects of business operations. Let's now explore further the psychological theories and strategies that can be deeply examined through this case. This will provide additional insights into how other companies can build and maintain investor trust in similar situations.

Expanding Psychological Approaches

1. Emotional Intelligence Theory: Developed by Daniel Goleman, Emotional Intelligence Theory emphasizes how important the ability to recognize and manage one's emotions is in building successful relationships. GYS can use this theory to train its management and team members to be more emotionally sensitive and responsive in communications with investors, helping minimize conflicts and deepen trust.

2. Relational Framing Theory: Relational Framing Theory focuses on how information is presented and interpreted within the context of relationships. GYS can apply this theory to frame information provided to investors in a way that encourages them to interpret it positively. This can guide investors to perceive company information positively and strengthen long-term relationships.

3. Social Proof Theory: Robert Cialdini's Social Proof Theory explains that people tend to determine their actions based on the behavior of others. GYS can use this theory to create positive social proof among investors. For example, by highlighting successful investment cases or positive feedback from existing investors, new investors can be influenced to make investment decisions.

These psychological approaches will play a crucial role in further developing GYS's investor relations and enabling the company to effectively respond to crises. Additionally, this approach provides valuable insights into building and maintaining trust with investors, helping other companies successfully overcome challenges in their business environments and pursue sustainable growth.

7. Emotional Investing and Behavioral Finance

Riding the Waves of Emotion: Psychological Insights in Behavioral Finance

This chapter focuses on the emotional factors affecting investors' decision-making processes and the fundamental principles of behavioral finance. Behavioral finance steps away from the perfect rationality assumed by traditional financial theories to explain the irrational behavior patterns of real investors. This field studies phenomena where investors are often swayed by emotions to make irrational investment decisions, and these insights can assist both companies and investors in devising effective investment strategies.

Emotional investing describes the impact of emotions such as fear, greed, and hope that investors experience in response to market volatility on their investment decisions. These emotions significantly influence how investors process information and assess risks, often leading them to either hold onto unstable investments despite losses or to make excessive investments based on overly optimistic forecasts. Such behaviors have a profound impact on how investors manage their investment portfolios.

Behavioral finance offers a variety of theories and models that focus on understanding and predicting these irrational behaviors. For example, the principle of 'loss aversion' explains that investors feel much greater pain from losses than the joy from gains of equivalent value. This principle helps understand why investors might choose conservative investments to minimize losses or fail to acknowledge losses and hold onto losing investments for extended periods.

This chapter will explore how emotional investing and theories of behavioral finance can be applied in real investment situations. This will enable companies and investors to more effectively tailor their investment strategies, understand the behaviors of investors, and minimize potential errors in the decision-making process. Additionally, these theories aim to reduce the tendency of investors to make decisions based on emotion and to develop strategies that increase the success rate of investments through more rational, scientific approaches.

Startup ABSNA, a company developing healthcare solutions based on advanced technology, initially succeeded in attracting significant funding from investors. The company's products, combining innovative medical devices and software, aim to revolutionally improve patient care management. However, as the market changes rapidly and competition intensifies, Startup ABSNA has found it challenging to achieve tangible results that meet investor expectations.

Startup ABSNA is particularly struggling with delays in product launches and lower-than-expected market acceptance rates. These issues have caused investors to feel uneasy, adversely affecting additional funding rounds. Initially, investors had high expectations for ABSNA's technology and vision, but they have become increasingly skeptical and reluctant to provide further financial support.

In this situation, ABSNA's management needs to manage investors' emotional responses and devise strategies to regain trust. The impact of emotional investing on investors' behavior can significantly affect the company's financial stability and long-term growth potential, making its proper management a crucial factor for the company's success. This scenario is particularly suitable for applying theories of emotional investing and behavioral finance to alleviate investor anxiety and promote more rational investment decisions.

When analyzing the root causes of the problems faced by Startup ABSNA, incorrect predictions about market acceptance rates and unexpected delays in the product development process are identified as major factors. The company anticipated rapid market acceptance of its innovative medical devices, but in reality, the presence of competitive products, lack of market readiness, and conservative attitudes of target customers slowed down acceptance rates. This discrepancy between initial investor expectations and actual market reactions caused significant investor unease and disappointment.

Furthermore, technical difficulties and regulatory approval delays in the product development process have postponed the launch timeline, causing investors to doubt ABSNA's execution capabilities and diminishing trust in the company. These situations triggered emotional reactions from investors, with behavioral finance factors such as aversion to uncertainty and risk aversion becoming more pronounced.

To address these issues, Startup ABSNA needs to apply behavioral finance theories to understand and manage the emotional decision-making mechanisms of investors. Specifically, utilizing concepts like loss aversion to mitigate investors' fear-induced hasty actions and help them assess the company's potential from a long-term perspective is crucial. Additionally, ABSNA must enhance communication with investors, sharing all critical updates and the company's progress transparently, and proactively presenting solutions and plans when problems arise. By doing so, ABSNA can reduce investor anxiety, gradually restore trust, and secure long-term support.

To solve these problems, Startup ABSNA developed strategies applying various psychological theories to adjust investors' emotional responses and rebuild trust. The focus is on utilizing various principles presented in behavioral finance to understand and predict investors' irrational behaviors and emotional decisions. Through this, ABSNA sought ways to mitigate the fears and anxieties investors might experience, promoting more rational investment decisions.

Understanding the principle of loss aversion is crucial in managing the emotional unease investors experience. ABSNA based its strategy on this principle to report business progress more transparently to investors, aiming to reduce potential loss-related anxieties. Moreover, the company strategically emphasized positive outcomes and market progress to encourage investors to focus on the long-term growth potential of the company.

ABSNA utilized regular investor meetings and informal communication channels to strengthen emotional connections with investors, ensuring they feel a greater personal connection to the company and maintaining their support over the long term. This human-centric approach has helped transform investors from mere capital providers into genuine partners rooting for the company's success.

By integrating theories of behavioral finance into the company's investor management strategies, Startup ABSNA has been better able to manage the unpredictable behaviors of investors. This strategic approach has helped anticipate potential behavioral biases among investors and adjust communication and management strategies accordingly. As a result, this approach has successfully contributed to restoring trust and stabilizing investment relationships.

This strategic execution has allowed Startup ABSNA to reestablish relationships with investors and lay the foundation for pursuing sustainable growth in a volatile market environment. This serves as a valuable case study for other companies in utilizing behavioral finance approaches in investor relationship management and decision-making processes during crises.

Startup ABSNA's strategies based on emotional investing and behavioral finance have effectively deepened and stabilized relationships with investors. This successful management practice is crucial for the company's continued growth and strengthening partnerships with investors. Moving forward, it is necessary to further explore strategies to overcome various challenges in investor relationships and minimize the impact of emotional factors on management decisions.

Additionally, Startup ABSNA has started to regularly hold performance review meetings and actively involve investors in all critical decision-making processes. This approach helps investors gain more insight into the company's operations and clearly understand how their investments are being managed. Moreover, involving investors in major decisions increases their satisfaction and attachment to their investments.

Startup ABSNA continues to develop strategies to respond swiftly and effectively in crisis situations. For this purpose, protocols have been established to immediately notify investors during crises and clearly present solutions to the situation. Regular training simulations are also conducted to ensure the entire team is prepared to respond effectively in actual crisis scenarios. This preparedness provides significant reassurance to investors, further strengthening the trust relationship.

To minimize the impact of emotional factors on investors' decision-making processes, Startup ABSNA has initiated educational programs for investors. These programs aim to enhance understanding of the fundamental principles of behavioral finance and the psychological errors that often occur in the investment decision process. Through education, investors can better recognize and manage the emotional factors that may influence their decisions, leading to more rational investment choices.

This strategic approach plays a crucial role in maintaining and strengthening Startup ABSNA's long-term relationships with investors. By enhancing investors' psychological stability and maintaining a strong partnership even in crisis situations, ABSNA can pursue sustainable growth in the market.

The continuous education and psychological stability resulting from these initiatives have enabled Startup ABSNA to build more robust trust with investors. Investors have been impressed by ABSNA's transparent communication and crisis response capabilities, leading to positive interactions that include additional funding opportunities. As investor trust is reinforced, they become more understanding and proactive in providing necessary support during difficult times.

As investor participation and support increase, Startup ABSNA has been successful in securing the resources necessary for product development and market expansion. This has played a crucial role in solidifying the company's position in the market and securing a competitive advantage. Additionally, the investor education program has enabled investors to become more deeply involved in ABSNA's long-term vision and strategy, providing broader insights and support for corporate management.

Startup ABSNA's experience is documented as a model case for successfully applying the principles of emotional investing and behavioral finance in business operations and investor management. This case offers important insights for other companies on understanding the role of emotions in investor relations and decision-making processes, and on developing more effective strategies based on this understanding.

Looking forward, Startup ABSNA plans to continuously observe and analyze the behavioral biases and emotional factors of investors to further strengthen and maintain these relationships and lay the foundation for maintaining robust trust even in crisis situations. These ongoing efforts are essential for Startup ABSNA to successfully grow in the global market and maintain a sustainable business model.

Several additional strategies and directions for exploring and applying the principles of emotional investing and behavioral finance are suggested for further advancing investor relationships and minimizing the impact of emotions on business decisions:

1. Development of Behavioral Finance Workshops: ABSNA can develop and offer behavioral finance workshops for investors, where key behavioral finance concepts influencing investment decisions are taught, and practical methods for applying this information to investors' strategies are explored.

2. Development of Emotional-Based Investment Tracking Tools: ABSNA can develop digital tools that allow investors to monitor the relationship between their emotional state and investment decisions. These tools help investors manage the impact of emotional factors such as stress or excessive optimism on their investment decisions in real-time.

3. Publication of Case Study Series: ABSNA can compile and publish research reports or a series of cases where behavioral finance theories have been successfully applied to improve investor relations. This material can serve as a useful reference for investors and financial professionals and can be used to highlight the company's expertise and leadership.

4. Investment Behavior Analysis Consulting Services: ABSNA can start providing consulting services offering investment behavior analysis and behavioral finance advice to other companies. This service can help companies more effectively manage their investor bases and minimize the negative impacts of emotional investing.

These strategies will contribute significantly to ABSNA's ability to more effectively utilize the principles of emotional investing and behavioral finance, continuously improving investor relations. This will enable ABSNA to maintain its competitiveness in the market and pursue successful long-term growth.

8. Cognitive Biases in Investment Decisions

The Mind's Maze:
Cognitive Biases in Investment Decisions

This chapter delves deeply into cognitive biases that occur during the investment decision-making process. Cognitive biases are unconscious errors that frequently occur as investors interpret information and make decisions. These biases encompass various cognitive errors that influence economic choices and are a significant topic of study in psychology and behavioral economics. Cognitive biases can distort an investor's judgment, increasing the likelihood of irrational investment decisions. Thus, understanding and managing these biases is crucial for investors to make more rational decisions. This chapter will identify major cognitive biases that affect investment decisions and analyze how they influence financial markets and individual investor behavior.

To broadly understand the impact of cognitive biases on investment decisions, it is essential to first identify how these biases manifest. For example, confirmation bias is the tendency of investors to selectively gather and pay attention to information that supports their beliefs or existing investment strategies. This bias can cause investors to overlook market changes or new risk factors, potentially leading to significant losses. Another bias, representativeness bias, refers to the tendency of investors to incorrectly assess the likelihood of an event or phenomenon by comparing it to similar past occurrences. This bias can lead investors to overgeneralize from past successful investment experiences and apply them incorrectly to future investment decisions.

There are several strategies to overcome these cognitive biases in investment decisions:

Firstly, educating and training investors to recognize their biased thought processes and cope with them is essential. Investment workshops, seminars, and online courses can be provided to help investors adopt a more objective and analytical approach in various market scenarios.

Secondly, introducing a structured investment process to minimize the emotional impact on decision-making and base decisions on objective data and analysis can be beneficial. This can be achieved by forming investment review committees or using automated decision-making tools.

These approaches will help investors reduce the impact of cognitive biases, leading to more rational and effective investment strategies. Such understanding and strategies are invaluable not only for individual investors but also for financial institutions and asset management companies, contributing to more efficient capital allocation and enhanced investment profitability.

Now, let's examine a specific scenario faced by a company.

Startup Mero developed an advanced big data analysis platform, aiming to bring innovation to the financial services market. Initially, its innovative approach and technological superiority attracted significant investment. However, over time, market changes and intensified competition began to slow its growth rate. This situation triggered various cognitive biases among the investors, ultimately undermining their trust.

Particularly, Mero faced issues of confirmation bias and post-purchase rationalization among its investors, who tended to emphasize only successful outcomes to justify their initial investment decisions, overlooking or downplaying negative information. This prevented Mero's actual issues from being properly assessed and timely addressed.

Moreover, Mero experienced an enhancement in investors' loss aversion tendency amid market uncertainty and rapid technological changes. This led investors to avoid greater risks and seek other investment opportunities that could offer stable returns. As Mero became less attractive for investment, investors began to halt further investments or withdraw their capital.

These challenges presented Mero with two primary tasks: rebuilding investor trust and securing financial stability. The company needed to enhance communication with investors and provide objective and transparent information to rebuild trust. Additionally, considering investors' cognitive biases, the management needed to emphasize the company's true value and long-term growth strategy through investor briefings and regular updates. These efforts would be crucial in alleviating investor anxieties and motivating them to maintain their long-term investments in Mero.

The root causes of Mero's challenges were investor cognitive biases and market volatility. Investors' confirmation biases led them to selectively interpret and accept information that supported their initial positive expectations, overlooking Mero's long-term issues. Additionally, their loss aversion tendency caused an overly reactive response to potential risks, leading to decisions to avoid further investment or withdraw existing investments, significantly weakening Mero's fundraising capabilities and market competitiveness.

To address these issues, Mero needed to develop strategies to manage and minimize the impact of investor cognitive biases. Particularly, implementing investor education programs to help investors recognize their cognitive biases and make more objective and rational investment decisions was considered. This education would introduce investors to various psychological errors that could occur during the investment decision-making process and ways to handle them, incorporating real market data and case studies to apply theoretical knowledge in real investment situations.

Furthermore, Mero strengthened efforts to provide accurate and transparent information to investors through regular communications and investment reports. This helped investors clearly understand the company's progress and evaluate potential risks in real time. Especially, Mero arranged times during investor meetings and conference calls for management to directly respond to investor questions and explain the company's long-term strategies and market position, focusing on alleviating investor anxieties and enhancing trust.

The strategic approaches based on prospect theory helped Mero predict and address behaviors like investors' loss aversion tendencies, providing psychological comfort to the investors. The company continuously monitored investors' reactions and behavior patterns, using this data to offer more personalized information and advice. These efforts significantly helped reduce investor cognitive biases and improve the quality of investment decisions.

Such approaches have gradually helped Mero rebuild trust with investors and successfully establish long-term partnerships. The enhanced communication and investor education strategies have laid the foundation for investors to confidently support Mero's long-term vision and growth strategy. These strategic approaches have ensured Mero's sustainable growth and maintained its competitiveness in an uncertain economic environment.

Mero's strategic approach to understanding and managing investor cognitive biases offers important lessons for other companies. Based on this experience, helping more investors understand psychological theories and apply them to their investment behavior can have a positive impact on the entire investment community.

Further exploration and providing additional educational opportunities are available. Mero can offer continuous education opportunities to investors to deepen their understanding of cognitive biases and their impact on investment decisions. This can be done by inviting expert instructors and psychologists to conduct workshops and seminars regularly, providing educational content that integrates the latest psychological research and market analysis.

And enhancing investor engagement and feedback is crucial. Encouraging investors to actively participate in the education and investment decision-making process enriches their experience and allows for substantial feedback. This plays a vital role in assessing and continually improving the effectiveness of the education program.

Next is the development of digital resources and tools. Developing digital tools and applications that help investors recognize and manage cognitive biases in real time can be a useful approach. These tools support investors in monitoring their investment behavior and making necessary adjustments promptly, helping them make more rational investment decisions.

Lastly, building community and strengthening networking is important. Mero can provide a platform for investors to share experiences and exchange knowledge within the investor community, fostering learning and collaboration. This community enables investors to learn from each other's experiences, discuss cognitive biases more deeply, and develop collective investment strategies.

These strategic activities play an essential role in maintaining and enhancing Mero's continuous trust relationship with investors and expanding their influence in the broader investment market. This ultimately ensures Mero's sustainable growth and success in the market.

Mero's approach has provided a deep understanding of managing investor cognitive biases, but further exploration of additional psychological theories can deepen this understanding and find ways to effectively support investors' decision-making processes and optimize their behavior in the financial markets.

1. Emotional Contagion Theory: This theory covers the concept that emotions can be transferred from one person to another. Understanding how positive or negative market sentiments spread among investors can enable Mero to develop strategies to predict and respond to large-scale emotional reactions in the market. This knowledge can help prevent market panic or overheating and maintain investor emotional stability.

2. Self-Efficacy Theory: Albert Bandura's theory explains how individuals perceive their capabilities and how this perception influences their goal-achieving behaviors. Developing programs to enhance investors' self-efficacy can help them make more confident investment decisions and respond more effectively to market fluctuations.

3. Social Learning Theory: This theory discusses the concept that individuals learn by observing and mimicking the actions of others. Mero can present cases of successful investors in its investor education programs, enabling investors to acquire effective investment habits and skills.

4. Groupthink Theory: This theory suggests that a strong motivation to reach consensus within a group can degrade the quality of decisions. Mero can develop

strategies to ensure that investors do not fall into the trap of groupthink, encouraging the reflection of diverse opinions and perspectives in the investment decision-making process.

By further exploring and applying these psychological theories, Mero can deepen its understanding of investor behavior and decision-making processes and based on this, establish more effective investor management strategies. This will contribute to optimizing investor psychological stability and investment performance.

9. Crowdfunding and Social Motivation

Leveraging Social Connections for Fundraising: The Psychology of Crowdfunding

In this chapter, we explore crowdfunding and the significant role of social motivation in the process. Crowdfunding is a method of gathering funds from a large number of people via the internet, where individuals or organizations contribute small amounts of money to support projects, ideas, or enterprises. During this process, social motivations play a crucial role as participants choose to contribute for reasons beyond financial gain, such as social recognition, contribution to the community, and support for innovative ideas.

The success of a crowdfunding campaign is not guaranteed merely by having a good idea. Understanding the psychological process that motivates participants to invest money is crucial, and this understanding can make a decisive difference in the design and execution of crowdfunding campaigns. Crowdfunding platforms serve as a venue for social interaction, where people adjust their behavior based on the activities of others. In this context, psychological concepts such as social proof, cognitive dissonance, and reciprocity play significant roles.

This chapter will deeply explore the psychological factors influencing individuals participating in crowdfunding and how these factors can be utilized in the design and strategy of crowdfunding campaigns. Additionally, by understanding investors' social motivations and their impact on investment decisions, we will present methods to more effectively manage and optimize crowdfunding campaigns. Such approaches are essential for establishing successful fundraising strategies in the dynamic environment of crowdfunding.

Let's examine a specific situation faced by a company. EcoGreen, a startup, aimed to reduce the use of disposable plastics by providing eco-friendly packaging solutions. The company decided to raise funds through crowdfunding but faced difficulties attracting as much interest as anticipated. Initially, some investors actively supported the campaign, but over time, interest waned, leading to a failure to gather the necessary funds and causing significant issues for the project's sustainability.

EcoGreen's crowdfunding failure was due to multiple factors:

1. The campaign's message was not compelling enough to motivate a broad audience.
2. In the highly competitive environment of the crowdfunding platform, EcoGreen's project did not stand out.
3. The lack of continued participation from initial investors failed to provide subsequent investors with social proof, which is crucial given the nature of crowdfunding where social motivation plays a significant role.

The primary issues EcoGreen faced were the lack of appeal in the campaign and insufficient social motivation. The success of crowdfunding largely depends on how emotional and psychological engagement is elicited from the public. Without providing sufficient investment incentives and motivations, it is challenging to achieve fundraising goals. EcoGreen overlooked these aspects and consequently failed to raise the necessary funds.

Upon analyzing EcoGreen's crowdfunding campaign failure, the identified causes were threefold:
1. The campaign's messaging and presentation were not persuasive or attractive enough to draw investors.
2. The initial lack of active participation failed to provide strong social proof for subsequent investors.
3. EcoGreen's project did not sufficiently stand out in the competitive crowdfunding platform environment, failing to generate overall visibility and interest.

To overcome these issues, applicable psychological theories include the 'Social Proof Theory' and the 'Principle of Reciprocity'. Social Proof Theory explains that people tend to determine their behaviors based on the actions of others. Applying this theory, EcoGreen could secure the participation of a few influential investors early on to send positive social signals to other investors. Additionally, by utilizing the Principle of Reciprocity, offering investors a form of reward can encourage their further participation and support.

By integrating these psychological approaches into their campaign strategy, EcoGreen could provide stronger motivational incentives for investors and foster interest and investment in the project. For instance, highlighting contributions from initial investors and actively promoting this on social media and campaign pages could provide strong social proof for subsequent investors. Creatively designing rewards for investors can also foster a personal connection and sense of belonging to the project. These strategies would play a crucial role in EcoGreen achieving its fundraising goals and ensuring the successful implementation of the project.

Such a psychological approach to reconstructing EcoGreen's crowdfunding campaign would proceed as follows. EcoGreen plans to leverage Social Proof Theory from the early stages of the campaign by securing the participation of influential investors, whose support would serve as a positive signal to other potential investors. This would involve building partnerships with influencers or industry leaders who would publicly endorse and promote the campaign.

Furthermore, applying the Principle of Reciprocity, EcoGreen would offer special rewards as a token of appreciation for investors' contributions. These rewards could be unique and valuable items relevant to the project's nature, providing exclusive experiences that encourage investors' continued participation and support. For example, offering limited edition EcoGreen products or opportunities to participate in the product development process would make investors feel more connected and personally invested in the project.

This approach considers investors' psychological factors to guide their behavior and stimulate investment in the project. By closely analyzing investors' responses at each stage of the campaign and making necessary adjustments promptly, the maximum effect can be achieved. Through this process, EcoGreen could successfully complete its crowdfunding and achieve its goal of introducing environmentally friendly packaging solutions to the market.

The reconstructed campaign provides investors with the satisfaction of contributing to a socially responsible project, serving as a crucial motivator for EcoGreen to pursue larger goals of social value and environmental protection. This strategic approach enables EcoGreen to pursue sustainable growth in the market, maintain competitiveness in an uncertain economic environment, and build trust with investors.

Several psychological theories significantly influence the motivational and behavioral aspects of investors in crowdfunding campaigns. Among these, Robert Cialdini's Social Proof Theory and the Law of Reciprocity, along with Abraham Maslow's Need for Belonging, play crucial roles in the success of crowdfunding. These theories provide a foundation for understanding and predicting investors' behaviors and are essential elements in effectively designing and executing campaigns.

According to Robert Cialdini's Social Proof Theory, people tend to imitate the actions they observe others performing. In the context of crowdfunding, this is particularly important because when a few influential investors fund a project early on, their actions serve as a strong signal to subsequent investors, indirectly proving the project's credibility and value. This signal helps other investors reduce uncertainty and make participation decisions.

The Law of Reciprocity explains the tendency of people to return favors or gifts in kind. In crowdfunding, the rewards that investors receive after contributing to a project activate this law, providing an additional incentive for them. For example, offering investors special rewards such as limited edition products, results of the project, or experiences in exchange for specific donation amounts deepens their personal investment and interest in the project.

Abraham Maslow's Need for Belonging is based on the human desire for social connections and belonging. Crowdfunding campaigns are often organized around specific communities or social causes, and by contributing to these shared goals, investors satisfy their desire to be part of a community. This process gives investors a sense of their contributions being part of a larger purpose, providing them with psychological satisfaction and motivation.

By integrating and applying these psychological theories, crowdfunding campaigns can effectively understand and predict investors' psychological motives and behaviors, allowing for more sophisticated campaign design and execution strategies. This approach increases the likelihood of campaign success and ensures the project's long-term sustainability.

The psychological approaches applicable to solving the issues faced by EcoGreen's crowdfunding campaign are detailed as follows. This approach is designed to positively influence the investment decision process by considering investors' social motives and psychological factors.

First, following the Social Proof Theory, EcoGreen secured the participation of influential investors early on to indirectly prove the campaign's trustworthiness and value through their support. EcoGreen organized an initial fundraising round targeting environmental advocacy groups, renowned environmental activists, and industry leaders. Their participation was promoted on the campaign page and social media, providing strong social proof to other potential investors. This strategy was particularly effective in the uncertain crowdfunding environment, encouraging subsequent investor participation.

Next, utilizing the Principle of Reciprocity, EcoGreen enhanced its reward system for investors. Offering special rewards as a token of appreciation for investors' contributions is a powerful way to create investment incentives. EcoGreen set up different reward tiers for donors, including unique eco-friendly products, opportunities to participate in the project's development process, and the right to test some successful project outcomes. These rewards motivated investors to engage more deeply with the project and continue their support.

Lastly, based on the Need for Belonging, EcoGreen worked to ensure that investors felt personally connected to the project and part of the community. EcoGreen issued regular newsletters to investors and hosted webinars sharing project progress. Additionally, online forums and social media groups were provided as platforms for investors to exchange opinions, share ideas, and provide feedback on the project. These activities facilitated interactions among investors and made them feel a greater sense of belonging to the project, positively influencing their investment decisions.

This psychological approach played a crucial role in reorganizing EcoGreen's crowdfunding campaign and maximizing investor participation. By enhancing investors' emotional and psychological engagement with the project, EcoGreen successfully raised the necessary funds and achieved its goal of launching a sustainable packaging solution in the market.

To further explore social motivations related to crowdfunding, additional psychological theories that can be discussed include:

1. Emotional Contagion Theory: This theory deals with the concept that emotions can be contagious from one person to another. In crowdfunding, the enthusiasm or positive emotions of participants can spread to other potential investors, contributing to the campaign's momentum. Projects like EcoGreen can foster positive emotions among investors, encouraging them to participate more actively and provide support.

2. Equity Theory: This theory explains that individuals assess the fairness of their contributions and the rewards they receive, and this perceived fairness determines their satisfaction and behavior. In crowdfunding, if investors feel a sense of fairness between their contributions to the project and the rewards they receive, they are more likely to be satisfied and continue their support. EcoGreen can encourage ongoing participation and support by offering investors rewards that are commensurate with their contributions.

3. Self-Determination Theory: This theory explains that people experience greater satisfaction and motivation when they have control over their actions. In a crowdfunding campaign, if investors feel that they have control over their choices and decisions, they are more likely to participate actively and feel a greater sense of responsibility for the outcomes. EcoGreen can engage investors more deeply by providing various ways to participate and choices that allow them to connect personally with the project.

By applying these psychological theories to its crowdfunding campaign, EcoGreen can further facilitate investor participation, secure their support, and increase the project's chances of success. This approach provides deeper psychological satisfaction for investors while securing the essential funds and support needed to achieve EcoGreen's goals.

10. Psychological Management After Raising Investment

Post-Investment Psychological Support: Sustaining a Lasting Partnership

This chapter explores psychological strategies for managing investors' expectations and relationships after raising investment. Even after successfully securing investment, companies must continually manage their relationships with investors and maintain their trust. Applying psychological theories during this process can effectively manage investors' anxieties and expectations, helping to secure long-term support and loyalty.

After securing investment, investors want positive reinforcement regarding their decision. They hope to see their choices validated and their expectations realized. The anxiety or satisfaction that investors feel during this period significantly impacts their relationship with the company and plays a crucial role in their continued engagement and future investment decisions.

Therefore, post-investment management requires an understanding and strategy that go beyond financial performance to satisfy investors' psychological needs. This chapter will discuss in depth how to identify and meet investors' psychological needs and how companies can continuously strengthen their relationships with investors. This approach will allow companies to deepen trust with their investors and secure their long-term support.

JayTech recently faced significant challenges in managing psychological relationships with investors after securing substantial venture capital investment. The company, aiming to develop innovative IoT solutions, encountered unexpected delays in project progress post-investment. These delays and market changes amplified anxiety and concern among investors, emerging as a critical psychological issue that JayTech needed to address swiftly.

The anxiety among investors primarily stemmed from two sources:

First, investors wanted continual reassurance that their investment was progressing as planned. As JayTech's projects failed to meet scheduled targets, investors began to doubt their decisions, which started to erode the trust between the investors and the company.

Second, there was growing tension between JayTech's long-term vision and short-term performance. While some investors expected immediate returns, JayTech's strategy focused on long-term growth and technological development, leading to a mismatch between investor expectations and company performance.

To address these issues, JayTech had to develop strategies through a psychological approach:

The first strategy was to ensure investors' psychological comfort. JayTech began using regular communication channels to transparently share updates on project progress, challenges, and achievements. This process helped investors understand and empathize with the challenges JayTech faced, keeping them informed about the company's status in real time.

Additionally, JayTech hosted workshops with investors to discuss the company's long-term strategy and market prospects in depth, actively incorporating investors' opinions and expectations. These workshops reaffirmed JayTech's vision and plans to the investors, strengthening their positive attitudes towards their investment decisions.

These psychological management strategies played a vital role in reducing investors' anxieties and enhancing their trust and satisfaction with JayTech. Investors responded positively as they observed JayTech's open and transparent approach to problem-solving, considering further investment and long-term support from a perspective of trust. Such approaches helped JayTech strengthen relationships with investors post-investment, laying a foundation for sustainable growth.

Key psychological theories applicable in JayTech's investor management strategy significantly impact investors' psychological states and behavior, enabling more effective relationship management.

Cognitive Dissonance Theory, developed by Leon Festinger, explains the psychological discomfort individuals experience when there is a lack of consistency between their beliefs and behaviors. Particularly, when there is a gap between investors' initial decision to invest in JayTech and the actual progress of the company, investors may adjust their beliefs or reinterpret information about the company to resolve this dissonance. By applying this theory, JayTech can minimize cognitive dissonance and maintain investor trust and satisfaction by providing regular updates and transparent information.

Expectancy Theory, developed by Victor Vroom, explains that an individual's behavior is motivated by the outcomes they expect and their belief in their ability to achieve those outcomes. JayTech applies this theory to motivate investors positively about the company's potential for success. By setting achievable short-term goals and successfully meeting them, JayTech can satisfy investors' expectations and strengthen their confidence in long-term success.

Social Identity Theory, developed by Henri Tajfel and John Turner, argues that individuals form their identities through pride and affiliation with their groups. JayTech enhances investors' social identity by making them feel that the company's success is their success. For this, the company organizes special events for investors, networking meetings, and exclusive information sessions, promoting a sense of belonging and participation within the investor community.

These theories enable JayTech to deeply understand investors' psychological states and maintain a close and continuous relationship with them. This approach plays a crucial role in engaging investors more deeply in the company's long-term vision and growth strategy, ensuring their ongoing support.

JayTech has implemented several strategic measures applying psychological theories, particularly Leon Festinger's Cognitive Dissonance Theory, Victor Vroom's Expectancy Theory, and Henri Tajfel's Social Identity Theory, to strengthen and sustain trust with investors.

Based on Cognitive Dissonance Theory, JayTech has established a system to provide investors with consistent and accurate information to prevent any mismatch between their initial investment decision and the current situation at JayTech. The company offers regular newsletters, a web-based update portal, and Q&A sessions to provide transparent updates on the project's progress, challenges, and achievements, helping investors maintain a positive attitude towards their investment and minimizing any discomfort due to cognitive dissonance.

Utilizing Expectancy Theory, JayTech has improved its goal-setting process to strengthen the relationship between the results investors expect and their belief in their ability to achieve these results. By setting and achieving short-term goals, JayTech realistically satisfies investors' expectations and provides them with experiences of success, enhancing their satisfaction and motivation. Each successful step reassures investors that their investment decisions are correct, positively influencing their willingness to make further commitments and provide support.

Through Social Identity Theory, JayTech fosters a strong sense of social connection among investors, encouraging them to view their investment as part of a larger community. The company invites investors to key company events and meetings and operates investor-exclusive social media groups. These platforms enable investors to communicate with each other, perceive the company's success as their own, and engage more deeply and commit further.

These methods have been crucial in reducing the psychological distance between JayTech and its investors, securing ongoing trust and support. This psychological approach contributes to JayTech's long-term success and strengthens investor relationships, helping the company achieve sustainable growth.

Additional psychological theories that can further explore managing investor relationships post-investment are also worth considering. These theories can help JayTech maintain and enhance investor expectations and trust:

1. Theory of Competence: This theory explains that people experience greater satisfaction and motivation when they are recognized for their abilities and feel that their actions significantly impact the outcomes. JayTech can use this theory to

emphasize to investors that they play a crucial role within the company. For instance, involving investors in meetings or decision-making processes related to specific projects can clarify how their opinions significantly influence the company's direction.

2. Basic Psychological Needs Theory: This theory argues that all humans have fundamental psychological needs for autonomy, competence, and relatedness. JayTech can apply this theory to find ways to satisfy these needs among investors. For example, providing investors with autonomous choices and organizing activities that make them feel they are forming meaningful relationships within the company.

3. Emotional Intelligence Theory: This theory highlights the critical role of an individual's emotional intelligence in their social interactions and relationship management. JayTech can integrate emotional intelligence elements into its investor management strategy by actively listening to and understanding investors' emotions and expectations and developing communication strategies to respond to these effectively.

By incorporating these additional psychological theories, JayTech can further develop and sustain deeper relationships with investors, finding ways to maintain their support and trust long-term. This not only surpasses the short-term success of raising investment but also lays the foundation for long-term partnerships and company growth.

V. Collaboration and Psychology

The Orchestra of Collaboration Tuned by Psychology: A Deep Understanding of Teamwork Within Organizations

In "Collaboration and Psychology," we deeply explore the notion that collaboration within organizations is not merely the sum of individual actions but a product of complex psychological interactions. This section clarifies that the success of organizational collaboration cannot be solely explained by the aggregation of individuals, thoroughly analyzing the psychological aspects of team interaction, motivation, communication efficiency, and leadership. Collaboration transcends simple task execution, demanding deep emotional connections and psychological harmony among team members, which has become an essential element for success in the modern business environment, not just an optional factor.

Today's companies are increasingly competing in global and diverse environments, where effective collaboration among team members enables creative problem-solving, the generation of innovative ideas, and the development of competitive business strategies. However, the success of such collaboration significantly depends on the psychological interactions among the members. Psychology provides essential insights for understanding and improving these interactions, offering specific strategies for team motivation, conflict resolution, and communication enhancement.

This chapter delves deeply into the significant psychological components of organizational collaboration through various psychological theories, such as Hackman & Oldham's Job Characteristics Model, Watzlawick's theory of communication, and Belbin's team roles theory. Each subsection centers on a specific psychological theory to analyze the psychological aspects of collaboration within organizations, exploring how organizations and individuals interact and how these interactions are linked to the organization's collaborative culture. This major theme does not merely view collaboration as team members working together; it explores how individual psychological factors combine to contribute to the overall organizational performance. This approach offers methods for developing beneficial collaboration strategies for both organizations and individuals, playing a crucial role in achieving sustainable success in today's business environment.

1. Team Motivation and Hackman & Oldham's Job Characteristics Model

Unlocking Team Energy: Motivation through Hackman & Oldham's Job Characteristics Model

Team motivation is a crucial component for successful collaboration within contemporary organizations. Notably, Hackman & Oldham's Job Characteristics Model offers a vital theoretical framework to enhance and understand team motivation. This model delves into how job design influences an employee's intrinsic motivation, job satisfaction, and performance, and examines how an individual's psychological state is linked to their work outcomes. The theory suggests that individuals are more motivated and satisfied when they perceive their tasks as enabling self-efficacy, autonomy, and meaningfulness.

To elevate productivity and creativity among team members, it's essential to manage five core job characteristics effectively: skill variety, task identity, task significance, autonomy, and feedback. Proper alignment of these traits ensures team members find greater meaning and satisfaction in their tasks, leading to enhanced overall team performance.

Building on this theoretical foundation, we will explore how Hackman & Oldham's model can be practically applied in various organizational scenarios. This examination not only deepens the psychological understanding of team motivation but also serves as a foundational resource for developing effective team management and composition strategies in modern organizations. Through this model, organizations can boost job satisfaction among team members, ultimately contributing to the achievement of organizational goals.

Techline, a global software development company, recently faced significant challenges, including delays in client projects and low team member satisfaction.

Surveys revealed that many employees felt a lack of control over their tasks and were unaware of their work's significance. These issues impeded project efficiency and hindered the production of creative outputs.

This situation led to a clear lack of motivation among team members, resulting in decreased job satisfaction. In particular, the development team did not fully understand how their roles impacted the final products, which significantly reduced their commitment and passion. Additionally, the absence of immediate feedback restricted personal growth opportunities, diminishing the team's sense of efficacy.

To address these issues, Techline's management decided to implement concrete and substantial changes. The company reassessed its work processes and team structures to increase autonomy for each team member and regularly clarified how each person's role contributed to the project's overall goals. These measures were crucial in helping team members recognize the importance of their work within the organization.

A deep analysis of Techline's challenges revealed two primary causes:
1. Team members lacked sufficient control over their tasks and did not fully recognize their work's importance, reducing job satisfaction and negatively affecting their motivation.
2. Immediate feedback was lacking, making it difficult for team members to see the impact of their efforts on final outcomes, which diminished their sense of the importance of their roles.

These factors led team members to perceive their tasks as mere jobs, significantly reducing their creativity and passion for work. Moreover, the lack of autonomy and control over their tasks decreased their sense of belonging and satisfaction, adversely affecting the overall project performance.

To address these root causes, Techline needed to redesign its work processes within the organization and introduce the Job Characteristics Model to clarify how each team member's tasks were connected to the bigger picture. These changes included measures to help team members recognize the importance of their roles and feel greater autonomy and control over their tasks.

Developed in the 1970s by psychologists Richard Hackman and Greg Oldham, the Job Characteristics Model explains how the nature of a job affects an individual's motivation, satisfaction, and performance. They argued that certain job design elements significantly impact employees' psychological states and performance, suggesting that well-designed jobs can enhance job satisfaction and intrinsic motivation.

The model centers on five core job characteristics:
1. Skill Variety: The degree to which a job requires a variety of skills and talents.
2. Task Identity: The degree to which a job involves completing a whole, identifiable piece of work.
3. Task Significance: The importance of the job's impact on others.
4. Autonomy: The degree of freedom and independence in carrying out the work.
5. Feedback: The clarity and directness of feedback about the effectiveness of one's performance.

When these traits are effectively managed and harmonized, employees experience high internal motivation, leading to increased job satisfaction and productivity. Hackman & Oldham's theory has significantly contributed to understanding the psychological mechanisms of job satisfaction and motivation and is widely applied in contemporary organizational job design and HR strategies.

Applying this theory allows organizations like Techline to help team members find greater meaning and satisfaction in their work, playing a crucial role in enhancing overall team performance and motivation. The Job Characteristics Model has proven to be an effective tool in real work environments for enhancing job satisfaction and performance, demonstrating its effectiveness in various organizational settings in maximizing team motivation and job satisfaction.

In implementing Hackman & Oldham's Job Characteristics Model at Techline, the primary issues addressed were the lack of team motivation and low job satisfaction. To improve these aspects, the company implemented various strategies to ensure team members could feel greater autonomy and significance in their roles. By increasing task variety, Techline provided opportunities for team members to experience and apply different skills and roles throughout projects, creating an environment for learning and applying new skills. This change offered team members opportunities to expand their skill sets and enhance their expertise, resulting in increased job interest and engagement.

Additionally, Techline ensured that each team member understood how their tasks were linked to the overall project goals, enhancing their sense of task identity. To emphasize the significance of their work, the company regularly conducted sessions introducing how their efforts impacted the final product. This process showed team members how their efforts contributed to the bigger picture, enhancing their job satisfaction and engagement.

In terms of autonomy, Techline allowed team members more control over their schedule and approach to tasks, enabling them to work in a style that suited them best, thereby increasing work efficiency and enhancing their sense of control over their work. Lastly, by establishing an effective feedback system, Techline ensured that team members could receive immediate reviews of their work performance, providing them with opportunities to understand their progress and make necessary adjustments, thus enabling them to perform their roles more effectively.

These measures led to successful outcomes at Techline, enhancing team motivation and job satisfaction. The systematic application of Hackman & Oldham's Job Characteristics Model played a critical role in making team members regard their roles as significant and engaging more deeply in their tasks, significantly boosting the overall team's performance. This model has demonstrated its effectiveness in various organizational settings in maximizing team motivation and job satisfaction.

Applying Hackman & Oldham's Job Characteristics Model in organizations like Techline also opens avenues for exploring additional psychological theories that can play a crucial role in understanding and enhancing team motivation and job satisfaction within organizations. Here are a few related psychological theories:

1. Self-Determination Theory (Developed by Edward Deci and Richard Ryan): This theory describes motivation as rooted in three basic psychological needs: autonomy, competence, and relatedness. By applying this theory in an organization, team members can be provided with an environment that fosters intrinsic motivation by allowing them to perform tasks autonomously. Additionally, providing opportunities for team members to exhibit and be recognized for their capabilities

can enhance their sense of competence, while fostering positive relationships among team members and with leaders can boost their sense of social belonging.

2. Goal-Setting Theory (Developed by Edwin Locke): This theory emphasizes that clear and challenging goals are crucial for enhancing individual performance. By applying this theory in an organization, specific and achievable goals can be set for team members, increasing their focus and dedication to their tasks. Goals provide team members with the opportunity to track their progress and experience a sense of achievement, clarifying the direction and purpose of their work.

3. Reinforcement Theory: Based on the principle that the consequences of behavior increase or decrease the frequency of that behavior, positive reinforcement can be used in an organization to motivate team members to repeat desired behaviors by providing appropriate rewards. This can help improve work performance, create a positive work environment, and promote positive interactions among team members.

By integrating these psychological theories with Hackman & Oldham's Job Characteristics Model, organizations like Techline can develop effective strategies to maximize team motivation and job satisfaction, ultimately enhancing the overall performance of the organization. This approach plays a vital role in creating an environment where team members can find greater meaning and satisfaction in their tasks and actively contribute to achieving organizational goals.

2. A Psychological Approach to Team Conflict Resolution

Creating Harmony through Conflict Management: Psychological Solutions for Team Conflicts

The psychological approach to resolving team conflicts is an essential component in modern organizations. Inevitably, conflicts within organizations occur, and understanding and applying effective management strategies can significantly impact team performance and organizational culture. If not managed properly, conflicts can lead to team division, reduced productivity, and increased employee turnover. Conversely, learning and implementing effective conflict resolution can strengthen relationships among team members, spur innovative solutions, and enhance overall organizational health.

The psychological approach to conflict resolution focuses on deeply understanding the roots of conflict and adjusting interactions among individuals and groups to yield positive outcomes. This approach encompasses various techniques and strategies that address the underlying causes of conflict and facilitate team members' understanding of each other's perspectives. Psychological strategies for conflict resolution aim to establish open communication channels within the organization, foster respect for differences, and encourage collaboration towards common goals.

This psychological methodology does not merely seek to eliminate conflicts but rather transforms them into opportunities for organizational growth and development. The application of various psychological theories and techniques during the conflict resolution process helps team members better understand each other's views and emotions, enabling constructive dialogue in conflict situations. Through this, organizations can build stronger and more harmonious teams and lay a solid foundation for long-term success.

Next, we will examine specific corporate cases to demonstrate how psychological approaches to conflict resolution can be applied in real organizational contexts. This examination will provide detailed insights into the analysis of actual problems, the application of theories, and the lessons learned in the resolution process. These insights are crucial for organizations to manage conflicts positively and enhance team collaboration.

Creative Solutions, a digital marketing company, recently faced significant challenges due to conflicts within its project management team. As project deadlines approached, frequent clashes of opinions within the team worsened the team's atmosphere. Some team members disagreed over project priorities, while others raised issues regarding the unequal distribution of resources and workload imbalance. These conflicts led to a decrease in team productivity and threatened the successful completion of the project.

Through analyzing the causes of the conflict, the management at Creative Solutions identified several key issues:

1. A lack of transparent communication during project management caused misunderstandings among team members.
2. The absence of clearly defined roles and responsibilities led some team members to feel overwhelmed by excessive workloads, while others felt their roles were undervalued.
3. Unclear criteria for fair resource distribution fostered resentment among team members.

To address these issues, Creative Solutions decided to implement a psychological approach to conflict resolution. The company conducted communication workshops to help team members effectively manage conflict situations and understand each other's positions. These workshops introduced Nonviolent Communication (NVC) techniques, allowing each team member to clearly express their needs and emotions and consider others' perspectives. Through these workshops, team members learned to understand each other's viewpoints more deeply and resolve conflicts constructively.

Furthermore, Creative Solutions utilized the Thomas-Kilmann Conflict Mode Instrument, a key psychological theory in conflict resolution, to analyze team members' conflict resolution tendencies. This tool helped identify each team member's style of resolving conflicts, enabling the development of customized strategies to improve communication and cooperation within the team. This approach helped team members respond more effectively in conflict situations and fostered a culture of respect for differences.

The psychological approach transformed the way Creative Solutions handled conflicts, turning them from a negative impact into an opportunity to enhance team creativity and collaboration. Through this method, the company learned to manage conflicts positively, strengthen team cooperation, and improve overall organizational performance.

To deepen understanding of the psychological approach to conflict resolution, we will further explore the Thomas-Kilmann Conflict Mode Instrument and Nonviolent Communication (NVC). These theories are deeply applied in organizational conflict resolution processes, playing a crucial role in fostering mutual understanding and cooperation among team members.

The Thomas-Kilmann Conflict Mode Instrument is a psychological tool used to analyze individuals' behavioral tendencies in conflict situations. It categorizes conflict resolution styles into five types: Competing, Collaborating, Compromising, Avoiding, and Accommodating.

This categorization helps understand how individuals react in conflict situations and develop more effective communication and resolution strategies within teams. Creative Solutions used this tool to identify each team member's tendencies and select the most appropriate conflict resolution methods for different situations.

Nonviolent Communication (NVC), developed by Marshall Rosenberg, is a communication technique that helps individuals express their needs and emotions clearly and non-critically in conflict situations. Centered around four components—observations, feelings, needs, and requests—NVC helps team members understand and respect each other's perspectives. Workshops conducted at Creative Solutions actively used this technique, enabling team members to empathize with each other and learn constructive conflict resolution methods.

The psychological approach implemented by Creative Solutions in designing and executing their conflict resolution process was centered around the Thomas-Kilmann Conflict Mode Instrument and NVC techniques. This approach helped team members understand each other's positions, manage emotions effectively, and develop productive solutions in conflict situations.

Initially, education sessions utilizing the Thomas-Kilmann Conflict Mode Instrument were conducted to identify each team member's preferred style of conflict resolution. This tool explained the advantages and disadvantages of each style (Competing, Collaborating, Compromising, Avoiding, Accommodating) and helped understand which style was most appropriate in different situations. These sessions provided team members with insights into their own and their colleagues' approaches to resolving conflicts, enhancing communication based on mutual respect and understanding.

Subsequently, NVC workshops taught team members how to clearly articulate their emotions and needs and listen to the perspectives of others. NVC, structured around the four stages of observations, feelings, needs, and requests, aided in handling conflicts more constructively. For example, during conflicts over project opinions, team members expressed their viewpoints using non-violent language like "I feel this way," which prevented the conversation from becoming defensive and focused more on the essence of the issues.

This psychological approach prevented team members from becoming emotionally charged in conflict situations and enabled clearer and more effective communication of individual needs and concerns. As a result, Creative Solutions' team turned conflicts into opportunities to strengthen teamwork and ensure the successful execution of projects. This process also improved the organization's communication culture and enhanced its long-term ability to manage conflicts.

To further develop and maximize the effectiveness of the psychological approach used at Creative Solutions, additional psychological theories and strategies can be considered:

1. Emotional Intelligence: In conflict situations, an individual's emotional intelligence is crucial for easing tensions and understanding the emotions of others. By implementing programs that develop emotional intelligence, team members can more effectively manage their own and others' emotions in conflicts, facilitating constructive resolutions.

2. Cultivating a Healthy Conflict Culture: Establishing a healthy conflict culture within an organization ensures that conflicts are not viewed merely as negative occurrences but as opportunities for growth and innovation. Enhancing leadership training and educating all employees on conflict resolution skills can encourage a culture that positively handles conflicts.

3. Integrative Negotiation Techniques: In conflict resolution, integrative negotiation techniques help team members with different interests find mutually satisfying solutions. This method focuses on an approach that does not view conflict as a 'win or lose' game but rather as a 'win-win' situation, emphasizing finding solutions acceptable to all parties involved.

4. Interpersonal Theory: This theory can be used to understand the underlying causes of conflict by analyzing patterns of interaction between individuals. Organizations can use this theory to assess the dynamics of relationships among team members, identify interaction patterns that may lead to conflicts, and work on improving these interactions.

By incorporating these additional psychological theories and strategies, Creative Solutions can further systematize its conflict resolution process and equip itself with the tools and skills necessary to turn conflicts into catalysts for organizational growth. This will contribute to creating an environment where team members understand and respect their differences and cooperate more effectively.

3. Communication Efficiency and Watzlawick's Theory of Communication

Delving into the Depth of Messages: Efficient Communication Through Watzlawick's Theory

Communication efficiency is one of the most crucial competencies within an organization. Effective communication contributes to clear information transmission among team members, prevention and resolution of conflicts, and overall organizational efficiency and satisfaction. Particularly, Watzlawick's theory of communication provides an essential framework for understanding and improving communication within organizations. This theory offers deep insights into how misunderstandings occur in the communication process and how they can be managed.

Watzlawick's theory views communication not as a single act but as a continuous interaction process, emphasizing the role of non-verbal signals and context. According to this theory, all communication includes two aspects: content and relationship. The content refers to the explicit information conveyed in communication, while the relationship indicates how the message should be interpreted through interactions between the messages. Both aspects must harmonize for communication to be successful.

This chapter will explore Watzlawick's theory of communication in depth, examining how it can be applied to solve contemporary organizational communication problems. Specific corporate cases will be analyzed to illustrate the application and effectiveness of the theory, and various methods and strategies to enhance communication efficiency will be presented. Through this process, the complexities of communication can be understood, and more effective communication methods within organizations can be developed.

Interactive Media, a digital communication company, was experiencing declines in efficiency due to challenges in their internal communication. The company managed multiple projects simultaneously and faced issues with smooth information flow between teams and departments. Project teams often found themselves on different pages, leading to necessary information not being shared timely, which caused delays in project progress.

Teams attempted communication using their own methods and tools, often leading to duplicated efforts and inconsistencies in information. For example, the marketing team had difficulties sharing updates on new campaigns with the tech team due to differences in file formats and platforms used, leading to ineffective information transfer. Additionally, the rapid growth and expansion of the company continually brought in new employees who struggled to adapt to the existing communication systems.

The rapid expansion also introduced cultural diversity, which led to variations in communication styles among employees from different backgrounds. These differences sometimes caused misunderstandings and conflicts, particularly in urgent tasks, causing confusion in decision-making processes and further reducing project efficiency.

These communication issues negatively impacted Interactive Media's overall workflow and teamwork, ultimately affecting customer satisfaction and the company's reputation. Unnecessary stress and tension built up among employees, often reflecting in their work performance. The company recognized these internal communication issues and sought effective approaches to address them.

Watzlawick's theory of communication, developed by Paul Watzlawick, is a significant theory in psychology and communication fields, providing vital insights into human communication patterns and especially useful in interpreting complexities and misunderstandings in organizational communication. Watzlawick distinguished communication into two main dimensions: content and relationship. The content dimension relates directly to the transmission of information, while the relationship dimension defines how the relationship between the communicators should shape the interpretation of that information.

Watzlawick's theory outlines five basic principles:
1. All behavior is communication: Humans cannot avoid communicating, and every action conveys some message.
2. Communication involves both content and relationship aspects: This means communication is not only about transmitting information but also defining the relationships between those who communicate.
3. People use different modes of communication (digital and analog): Digital communication occurs mainly through language, while analog communication happens through non-verbal signals.
4. Humans engage in different interaction patterns (complementary and symmetrical): Complementary interactions occur between two people with different power or roles, while symmetrical interactions happen between people with similar power or roles.
5. Communication is circular: Communication is not linear but circular, where each act is influenced by previous acts and influences subsequent acts.

These principles play a crucial role in understanding and resolving communication issues within organizations. Watzlawick's theory is particularly useful for identifying causes of misunderstandings and conflicts and developing effective communication strategies. By applying this theory, organizations can manage communication complexities and foster healthy relationships among organizational members.

Interactive Media applied Watzlawick's theory of communication to improve their internal communication challenges through a complex and multilayered approach. The company initially conducted a comprehensive communication audit across the entire organization to identify existing communication patterns and their associated problems. The insights gained from this audit provided critical foundational data that helped the company clarify areas for improvement and plan necessary changes.

Subsequently, Interactive Media developed and implemented a customized training program to enhance employees' communication skills based on Watzlawick's theory. This program educated employees on the importance of content and relationship in communication and how to apply effective communication strategies in different situations. It included training on the use of various communication channels and tools, enabling employees to select the most appropriate means of communication for each context.

Moreover, Interactive Media standardized communication protocols across all teams and departments, ensuring consistent information sharing that guaranteed accurate transmission and minimized duplication or omissions. The company regularly monitored the effectiveness of this new communication strategy through feedback sessions and made prompt adjustments as needed.

Through these efforts, Interactive Media significantly improved the quality of internal communication, leading to increased efficiency in project management, improved relationships among employees, and positive changes in the overall work environment. The application of Watzlawick's theory of communication played a crucial role in reducing misunderstandings, effectively managing conflicts, and enhancing teamwork and cooperation within the organization. This process helped the organization structurally solve and continuously improve internal communication issues, laying the foundation for ongoing enhancement.

Now, let's explore additional psychological theories that could further investigate the improvements in internal communication at Interactive Media. These theories can contribute to developing effective communication strategies within the organization and making interactions among employees more efficient, ultimately boosting the overall productivity and efficiency of the organization.

1. Transactional Analysis (TA): Developed by Eric Berne, this theory analyzes human interactions through three ego states: Parent, Adult, and Child. This helps understand how individuals respond to each other in an organization and behave in specific situations. Applying this theory, employees can better understand each other's communication styles and behavioral patterns, resolving conflicts more constructively.

2. The importance of non-verbal communication, including gestures, postures, and facial expressions: Non-verbal signals often play a crucial role in conveying meanings in communication but can be easily overlooked. Gestures, facial expressions, eye contact, and tone of voice are essential for effectively transmitting intentions and emotions. By educating employees on these non-verbal elements,

organizations can enable them to accurately interpret and appropriately respond to each other's non-verbal cues.

3. Understanding and managing cultural differences: Communication among employees from various cultural backgrounds can sometimes lead to misunderstandings and conflicts, as each culture has its own communication style and customs. By conducting communication training that considers these cultural differences, organizations can ensure that all employees recognize and respect each other's differences, creating an environment conducive to effective communication.

These psychological theories and approaches can help Interactive Media enhance the quality of internal communication, fostering cooperation and understanding among employees. This will ultimately contribute to improving the organization's overall productivity and efficiency.

4. Teamwork and Belbin's Team Role Theory

Harmonizing Roles: Optimizing Teamwork through Belbin's Team Role Theory

Teamwork is a vital element for organizational success. Strong teamwork facilitates efficient task completion, fosters creative problem solving, and promotes close cooperation among employees. However, a common challenge organizations face in implementing teamwork is finding ways for members with diverse personalities and roles to collaborate harmoniously. Addressing this challenge effectively requires the application of psychological theories.

This chapter explores the psychological aspects of teamwork through the lens of Belbin's Team Role Theory. This theory aids in understanding individual roles within a team and maximizing each member's strengths, thereby enhancing organizational function. Notably, the theory elucidates how various roles contribute to team performance and suggests ways to improve teamwork quality through role interactions.

We will analyze specific corporate cases to demonstrate how Belbin's Team Role Theory can be applied in real business contexts. This analysis will help each team member understand their role clearly and explore methods to function more effectively within the team. This process plays a crucial role in strengthening teamwork and maximizing organizational performance.

TechnoByte, a software development company, comprises team members from diverse backgrounds and expertise, collaborating on complex projects. The company has recently faced challenges, particularly project delays due to poor cooperation among teams. Although each team performs its tasks with specialized skills and expertise, the lack of smooth communication and information sharing leads to several issues.

For instance, significant communication gaps exist between the UI design team and the backend development team. The UI design team focuses on optimizing user experience, while the backend team prioritizes system functionality and performance. Differences in goals and priorities between these teams degrade understanding of project requirements and disrupt key project milestones.

These issues stem from a failure to coordinate tasks among teams, and a lack of awareness among team members about how their work impacts the overall project. In particular, some team members are unaware of their contributions and roles, negatively affecting their engagement and motivation. Furthermore, this lack of awareness is a primary factor in reducing overall team cooperation and efficiency.

TechnoByte needs to enhance communication between teams and ensure all team members clearly understand the overall project goals and their roles. The company considers establishing effective communication channels and introducing training programs, anticipating that these efforts will significantly enhance team cooperation and ensure project success.

We will conduct an in-depth analysis of the communication issues and teamwork decline at TechnoByte. The root causes of project delays and lack of team cooperation include:

First, the absence of a communication protocol has emerged as a significant issue. Each team works independently without a consistent communication method or standard, leading to improper information transmission. Important information either does not reach all teams on time or gets distorted.

Second, conflicts in goals and priorities between teams, especially between the UI design and backend development teams, have been particularly severe. Each team pursues goals related to their expertise without adequately considering the needs or objectives of other teams, which ultimately impedes the achievement of integrated project goals.

Third, a lack of management of cultural diversity and individual differences has also caused problems. Naturally, team members from various backgrounds exhibit differences in communication styles and work processes. Failing to manage these effectively has led to misunderstandings and decreased teamwork.

Fourth, inadequate leadership and management have complicated the communication and cooperation issues among teams. Team leaders often fail to understand or appropriately coordinate the roles and contributions of team members, negatively impacting overall team performance.

These issues represent significant challenges that TechnoByte must overcome to strengthen teamwork and efficiently manage projects. Accurately identifying and addressing these problems is essential for the company's successful operation.

Belbin's Team Role Theory, developed by British psychologist Meredith Belbin, is a critical theory based on the research of Henry Fayol, aiming to understand how to maximize team effectiveness. Belbin observed how team performance changed when members assumed different roles during management training courses at the Henry Fayol College in the 1970s. This led him to identify specific roles within teams that significantly impact team performance.

Belbin's theory categorizes individual behavioral tendencies within a team into nine team roles. Each role contributes uniquely to the team, enhancing the overall likelihood of success. Below are the nine key roles and their characteristics identified by Belbin:

1. Coordinator: Coordinators lead the team, setting objectives and harmonizing members' efforts. They play a central role in decision-making and effectively integrate other team members' activities.
2. Shaper: Passionate and motivated, Shapers energize the team. They thrive on challenges and can deliver results under pressure.
3. Implementer: Implementers are reliable and organized. They excel at turning plans into action, playing a crucial role in transforming ideas into reality.
4. Completer-Finisher: Completer-Finishers pay close attention to detail and focus on completing tasks precisely and thoroughly. They are skilled at identifying and correcting errors.

5. Specialist: Specialists bring deep knowledge and expertise to the team, providing essential technical skills or specialized knowledge.
6. Teamworker: Teamworkers foster harmony and mediate conflicts within the team. They facilitate communication and cooperation among team members.
7. Resource Investigator: Resource Investigators are adept at exploring opportunities and acquiring resources. They bring fresh ideas and opportunities to the team through external networking.
8. Plant: Creative and innovative, Plants provide creative solutions and original approaches that enhance the project's innovative aspects.
9. Monitor-Evaluator: Monitor-Evaluators possess objective and critical thinking skills. They analyze and evaluate proposed plans or ideas, helping the team make realistic and rational decisions.

By understanding and appropriately assigning these roles within the team, organizations can maximize each member's strengths and optimize overall team performance. Belbin's Team Role Theory assists each team member in clearly understanding their role and finding more effective ways to function within the team. This helps organizations enhance teamwork and improve overall organizational performance.

In the case of TechnoByte, we will closely examine how Belbin's Team Role Theory was specifically applied to address their challenges. By implementing this theory, TechnoByte was able to clarify each team member's role and effectively improve communication and cooperation between teams.

Firstly, an initial assessment was conducted according to Belbin's Team Role Theory to evaluate each team member's fundamental tendencies and roles. This assessment helped each member recognize their strengths and weaknesses and identify which roles they could best perform. For example, natural Coordinators took on leadership and coordination among team members, while Resource Investigators were responsible for securing external resources and exploring new opportunities.

Secondly, team composition was realigned to optimize each member's role, maximizing the potential of each team member and balancing role distribution to enhance everyone's contributions. For instance, those with the Plant role were positioned to focus on providing creative ideas, strengthening the project's innovative elements.

Thirdly, regular team-building sessions and workshops were used to enhance interactions and communication skills among team members. These activities educated the team about Belbin's theory and helped members understand the importance and roles of others. This built trust among team members and clarified how each person's role contributed to the team's overall success.

Fourthly, mechanisms for managing conflicts that could arise from role distribution and adjustments were improved. Teamworkers and Coordinators played mediator roles, addressing potential conflicts early and contributing to maintaining team harmony.

These approaches ensured that each member of TechnoByte faithfully fulfilled their role, contributing to the team's objectives. By clearly defining and optimizing roles through Belbin's Team Role Theory, TechnoByte was able to increase project efficiency, strengthen teamwork, and improve the overall performance of the organization. This process also brought about positive changes in the organization's communication and collaboration culture.

Further exploration of Belbin's Team Role Theory in TechnoByte's case will examine additional psychological theories and strategies. These can optimize role distribution and interaction within the team and enhance cooperation and communication within the organization.

1. Emotional Intelligence: This theory plays a crucial role in managing conflicts and enhancing teamwork. Widely recognized by Daniel Goleman, emotional intelligence emphasizes an individual's ability to recognize and manage their own and others' emotions. When team members understand and appropriately respond to each other's emotional reactions, it reduces conflicts and enables more constructive problem-solving within the team.

2. Management of Diversity and Inclusion: Properly managing diversity within an organization is essential for strengthening teamwork. When a culture that respects and includes the diverse backgrounds and experiences of team members is

cultivated, the team's creativity and innovation improve. This management approach helps team members recognize and utilize each other's unique skills and knowledge.

3. Cultivating a Feedback Culture: Feedback provides team members with opportunities to perform their roles more effectively and make improvements. An open and regular feedback culture builds trust within the team and promotes continuous learning and growth. This ensures that all team members have a clear understanding of their roles and continuously improve their performance.

4. Role-based Training: Providing customized training for each team role identified through Belbin's theory helps team members perform their roles more effectively. This training enhances understanding of the roles and optimizes functioning within the team.

These psychological theories and strategies enable TechnoByte to effectively manage team role distribution and interactions, further strengthening teamwork and cooperation within the organization. This approach plays a vital role in enhancing the organization's overall performance and efficiency, increasing employee satisfaction and engagement.

5. Project Management and Psychological Factors

The Psychological Keys to Project Success: The Importance of Psychological Elements in Project Management

Project management is not merely a technical task of coordinating schedules, budgets, and scopes. Psychological factors significantly influence project success, with elements such as team motivation, stress management, and communication styles playing critical roles in project outcomes. This chapter explores the importance of psychological factors in project management and presents methods to maximize efficiency through these insights.

A psychologically informed approach to project management helps project leaders and team members perform their roles more effectively. It also facilitates understanding the causes of team conflicts and developing effective solutions, thus minimizing problems that may arise during the project. This approach enhances the project's success rate and improves team cooperation and satisfaction.

This chapter will analyze the psychological challenges faced during project management processes through specific corporate cases and introduce psychological strategies and techniques to address them. Readers will gain useful insights into the psychological aspects of project management and apply them in practical work settings.

NextSolutions, a global IT consulting firm, is experiencing difficulties with coordination and cooperation among teams during a large-scale digital transformation project. This complex task involves integrating systems across offices in various countries, with teams participating from different time zones and cultural backgrounds, leading to significant differences in communication and work styles among team members.

Initially, there was high enthusiasm and cooperation among team members, but as the project progressed, unclear communication and ambiguous task allocations increased stress and conflict. In particular, delays in sharing critical decision-making information led to redundant work by several sub-teams. Additionally, some teams faced excessive overtime and weekend work to meet deadlines due to difficulties in grasping the overall progress of the project.

These issues fostered distrust among team members and significantly reduced project efficiency. The cultural differences and communication style variations among teams have emerged as major obstacles to project success, necessitating proactive measures by project managers. These challenges highlight the need for NextSolutions to consider psychological factors in managing global projects to improve teamwork and communication quality.

An analysis of the issues faced by NextSolutions' project management has identified several key factors that hinder project efficiency and success. These issues require a psychological approach to resolution.

The first problem is the absence of communication. There is no systematic and consistent communication mechanism among project teams, leading to frequent delays and omissions in important information sharing. This causes teams to work without a clear understanding of the project's overall goals and progress, leading to redundant tasks and reduced work efficiency.

Secondly, conflicts due to cultural differences have arisen. Team members from various countries work together, and their cultural backgrounds and work styles have caused conflicts. These cultural differences make it difficult to build trust and cooperate among team members, sometimes amplifying misunderstandings about work methods.

The third major cause is the failure to manage stress. The pressure of project deadlines and performance expectations has caused excessive stress among team members, negatively affecting their work quality and personal health. Team members have been working under continuous pressure, adversely affecting the overall team atmosphere and motivation.

These issues underscore the need to include important psychological factors in NextSolutions' project management strategy. Establishing effective communication channels between teams, conducting training to understand and respect cultural differences, and enhancing stress management skills are part of the solution. These measures will enable the project team to cooperate better and significantly increase the likelihood of project success.

This chapter will provide an in-depth look at the psychological approaches that can be applied to resolve the communication issues and cultural conflicts experienced by NextSolutions. The strategies for reducing team stress and conflicts and promoting efficient project management include:

1. Conflict Resolution Strategy Development: Develop strategies that consider the cultural differences and communication styles of team members to prevent and resolve conflicts. For example, regularly holding workshops among teams to foster understanding of each other's cultural backgrounds and work styles, creating an environment where everyone's opinions are respected.

2. Communication Skills Enhancement Program: Implement a systematic communication training program to enable team members to communicate clearly and effectively. This program includes various communication skills, such as clear messaging, effective listening, and non-verbal communication skills.

3. Emotional Intelligence Enhancement: Conduct training to improve team members' emotional intelligence, enabling them to better understand and manage their own and others' emotions. This is particularly useful in high-stress project environments to reduce conflicts and enhance team motivation.

4. Cultural Diversity Management Training: Provide training for team members to understand and respect various cultural backgrounds, helping to ensure cultural differences contribute positively to team performance and minimize cultural conflicts.

5. Stress and Time Management Skill Enhancement: Educate team members on effectively managing stress and using time efficiently under project deadlines and

pressures. This will improve the overall efficiency of the project and increase job satisfaction among team members.

Through these psychological approaches, NextSolutions can strengthen collaboration among project teams and enhance communication efficiency. Consequently, this will greatly improve the likelihood of project success and contribute to overall organizational satisfaction.

Additional areas of project management worth exploring for their psychological aspects include:

1. Motivation Theories: Maintaining and enhancing team members' motivation in project management is crucial. Herzberg's Motivation-Hygiene Theory and Maslow's Hierarchy of Needs provide insights into what factors motivate team members and how they experience job satisfaction. Understanding and applying these theories can help managers create an environment that appropriately stimulates both intrinsic and extrinsic motivations among team members.

2. Leadership Styles: The impact of a leader's style on team atmosphere and performance is significant. Daniel Goleman's Leadership Styles Theory describes how leaders influence their teams and which styles are most effective in certain situations. Adjusting and developing leadership styles can maximize team members' engagement and performance.

3. Preventing Groupthink: Groupthink in decision-making within groups can inhibit a project's creativity and innovation. Irving Janis's Groupthink Theory provides strategies to recognize and prevent this phenomenon, enabling teams to maintain a more open and critical decision-making process and manage potential risks and issues more effectively.

4. Applying Emotional Intelligence: Emotional intelligence is essential for managing conflicts and building effective teamwork. Developing team members' abilities to understand and respond appropriately to each other's emotions can create a more harmonious and productive work environment.

5. The Importance of Feedback and Reflection: Continuous feedback and reflection are crucial for enhancing performance in project management. Providing regular feedback at each project stage and creating opportunities for team members to reflect on their work and personal growth is necessary.

By applying these psychological theories and strategies, project managers and team members can perform their projects more effectively, increasing the chances of project success and improving the overall efficiency and satisfaction of the organization.

6. Psychological Strategies for Facilitating Collaboration

The Psychology of Teamwork: Mastering Psychological Strategies for Enhancing Collaboration

Collaboration is a pivotal element in the modern business environment. The success of an organization depends not just on the abilities of individual members, but on how effectively they can work together. Facilitating and optimizing collaboration through psychological strategies is a crucial method for maximizing organizational productivity and innovation. This chapter will explore methods to strengthen cooperation within teams and foster positive interactions among team members by applying various psychological theories.

The psychology of collaboration focuses on understanding individual behaviors, attitudes, and team dynamics. This understanding enables organizations to prevent potential issues that individuals and teams may encounter and develop efficient strategies for their resolution. Beyond theoretical approaches, this chapter will demonstrate how these strategies can be practically applied in the field.

Particularly, this chapter will detail how psychological understanding within organizations can facilitate collaboration, minimize conflicts, and strengthen organizational culture. It will analyze collaboration-related issues faced by real companies as case studies, presenting psychological approaches and solutions to these issues. Throughout this process, the importance of understanding each team member's role and respecting individual differences will be emphasized, exploring how each member can contribute to achieving organizational goals.

CodeBridge, a global software development company, is conducting a complex multi-team project involving development centers across several countries, with each center responsible for specific parts of the project. While this structure holds potential for enhancing project efficiency, it poses significant challenges in team collaboration.

From the outset, each team focused on its own goals and worked independently. While this initially appeared to promote autonomy, it led to redundant work and scheduling failures over time. Communication issues among teams located in different regions became a serious obstacle to project progress. Incomplete information transmission and delayed updates disrupted the entire project schedule, inevitably leading to integration problems among different modules.

Moreover, the lack of internal communication within teams made it difficult for project managers to understand the overall project status. This situation delayed critical decisions and affected the quality of the final product. Communication problems among team members were also due to time zone differences, language barriers, and cultural differences, all of which exacerbated tensions and misunderstandings between teams.

These communication barriers caused various forms of stress among the project teams and led to dissatisfaction and conflict among team members. CodeBridge urgently felt the need to develop strategies to improve interactions and communication between teams. A strategic and systematic approach is required to address these issues, with project managers and team leaders actively seeking concrete solutions to enhance the chances of project success and improve overall organizational efficiency and team satisfaction.

A thorough analysis of the collaboration issues in CodeBridge's global software development project shows that these problems primarily stem from lack of communication and cultural differences. Time differences and language barriers due to the geographic dispersion of teams complicated communication further, and the tendency of each team to push work independently significantly hindered the project's consistency and efficiency.

The first issue is the absence of clear communication channels and standardized procedures. Each team had its own way of managing and sharing information, which led to delays or distortions in important information transfer. This hindered necessary integration between various parts of the project, ultimately having a severe impact on overall project progression.

The second issue is cultural differences and the conflicts they cause. Interactions between team members from diverse cultural backgrounds sometimes led to misunderstandings and conflicts. For example, the differences between cultures that prefer direct communication and those that prefer indirect communication caused discrepancies in decision-making processes within the project. Additionally, differing approaches to work prioritization and project management methods caused additional tension within the project teams.

The third issue is a lack of project management skills. Project managers and team leaders lacked sufficient skills to maintain team motivation, efficiently allocate resources, and manage conflicts appropriately. Despite being essential for fostering cooperation between teams and leading the project to success, they failed to provide the necessary support for team members to effectively perform their roles.

To address these issues, psychological approaches are needed to facilitate effective communication between teams, create an environment that acknowledges and respects cultural differences, and enhance team members' competencies. These approaches can fundamentally solve collaboration issues in the project and improve overall organizational performance.

One psychological theory that can be applied to facilitate collaboration in the CodeBridge project is Bruce Tuckman's stages of team development. This theory describes how teams evolve through five stages: Forming, Storming, Norming, Performing, and Adjourning. Introduced by Tuckman in 1965, his research has significantly contributed to understanding team dynamics and their development processes.

Bruce Tuckman, a psychologist and educator, is widely recognized in the fields of organizational and group psychology. His theory provides deep insights into how teams change and grow over time, offering methods for leaders and team members to recognize specific challenges that can arise at each stage and respond appropriately.

Tuckman's theory consists of the following stages:

1. Forming: In this initial stage, team members get to know each other and begin to understand the team's goals and structure. This period is characterized by uncertainty and anticipation, and the role of the leader is crucial.

2. Storming: At this stage, conflicts and disagreements among team members can arise as they try to establish their roles and positions within the team. Effective communication and conflict resolution strategies are essential during this period.

3. Norming: Team members accept each other's differences, and team norms and policies are established. During this period, the team becomes more cohesive, and members start to cooperate towards a common goal.

4. Performing: The team operates efficiently and performs at a high level. Team members trust each other's abilities and can effectively handle complex tasks.

5. Adjourning: The final stage occurs as the project concludes and the team disbands. This period involves evaluating the project's outcomes and preparing team members for their next roles.

By understanding and applying Tuckman's stages of team development, organizations can effectively manage challenges that arise at each stage and foster team collaboration, promoting successful project completion. This theory provides team leaders and project managers with insights to plan appropriate strategies and interventions for each stage, supporting team growth and development.

Further exploration of psychological strategies for facilitating collaboration is necessary. This is crucial for ensuring close cooperation among team members and effective project progression. Additional psychological theories and strategies that can be considered include:

1. Systems Theory: This theory views organizations as complex systems and analyzes how various parts of the system interact with each other. By understanding the role of each team member and their contribution to achieving overall goals, team leaders can develop strategies for harmonious functioning of the entire team.

This theory emphasizes the interdependence of team members and is useful for developing strategies to ensure the team functions harmoniously.

2. Social Identity Theory: This theory explains how individuals form their identities as members of a group. By enhancing individuals' sense of belonging within the team and strengthening group identity, cooperation and motivation within the team can be increased. Team leaders can use this theory to foster a positive culture within the team and motivate members to work towards a common goal.

3. Conflict Resolution Theory: Conflict is one of the main factors that can hinder teamwork. Conflict resolution theory provides strategies for effectively managing and resolving conflicts within the team. By constructively resolving conflicts, leaders can improve relationships between team members and facilitate successful project execution.

4. Motivation Theories: Various motivation theories, such as Herzberg's Motivation-Hygiene Theory and Deci and Ryan's Self-Determination Theory, provide methods for motivating team members. These theories help understand the intrinsic and extrinsic motivations of team members and appropriately stimulate them to actively participate in the project.

These psychological approaches can play a significant role in maximizing collaboration within the organization, enhancing project efficiency, and improving relationships among team members. Each theory and strategy must be applied according to specific situations, and team leaders and project managers can develop concrete plans for motivating the team, resolving conflicts, and strengthening teamwork through these strategic approaches. These strategies will contribute to the success of the project and improve overall organizational satisfaction and performance.

7. Preventing Groupthink and Janis's Theory

Avoiding the Pitfalls of Thought: Janis's Groupthink Theory and Its Prevention Strategies

Groupthink is a psychological phenomenon that can occur in the decision-making processes of organizations or teams, where the members of a group prioritize consensus over critical thinking, often leading to suppressed dissent and potentially serious errors. Understanding and preventing groupthink is crucial for maintaining the health and efficiency of an organization.

Theoretical background and various case studies indicate that groupthink can particularly impair decision-making efficiency in situations requiring high-risk decisions. To prevent and resolve such issues, it is essential to encourage open and critical dialogue within teams and cultivate a culture that embraces diverse perspectives. Additionally, the approach of leadership and organizational structure should be designed to support this culture.

In this chapter, we will explore psychologist Irving L. Janis's theory of groupthink in depth, examining how organizations and teams can overcome the various challenges they may face through this lens. By understanding the mechanisms of groupthink, we can create a healthier decision-making environment within organizations. We will look closely at specific corporate cases to see how groupthink actually occurs and what impact it has had on organizations, thereby aiding a practical understanding of how psychological theories can be applied in real business scenarios.

TechCompany recently undertook a major project to launch a new product, aiming to maintain its leading position in the market by developing innovative technologies and commercializing them. However, groupthink phenomena in the decision-making process within the project team led to several serious errors in crucial technical decisions.

Despite the team's composition of experts with diverse technological backgrounds, members hesitated to challenge the opinions of superiors, leading to the promotion of inefficient designs from the early stages. Particularly, the project leader's strong personality and a lack of openness to criticism were major factors suppressing dissent within the team. This environment stifled team members from expressing their true opinions and concerns, leading them instead to support 'safe' decisions.

As a result, this groupthink prevented the team from thoroughly discussing and examining specific technical issues. For example, the lack of critical review of important design decisions meant that when significant problems were discovered during the testing phase, the project schedule and budget had already been severely impacted. This not only delayed the product launch but also affected the company's competitive position in the market, forcing the company to allocate additional resources to correct these errors.

This case exemplifies how groupthink can lead to inefficient decision-making in technology-focused organizations. If an environment where team members can freely communicate and listen to each other is not fostered, it can lead to serious project failures.

Irving L. Janis's theory of groupthink provides psychological insights into the major pitfalls that can occur in organizational decision-making processes. Introduced in 1972, Janis's theory presents essential concepts for preventing organizations from making grave errors. Groupthink occurs when the strong desire of group members to achieve consensus suppresses critical thinking. This phenomenon is especially likely when the group is homogeneous, works in isolation, and is under the influence of strong leadership.

Janis also proposed several strategies for preventing and overcoming groupthink. One of his key recommendations is that leaders should not express their opinions early in the decision-making process, creating an environment where team members can freely express their views. Additionally, Janis encouraged organizations to actively seek external expert opinions during the decision-making process and to create independent subgroups to explore different alternatives.

These measures enhance the diversity and depth of decision-making within teams, helping each member to adopt a more open and critical perspective. Janis's theory also provides an important framework for understanding various psychological factors that can occur during the decision-making process, helping organizations to develop more effective and sound decision-making cultures.

The theory of groupthink has been validated in many historical events and organizational failures, such as the attack on Pearl Harbor, the Cuban Missile Crisis, and the Challenger space shuttle disaster. These cases help us better understand the severe impact of groupthink on organizations and explore ways to create a healthier and more objective decision-making environment.

The process of applying Irving L. Janis's theory to solve the problem of groupthink at TechCompany involves encouraging each team member to actively participate in the decision-making process and creating an environment where they can freely express their opinions.

Firstly, by not disclosing their preferences or opinions in the early stages of decision-making, leaders foster an atmosphere where team members can express their true thoughts. This ensures that team members do not feel pressured to conform to the leader's views. Instead, leaders focus on posing open questions and gathering diverse opinions, facilitating an equal collection of information necessary for decision-making and ensuring all team members can share their views.

Secondly, during team meetings, leaders introduce the role of an 'evaluator,' ensuring that each opinion is fairly assessed and reviewed. The evaluator provides a critical perspective throughout the meeting, pointing out potential biases that could arise during decision-making. Often, this role is taken on by someone outside the team, playing a crucial part in challenging common assumptions and conjectures that may exist within the team.

Thirdly, leaders actively encourage the exploration of various decision-making alternatives. At each stage of the project, leaders prompt team members to propose alternative approaches and discuss the pros and cons of each, preventing the focus on a single solution and fostering more creative and innovative solutions.

Fourthly, the team regularly seeks opinions from external experts as part of the decision-making process. These experts provide new perspectives and challenge the fixed ways of thinking that may exist within the group, prompting the team to reassess their assumptions and consider problems from a broader viewpoint.

Finally, leaders manage regular reviews and feedback sessions following major stages of the project. These sessions allow team members to reflect on their decisions and the rationale behind them and make adjustments if necessary. Such reflection encourages the team to maintain a self-critical attitude and fosters continuous improvement in decision-making.

Through such strategic approaches, TechCompany minimizes the risks of groupthink, effectively prevents errors in the decision-making process, and promotes the successful completion of projects. This builds trust among team members and significantly contributes to enhancing innovation and efficiency across the organization.

TechCompany needs to apply various psychological theories and strategies to overcome groupthink and improve its decision-making process. This promotes cooperation within the team and fosters more efficient and creative decisions. Here is a detailed explanation of additional psychological approaches and their application methods that TechCompany should consider:

1. Complex Decision-Making Theory: This theory emphasizes that decision-making results from the interaction of various cognitive, emotional, and situational factors. TechCompany should apply this theory to thoroughly analyze and consider all relevant factors in the decision-making process. For example, when making significant project decisions, decision-makers should not only consider technical factors but also the market situation, the emotional state of the team, and possible risks.

2. Team Role Theory: According to Belbin's theory, each team member can contribute to the team's performance by fulfilling a specific role. TechCompany

should analyze each member's strengths and roles when forming teams, placing them in positions where they can perform most efficiently. This prevents groupthink and ensures that diverse perspectives are reflected in team decision-making.

3. Information Exchange Theory: Effective information exchange can significantly improve the quality of decision-making. TechCompany should actively encourage all members to share critical information during meetings and throughout the project's progression. Transparent sharing of information ensures that all relevant data and opinions are fully considered in the decision-making process, reducing the risk of incorrect decisions.

4. Group Dynamics Theory: Understanding and managing the interactions and social structures within a group is crucial for maintaining healthy team functioning. TechCompany can use this theory to understand and manage the dynamics between team members, reducing tension, fostering cooperation, and enhancing the overall performance of the team.

5. Psychological Safety Theory: In an environment where psychological safety is secured, team members can take risks and freely propose creative ideas. TechCompany should create such an environment through its leadership, allowing team members to honestly share their genuine opinions and ideas. This prevents groupthink and ensures that diversity and creativity positively influence the decision-making process.

Applying these theories helps TechCompany effectively prevent groupthink and strengthen its decision-making process. The organization's leaders and managers should develop and implement concrete plans for motivating the team, resolving conflicts, and enhancing teamwork through these psychological approaches. This process not only contributes to the success of projects but also enhances overall organizational satisfaction and performance. These strategic approaches play a crucial role in building trust among team members and boosting innovation and efficiency across the organization.

8. Leadership and Group Dynamics

The Organizational Compass: How Leadership Shapes Group Dynamics

Leadership is a crucial element in the success of any organization. Particularly in complex organizational structures and dynamic market environments, the role of a leader is central in shaping group dynamics and leading the organization toward achieving its goals. Leadership extends beyond mere instruction and supervision; it involves motivating team members and helping them realize their full potential. This chapter delves deeply into how the interaction between leadership and group dynamics functions within organizations and will examine the elements that effective leadership must possess in contemporary organizations.

Leadership is exercised at various levels within an organization, from top executives to middle managers and project team leaders, encompassing all organizational strata. Each leader has the responsibility to understand group dynamics and manage them appropriately to maximize team performance. This includes resolving conflicts within the group, setting goals, allocating resources, and fostering cooperation among team members. Additionally, leaders play a pivotal role in conveying the organization's vision and values to team members and creating an environment where these can be actualized.

This chapter will analyze the various aspects of leadership through specific case studies and explore how leadership theories can be applied in real organizational settings. Through this exploration, we will provide a deeper understanding of how leadership effectively fosters group dynamics within organizations and the impact this has on overall organizational performance. This will aid in discovering ways for leaders and team members to cooperate more effectively and advance toward shared goals.

BlueWave, a global technology company, has acutely felt the importance of team leadership while pushing forward with innovative projects. The company recently initiated a new software development project that required collaboration across multiple departments. However, in the early stages of the project, a lack of leadership led to unclear goal-setting and inadequate inter-departmental cooperation.

The project team consisted of members with diverse technical backgrounds and expertise. While this diversity had the potential to enhance innovation, initially, it caused confusion and conflict due to undefined roles and responsibilities for team members. Moreover, a lack of interaction slowed down the project's progress and increased the risk of errors in crucial decision-making.

These problems were closely related to the project leader's style of leadership. The leader lacked effective communication skills and the experience needed to act as a bridge among team members. This inadequacy prevented the leader from meeting team expectations and building trust within the team. The leader's deficiencies negatively impacted team motivation and productivity, ultimately hindering the project's chances of success.

This situation highlighted the importance of leadership within the organization and the skills and qualities that leaders must possess. To address these issues, BlueWave decided to implement a leadership development program to support team leaders in developing effective communication, conflict resolution, and team management skills. The program was designed to help leaders perform their roles more effectively and optimize team performance.

One of the key psychological theories providing deep insights into leadership and group dynamics is the leadership behavior theory by Ruth W. Bennies and Ronald S. Bales. This theory explains how a leader's behavior affects group dynamics and organizational performance, offering an essential framework for developing effective leadership styles.

Bennies and Bales categorize leadership into three main behavioral categories: task-oriented behavior, people-oriented behavior, and transformative behavior. Task-oriented leadership focuses on achieving goals and task performance. Leaders of this style concentrate on maximizing work efficiency and productivity, emphasizing specific goal setting and stringent schedule management. In contrast, people-oriented leadership values the welfare and development of team members, striving to foster positive relationships within the organization and motivating team members. This leadership style effectively enhances team members' satisfaction and loyalty.

Transformative leadership seeks to pursue organizational change and innovation through interactions between the leader and team members. A transformative leader inspires passion for the vision among team members, utilizing their charisma, inspirational motivation, intellectual stimulation, and personal attention to draw out the maximum potential of team members.

In BlueWave's case, applying the leadership behavior theory could strengthen the leader's capabilities and improve group dynamics. Project leaders could enhance cooperation and performance by understanding each team member's needs and expectations and adjusting their leadership style accordingly. Moreover, leaders could effectively manage conflicts within the team and develop capabilities to adapt to changes, thus enhancing the organization's overall flexibility and adaptability.

This theory enables BlueWave to design its leadership development program more effectively, strengthening interactions between leaders and team members and increasing the likelihood of project success. Such an approach allows leaders and team members to collaborate more effectively and advance towards shared goals.

The leadership development program implemented at BlueWave focused on understanding various leadership styles and group dynamics, emphasizing developing transformative leadership skills to enable leaders to motivate their teams and lead innovations within the team.

During this process, leaders deeply learned about their behavior and its impact on team dynamics, participating in various simulations and workshops that allowed them to apply theories in real situations. These activities helped leaders critically evaluate their leadership styles and develop the ability to adjust as needed.

The program also taught leaders to respect team members' opinions and integrate diverse perspectives, contributing to creating an environment that fosters team members' creativity and innovation and effectively managing conflicts within the group. Leaders also learned how to use their charisma and influence to boost team members' enthusiasm and strengthen the team's motivation towards shared goals.

Through this development program, BlueWave's leaders acquired practical skills and knowledge necessary to improve team dynamics and increase the project's success rate. As a result, leaders were able to enhance their leadership capabilities, which led to improved overall organizational performance and efficiency.

This process provided BlueWave with a crucial lesson: effective leadership development involves more than just transferring skills—it includes helping leaders understand their behavior and its impact on the team and developing the ability to adjust it. Such an approach plays a decisive role in driving continuous growth and development within the organization and successfully leading change and innovation.

It is crucial to explore additional psychological theories that can provide deeper insights into the psychological aspects of leadership and team members. These theories can strengthen relationships between leaders and team members and promote better cooperation and communication within the organization.

1. Interdependence Theory: This theory explains how the interdependence among team members affects group performance. The more team members depend on each other, the more they cooperate, which can enhance the overall team performance. Leaders can use this theory to help team members recognize each other's roles and the importance of their contributions to achieving overall goals.

2. Emotional Intelligence: The emotional intelligence of leaders and team members greatly impacts the team's atmosphere and productivity. A leader's ability to understand and appropriately respond to team members' emotions is essential for reducing tension within the team and effectively managing conflicts. This enables the leader to create a more positive and supportive team environment.

3. Leader-Member Exchange Theory (LMX): This theory explains how the relationship between a leader and each team member shapes the team's dynamics. Strong LMX relationships are characterized by high levels of trust and mutual respect, which are key factors in enhancing team members' satisfaction and

performance. Leaders can use this theory to strengthen individual relationships with team members and better understand and meet their individual needs and expectations.

Applying these psychological theories can help leaders more effectively manage the team and foster positive changes within the organization. By educating and applying these theories in leadership development programs or team-building workshops, leaders and team members can enhance their understanding of each other and engage in more effective cooperation. This will ultimately improve the overall performance and efficiency of the organization.

9. Remote Work and Organizational Psychology

Psychological Perspectives on Remote Work: Understanding the New Work Environment through Organizational Psychology

Remote work has long been a norm in modern organizations. This model offers flexibility and the ability to leverage top talent from various geographical locations, yet it presents new challenges to organizational psychology. Successful management and teamwork in a remote work environment are directly linked to the psychological health of the organization, profoundly impacting employee productivity and job satisfaction. This chapter explores the unique psychological challenges arising in remote work environments and details psychological approaches and strategies to overcome them.

The recent pandemic accelerated the adoption of remote work globally, prompting many organizations to move from traditional office environments to virtual workspaces. This shift has introduced new demands on organizational leadership and teamwork. Remote work can lead to physical isolation and heighten barriers to communication and collaboration among team members. Additionally, the blurring of boundaries between work and personal life can negatively impact work productivity and job satisfaction.

This new work environment presents various psychological challenges from an organizational psychology perspective. The success of remote work heavily relies on effective communication, motivation of employees, and the maintenance of a strong organizational culture. This chapter will examine how organizational psychology can be applied in a remote work environment and how organizations can overcome the challenges they face. Organizational leaders and managers need to develop strategies based on this psychological understanding to manage remote teams more effectively and enhance employee well-being and productivity. This will create conditions where employees can be more satisfied and productive even in a remote work environment.

Infotech, a digital solutions company with employees in various global locations, has recently transitioned to a remote work model. Although the company is rich in technological resources, the introduction of remote work brought significant changes to the communication patterns and workstyles within the organization. Initially, many employees experienced a sense of isolation due to physical separation, impacting collaboration between teams and the efficiency of projects.

The lack of regular face-to-face communication among team members caused confusion about work clarity and priorities, directly affecting project schedules and quality. In this scenario, Infotech's management sought to understand how the changed work environment due to remote work was impacting the organizational culture. In particular, the balance between work and life, job satisfaction, and work continuity were significantly challenged.

This transformation motivated Infotech to introduce new management strategies and tools. To enhance interaction and a sense of belonging among employees in a remote environment, the company began to actively use virtual communities and team-building sessions. These efforts helped employees feel connected and aided in sharing work objectives.

Furthermore, Infotech implemented flexible working hours and provided regular wellness programs to support employee well-being. These changes were designed to ensure that remote work could have a long-term positive impact on the organization. Employees, through this support, managed their work more effectively, leading to improved overall work performance.

To deeply analyze the unique psychological issues that arise in a remote work environment, various theories of organizational psychology can be applied. Particularly important are the Social Exchange Theory and Self-Determination Theory. These theories explain factors that significantly impact employee motivation and satisfaction in a remote work environment.

Social Exchange Theory posits that human relationships are governed by the principle of mutual reward. According to this theory, employees respond more positively and their loyalty and commitment to the organization increase when the rewards they receive from interactions with the organization exceed the effort and costs involved. In a remote work environment, the opportunities for such interactions can decrease due to physical isolation. Therefore, leaders must find ways to maintain and enhance positive interactions with employees in a virtual setting. For example, regular virtual meetings, team-building activities, and establishing a fair and transparent reward system are crucial.

Self-Determination Theory explains that an individual's motivation is affected by the fulfillment of three basic psychological needs: autonomy, competence, and relatedness. In remote work, employees often experience higher autonomy, but the needs for competence and relatedness may not be sufficiently met. Organizations should provide a supportive feedback system, work-related training and development programs, and tools that promote communication and collaboration among team members to meet these needs.

As seen in the Infotech case, the company implemented various strategies based on these theoretical approaches to support employee well-being and overcome the psychological challenges of remote work. These strategies improved employee job satisfaction and overall commitment to the organization. Thus, theories of organizational psychology are invaluable tools for understanding and responding to the challenges in a remote work environment.

The specific measures applied to overcome the psychological challenges of remote work can be thoroughly examined through the case of Infotech. The company implemented several important strategies to maintain employee motivation and connectivity.

Firstly, Infotech established a robust virtual communication system to ensure all employees could communicate and collaborate effectively. This system included regular video conferences, real-time chat functions, and project management tools. These tools allowed team members to share information quickly and participate in decision-making processes, minimizing the negative impact of physical distance on teamwork.

Secondly, the company respected employees' autonomy while continuously supporting their work performance. It provided personalized training programs and career development plans, helping employees enhance their skills and manage their tasks autonomously. Additionally, the mentoring system was strengthened to assist employees in overcoming difficulties in their work.

Thirdly, Infotech introduced several welfare programs to enhance employee well-being and job satisfaction. These included virtual yoga classes, online wellness workshops, and mental health support services. These programs supported employees in maintaining a balance between work and personal life and helped reduce the stress and isolation that can arise from remote work.

These measures successfully practiced the principles of organizational psychology in a remote work environment, enhancing employee work efficiency and satisfaction. Infotech's case provides insights for other organizations on how to meet the psychological needs of employees in a remote work environment, which is considered a crucial strategy for long-term organizational success. This approach presents an effective model for turning the challenges brought by remote work into opportunities.

Further exploration of organizational psychology in the remote work environment is essential. This ensures close cooperation among team members and effective project progression. Additional psychological theories and strategies to consider include:

1. Systems Theory: This theory views organizations as complex systems and analyzes how various parts of the system interact with each other. Through Systems Theory, team leaders can understand the role of each organizational member and how they contribute to achieving overall goals. The theory emphasizes the interdependence of team members and is useful for developing strategies for the harmonious functioning of the team.

2. Social Identity Theory: This theory explains how individuals form their identities as members of a group. By enhancing individual belonging and strengthening group identity within the team, team members' cooperation and motivation within the

team can be increased. Team leaders can use this theory to create a positive culture within the team and motivate team members to work towards shared objectives.

3. Conflict Resolution Theory: Conflict is one of the main factors that hinder team collaboration. Conflict Resolution Theory provides strategies for effectively managing and resolving conflicts that occur within the team. Through this, leaders can constructively resolve conflicts and improve relationships between team members, assisting in the successful execution of projects.

4. Motivation Theories: Various motivation theories, such as Herzberg's Motivation-Hygiene Theory or Deci and Ryan's Self-Determination Theory, provide methods for motivating team members. These theories help understand the intrinsic and extrinsic motivations of team members and appropriately stimulate them to actively participate in projects.

These psychological approaches play a significant role in maximizing collaboration within the organization, enhancing project efficiency, and improving relationships between team members. Each theory and strategy must be applied according to specific situations, and team leaders and project managers can develop concrete plans for motivating the team, resolving conflicts, and strengthening teamwork through these. These strategic approaches contribute not only to the success of projects but also to enhancing overall organizational satisfaction and performance.

10. The Psychological Impact of Collaboration Tools

The Psychology of Digital Collaboration: The impact of collaboration tools on team interactions

Exploring the psychological impact of collaboration tools is one of the important issues that modern organizations face. With the development of digital technology, various collaboration tools have innovatively transformed communication and teamwork within organizations. In this chapter, we will examine the effects of these tools on the psychology of individuals and teams, and discuss how to resolve the potential psychological issues while facilitating effective collaboration. Collaboration tools greatly enhance communication among team members, facilitate project management, and optimize work processes, but they can also lead to problems due to excessive reliance on technology.

Globally, companies are adopting various collaboration tools like Slack, Microsoft Teams, and Zoom, which are transforming the ways employees interact. These tools enable team members to share information in real-time and collaborate effectively without being constrained by time and place. However, these changes also pose new psychological challenges to employees. Constant interaction in virtual spaces can blur the boundaries between work and personal life, potentially leading to increased work-related stress.

The continuous and immediate communication features provided by collaboration tools can make employees feel pressured to be always connected, promoting an 'Always On' culture that can lead to burnout. These issues can undermine psychological stability within the organization and lower trust among team members.

This chapter will deeply analyze the various impacts these tools have on organizational psychology and provide strategies on how organizations should manage them. In particular, we will discuss the appropriate ways to use collaboration tools and how to minimize the psychological issues they may cause, exploring solutions that can benefit both the organization and its employees. Through this, organizations can find a balance between leveraging digital tools to increase work efficiency and protecting the psychological health of employees.

Novatech is pushing for global business expansion and has adopted various digital collaboration tools to connect teams across different regions. The company has introduced platforms like Microsoft Teams, Slack, and Asana in its various branches in North America, Europe, and Asia, enabling hundreds of employees to collaborate without the constraints of time zones and geography. These tools have been focused on enhancing efficiency and transparency in remote work environments by enabling project management, file sharing, real-time communication, and tracking of work progress.

The adoption of collaboration tools initially elicited many positive responses. Employees were thrilled with the work environment that was accessible from anywhere and felt that these tools provided flexibility in work and strengthened connections among team members. However, over time, new challenges brought by these tools began to emerge. Employees experienced an overload of communication and information, which decreased work efficiency. The constant flow of information caused important messages to get buried or unrelated conversations to intrude into work hours.

Additionally, issues with integration between various tools and platforms led to duplication of data or discrepancies. Employees had to check and manage the same data across multiple platforms repeatedly, leading to work duplication and time wastage. This confusion negatively affected project schedules and performance, and caused unnecessary tension and stress among employees.

Novatech's management team recognized the need to actively gather feedback from employees and enhance training on the use of collaboration tools. Employees felt the need for continuous support and training to adapt to the constantly changing digital tool environment. To address this, the company started considering measures such as improving user-friendly interfaces, activating the use of integrated platforms, and clearly distinguishing between work and non-work hours to promote work-life balance. These efforts are expected to be a crucial step in increasing overall productivity and enhancing job satisfaction among employees.

The problems Novatech faced with collaboration tools arose from broad and layered factors. The company adopted these tools to connect globally distributed teams, but several issues with their integration and management emerged. Technically, insufficient integration among collaboration tools resulted in duplicated or varying information across systems, causing inconvenience and reducing work efficiency. Furthermore, the user interfaces (UI) and user experience (UX) designs of the collaboration tools were not intuitive, posing significant barriers especially for users who were not familiar with new technologies. This fueled resistance to new tools and a tendency to revert to familiar manual processes.

Organizationally, Novatech had not adequately established a training and support system. Adopting collaboration tools involves more than just purchasing and installing technology; it includes providing adequate training for employees and continuous support for effective use of the tools. However, these processes were neglected at Novatech, resulting in employees not being able to fully utilize the new tools.

Psychologically, the 'always connected' environment provided by collaboration tools blurred the boundaries between work and personal life, leading to employees feeling pressured to respond to work communications even outside of work hours. This led to increased work burnout and stress, negatively impacting employee job satisfaction and productivity.

Recognizing these various issues, Novatech began addressing them by effectively integrating collaboration tools and improving employee training programs, enhancing user interfaces, and implementing policies to clearly define the boundaries between work and personal life. These measures are expected to enable employees to use new tools more effectively, enhance job satisfaction, and increase overall organizational productivity. This is a significant step towards comprehensively solving the problems faced by Novatech, offering important lessons in the digital transformation process of the organization.

The psychological theories related to the adoption of collaboration tools play a critical role in understanding and solving the problems faced by the company. Fred Davis's Technology Acceptance Model (TAM) explains how users accept technology. This model emphasizes that the perceived usefulness and ease of use of technology significantly influence the user's decision to adopt technology. If usefulness is perceived as high, employees are more likely to accept and actively use the technology. On the other hand, if the tool is complex and difficult to understand, employees may resist adopting the new system and stick to their existing work methods.

Kurt Lewin's change management theory describes the organizational change process in three stages: 'unfreeze-change-refreeze'. In the case of Novatech, the adoption of collaboration tools starts in the unfreezing stage, where employees are encouraged to move away from existing work methods and accept new tools and procedures. In the change stage, sufficient training and support should be provided so that employees can apply the new system to actual work, and finally, in the refreezing stage, the new work methods should be solidly established within the organization. Through this process, the organization can minimize resistance to change and encourage active participation from employees.

Joseph Walther's Social Information Processing Theory (SIP) explains social interactions in communication via collaboration tools. This theory analyzes how information is conveyed and interpreted in the context of communication, and how this process shapes individual attitudes and behaviors. The issue of information overload experienced by Novatech employees can be approached through SIP theory. By regulating the quality and quantity of information, the theory suggests that it's possible to optimize employees' information processing capabilities and reduce work stress. This presents a way to adjust the use of collaboration tools to improve work efficiency and overall communication effectiveness within the organization.

These theories provide an essential framework for comprehensively understanding and solving the problems faced by Novatech during the adoption of collaboration tools. By considering the psychological aspects of technology acceptance, effectively managing organizational change, and optimizing psychological factors in the communication process, the organization can successfully overcome challenges related to technology adoption. During this process, the organization's leaders and managers need to develop strategies to foster employees' acceptance of technology, reduce resistance to change, and maintain psychological stability.

The psychological theories applied to solve the problems arising from the adoption of collaboration tools at Novatech have provided practical improvement measures and successfully led organizational changes. The focused theories included the Technology Acceptance Model (TAM), the three stages of organizational change, and the Social Information Processing Theory (SIP). Each theory offered specific solutions to respond to the psychological, organizational, and technical issues faced during tool adoption.

Novatech has focused on enhancing the perceived usefulness and ease of use of collaboration tools based on the Technology Acceptance Model. To this end, the company held workshops and seminars to explicitly explain to employees how each tool can enhance work efficiency. These educational sessions have helped clearly convey the advantages and effective methods of using the tools, contributing to fostering a positive attitude and acceptance among employees. Additionally, to enhance ease of use, the company simplified the user interface and introduced an intuitive design to make it easier for employees to learn and adapt to new tools.

Following the change management theory, Novatech conducted the adoption of collaboration tools within the organization through the stages of unfreezing, changing, and refreezing. In the initial unfreezing stage, the need for new tools was shared across the organization to change employees' perceptions. In the change stage, the actual introduction of tools was carried out, and problems arising during this process were quickly resolved to minimize employees' anxiety and resistance. Finally, in the refreezing stage, continuous support and reinforced training were provided to fully integrate the new tools and work methods into the organizational culture.

Applying the Social Information Processing Theory, Novatech addressed the issue of information overload through collaboration tools by regulating the quality and quantity of information. The company introduced information filtering mechanisms to ensure that employees only received the information they needed. Additionally, informal communication channels within the tools were activated to promote social interactions among employees, allowing them to share experiences and knowledge. These measures helped employees effectively process information and manage stress, thereby enhancing job satisfaction and teamwork.

Novatech's approach has played a significant role in effectively resolving various psychological and organizational issues related to technology adoption, enhancing overall productivity and satisfaction across the organization. Through this process, the organization has deeply recognized the importance of managing psychological changes, contributing to sustainable growth and improvement of the work environment for employees.

Further psychological approaches are needed to deepen the understanding of the impact of collaboration tools on organizational psychology. In particular, efforts to improve the interaction and communication patterns among organizational members can be supported by various theories in organizational psychology. Among these theories, the following can be specifically applied:

1. Interpersonal Theory: This theory explains how interactions between individuals shape each other's behavior and attitudes. By promoting effective interactions among organizational members through collaboration tools, positive interpersonal relationships can be developed, thereby strengthening organizational culture.

2. Group Dynamics Theory: This theory explores various psychological phenomena that occur within a group. Understanding how collaboration tools can influence the group's decision-making process, conflict resolution, and goal setting can be useful. Through this, the organization can use collaboration tools more effectively to maximize group productivity and efficiency.

3. Organizational Learning Theory: This theory deals with how an organization acquires, transmits, and applies knowledge. By using collaboration tools to promote continuous learning and knowledge sharing within the organization, members' personal growth and overall innovation of the organization can be supported.

Integrating these theories into the application of collaboration tools allows the organization to maximize the positive effects of these tools on employees' psychological health, job satisfaction, and overall performance. Additionally, this comprehensive approach can minimize the potential negative psychological impacts and support the sustainable growth of the organization. This integrated approach enables collaboration tools to function not just as technical means, but as significant psychological resources within the organization.

VI. Alliance Strategies and Psychology

The Mind's Map of Alliances: The profound impact of psychological strategies in alliances

Alliance strategies and psychology extend beyond the mere expression of contractual terms, focusing on understanding complex human interactions and deep relationship building. The "Alliance Strategies and Psychology" chapter delves deeply into the psychological foundations of the alliance process, analyzing subtle psychological interactions during negotiations, the process of building trust, and methods for resolving conflicts to broadly explain the various psychological elements that lead to the success of an alliance. Alliances are not just formed through legal documents but are based on each individual's psychological elements and deep human relationships. This chapter emphasizes that the flow of emotions and the need for mutual understanding play a crucial role in evolving alliances beyond mere functional relationships.

Starting with the psychological foundations of alliance negotiations, the chapter extensively covers the roles of trust and emotion, which are essential for forming and maintaining partnerships. Psychological movements occurring at the negotiation table often determine the success of an alliance and provide practical methodologies for building and maintaining trust and mutual understanding in long-term business relationships. Additionally, it explores how to effectively manage and resolve inevitable conflicts during the alliance process and how these conflict resolution methods contribute to strengthening partnerships. Managing conflicts within alliance relationships enhances the capacity to solve potential problems between or within organizations, strengthening relationships between partners and fostering long-term cooperation according to the principles of collaborative negotiation.

This chapter also explores how to manage the psychological disturbances and emotional management associated with the dissolution of alliances and tackles the psychological challenges that can arise when collaborating with partners from different cultural backgrounds, such as in international alliances. International alliances require the ability to understand and harmoniously integrate diverse cultural values and behavioral norms, enabling the formulation of successful strategies in the global business environment. This chapter elucidates the importance of deep human relationships that go beyond mere transactions in alliances, offering ways to more effectively manage and develop relationships both within and outside organizations. This psychological approach provides powerful insights and strategic advantages in business relationships, offering invaluable knowledge to all business leaders and negotiators.

1. Psychological Foundations of Alliance Negotiations

The Psychology of Negotiation: Understanding the Beginnings of Alliances

The psychological foundations of alliance negotiations play a central role in understanding and successfully managing partnerships in the business world. Negotiation is more than mere conversation; it requires careful strategy, deep human understanding, and strong psychological awareness.

Building trust and mutual understanding between parties during negotiations is crucial for forming long-term business relationships. Negotiators must clearly communicate their own needs and objectives while understanding and respecting the needs and objectives of their counterparts.

Deeply understanding the psychological aspects of business negotiations is a key skill for negotiators. This includes managing emotions, resolving conflicts, and reading the psychological cues of others. Emotions can run high during negotiations, and tensions may escalate due to conflicting interests. By applying psychological principles, negotiators can lead discussions more effectively and find amicable resolutions.

The success of negotiations does not solely depend on technical or economic conditions but is significantly influenced by the psychological connection and the quality of interaction between the parties. Useful psychological approaches include recognizing interdependence, utilizing empathy, and understanding the importance of non-verbal communication.

These approaches humanize the negotiation process and support each party in successfully achieving their goals.

This chapter introduces various psychological theories and models, detailing how they can be applied in real business negotiation scenarios. Through this, readers will solidify their understanding of the psychological foundations of alliance negotiations, which will greatly assist in developing strong negotiation skills. Armed with this knowledge, readers can confidently express their positions at the negotiation table and learn methods to build trust with counterparts. These abilities are crucial not only in business but also in personal relationships.

Global tech company Blue Ocean Technologies is exploring various strategic alliances to maintain a competitive edge in the rapidly changing market, particularly aiming for expansion and technological innovation in emerging markets through partnerships with several local and international firms. Through these alliances, the company hopes to strengthen its product portfolio, increase access to new technologies, and enhance brand recognition in the global market.

Recently, Blue Ocean considered an alliance with AsianTech to enter the Asian market. This alliance is expected to provide Blue Ocean with deep insights and networks in the local market, and offer AsianTech access to Blue Ocean's cutting-edge technology and international brand exposure. Both companies see mutual benefits in this alliance and have begun preliminary discussions.

However, some issues have arisen during the negotiation process. Contrary to Blue Ocean's expectations, AsianTech has taken a more cautious approach to technology sharing and has expressed concerns about some of Blue Ocean's demands. These differences have hindered trust-building between the companies and slowed the overall progress of the alliance. Additionally, it became apparent during the negotiations that Blue Ocean had underestimated the complexity of AsianTech's internal decision-making processes, which further complicated the negotiations.

This situation provided Blue Ocean with a challenging psychological moment, emphasizing the importance of psychological understanding and strategy in negotiation processes. The company has realized how crucial a psychological approach is in alliance negotiations and has begun exploring more effective ways to handle similar situations in the future. This case is a prime example of how identifying and understanding the psychological elements in alliance negotiations can play a decisive role.

Analyzing the issues that arose between Blue Ocean Technologies and AsianTech during their alliance negotiations, it appears that the main problems stemmed from a lack of trust between the companies, cultural differences, and differences in communication styles. These problems include important psychological elements that influence the success of alliance negotiations, and effectively resolving them requires a deep understanding and appropriate management of these elements.

Firstly, a lack of trust emerged as a major issue. During the negotiation process, Blue Ocean interpreted AsianTech's conservative stance on technology sharing as insincerity in the negotiations. On the other hand, AsianTech felt that Blue Ocean's aggressive demands for technology sharing could threaten its intellectual property. This mutual distrust significantly hindered the progress of the negotiations.

Secondly, cultural differences also played a crucial role. The differences between Blue Ocean's Western negotiation style and AsianTech's Eastern approach led to misunderstandings in several instances. The differences in decision-making processes were particularly stark; Blue Ocean preferred quick decisions, while AsianTech valued internal coordination and consensus. These differences slowed the negotiation process and sometimes led to conflicts.

Thirdly, differences in communication also caused problems. Communication between the companies was primarily conducted via email and video conferencing, but non-verbal signals and cultural context differences often led to misinterpretations of the messages. This accumulation of misunderstandings decreased the efficiency of the negotiations.

These issues have underscored the importance for Blue Ocean and AsianTech to understand and appropriately manage psychological elements in the alliance negotiation process. A psychological approach to preventing and resolving these issues will benefit both companies. This experience will also provide a strategic foundation for achieving better outcomes in similar international negotiation situations in the future.

The psychological theories that can be applied to negotiations between Blue Ocean Technologies and AsianTech provide important tools for understanding and overcoming psychological barriers that arise during the negotiation process. The theory of trust emphasizes the importance of trust in negotiations, explaining that trust is based on the perception of each party's honesty, reliability, and competence. Referring to Mayer, Davis, and Schoorman's trust model, negotiators can explore ways to build trust with each other. This creates an environment where both parties can positively assess each other's intentions and capabilities, facilitating a smooth alliance.

Additionally, understanding cultural differences is critically important in international negotiations. Geert Hofstede's cultural dimensions theory analyzes the cultural differences of countries across various dimensions and suggests how these can be integrated into negotiation strategies. Through this theory, negotiators can understand the cultural backgrounds and decision-making styles of their counterparts and apply cultural sensitivity to minimize cultural conflicts during the negotiation process.

The role of non-verbal communication is also crucial in negotiations. Albert Mehrabian's research emphasizes how important non-verbal elements are in communication, explaining how gestures, facial expressions, and tone of voice can affect the other party during the negotiation process. By consciously managing their non-verbal signals and correctly interpreting the non-verbal signals of their counterparts, negotiators can communicate more effectively.

By applying these psychological approaches, Blue Ocean and AsianTech can overcome initial uncertainties and conflicts, gradually increasing understanding and trust between them. Ultimately, these efforts led to the successful establishment of a mutually beneficial alliance, significantly contributing to the long-term business goals of both companies. This process left important lessons for Blue Ocean and AsianTech and will make these psychological strategies a valuable asset in future similar international negotiation situations.

Beyond the psychological theories related to collaboration and alliances, there are additional areas of psychology that can be explored to provide fresh insights into understanding and utilizing the psychological elements of collaboration and alliances.

1. Conformity in Groups: This theory explores how individuals conform to the opinions or behaviors of the majority within a group. Studies like Solomon Asch's conformity experiments show how group pressure affects individual judgment and behavior. This is useful for understanding group decisions in negotiation and alliance processes and for exploring ways to maintain diversity of opinion within groups.

2. Interpersonal Attraction Theory: This theory explains the factors that make people feel attracted to each other. Similar to social exchange theory, this theory analyzes how liking, compatibility, and similarity in human relationships influence the formation of cooperative relationships. This can help build strong relationships in alliance negotiations.

3. Psychological Contract Theory: This theory deals with the implicit expectations and promises between an organization and its employees, beyond formal contracts. Similar psychological contracts exist in alliance negotiations, and they are important for managing expectations and trust between parties. By understanding this theory, negotiators can manage informal expectations and prevent potential disappointments or misunderstandings.

4. Ego Defense Mechanisms: Psychologist Sigmund Freud presented several mechanisms that humans use to manage internal conflicts and stress. Understanding these defense mechanisms can help manage emotions in negotiation processes and interpret the defensive behaviors of counterparts. This enables negotiators to develop a more rational and less emotionally driven approach.

By further studying and understanding these areas, negotiators and alliance managers can more effectively handle the complexities of human psychology and flexibly respond to various situations. This psychological knowledge will provide deep insights and practical strategies not only for alliance negotiations but also for managing various human relationships both within and outside the organization.

2. Building Partnerships and Psychological Trust

The Essence of Partnership: Building and Maintaining Psychological Trust

Building partnerships and psychological trust is a crucial component for the success of all business alliances. This chapter deeply explores the psychological foundations that lead to successful partnerships, providing an understanding of how trust is built, maintained, and sometimes broken. Trust is more than just a positive feeling or belief; it is the result of complex psychological processes and interactions. Through trust, partnerships can be strengthened, thereby sustaining business success.

Throughout this process, we will examine various cases to understand the mechanisms through which psychological trust is formed, and analyze how this trust is tested, damaged, and restored in real business environments. Building trust heavily relies on the behavior, communication, and transparency in the decision-making processes of the involved parties. Psychological theories and research provide essential tools to understand, predict, and improve these processes.

We will specifically review negotiation and alliance cases across different industries to illustrate how psychological trust is formed and managed in crisis situations. This will deepen our understanding of the psychological foundations of trust and derive key psychological concepts and strategies in partnership management. This chapter will offer practical guidance to business leaders, negotiators, and managers, aiding them in building strong, trust-based partnerships that will enable readers to develop more effective alliance strategies and achieve long-term business success.

TechnoRise is currently seeking international alliances to introduce products to emerging markets. This company excels in developing innovative software solutions and is exploring partnerships with several companies in Asia and Europe to expand into global markets. Their goal is to provide customized solutions that meet the needs and regulations of local markets through alliances with local companies.

Recently, TechnoRise considered partnering with DigiCoa, a local company with significant potential for entering the Asian market. DigiCoa seemed a perfect partner that could combine TechnoRise's technological capabilities with local market knowledge to create mutual benefits. Both companies found considerable common ground during initial meetings and received positive impressions of each other.

However, several issues began to emerge during the partnership negotiations. TechnoRise had hoped for rapid market entry through the alliance with DigiCoa, but DigiCoa's internal decision-making process turned out to be slower than expected. DigiCoa had to undergo a careful decision-making process and complex internal approval procedures, which conflicted with the pace TechnoRise had anticipated. Additionally, differences in communication styles emerged between the two companies. TechnoRise's direct and goal-oriented communication style did not align with DigiCoa's emphasis on harmony and relationship-focused approach.

These differences led to delays in the alliance process, increasing uncertainty and tension between the parties. Despite initial optimism, TechnoRise and DigiCoa faced unexpected challenges as they adapted to each other's corporate cultures and operational styles. This situation highlighted the need for both parties to build mutual trust and improve effective communication, suggesting that additional efforts were necessary to successfully lead the alliance.

The causes of the delays and tensions in the negotiations between TechnoRise and DigiCoa stemmed from several psychological and organizational factors. The main issues between the two companies primarily arose from differences in communication styles, clashes in corporate cultures, and failures in managing expectations. By analyzing each factor in-depth, we can explore ways to overcome these issues.

First, the significant impact of differences in communication styles was evident. TechnoRise follows a Western business model, preferring concise and goal-oriented communication. In contrast, DigiCoa, rooted in Asian business culture, values harmony and the collective opinion in decision-making processes and prefers an indirect and relationship-centered communication style. These fundamental differences in communication styles caused misunderstandings in message interpretation and unnecessarily amplified tensions and misunderstandings during the negotiation process.

Second, the clash of corporate cultures also emerged as a critical issue. The swift decision-making and execution-oriented culture of TechnoRise and DigiCoa's cautious and hierarchical decision-making structure often clashed during their interactions. TechnoRise's employees felt frustrated by DigiCoa's slow decision pace, which weakened the project's momentum.

Third, the failure in managing expectations hindered the progress of the alliance. The inability to set and manage clear and specific expectations between the parties early in the alliance led to misunderstandings about each other's business goals and roles within the partnership. These misunderstandings eventually led to mistrust in each other's intentions and capabilities, further escalating tension and uncertainty during the negotiations.

Through this analysis, TechnoRise and DigiCoa can take the necessary measures to lead the alliance to success. Improving communication styles, acknowledging and adapting to cultural differences, and setting and managing clear expectations are crucial elements for both companies to move toward a common goal. By fully considering and applying these elements, the two companies can build a strong and sustainable partnership.

The application of various psychological theories can help TechnoRise and DigiCoa overcome the challenges encountered during their partnership negotiations. These theories play an essential role in understanding and managing the psychological factors that occur during the negotiation and relationship-building process. Such approaches can help the two organizations better understand each other and interact effectively in situations where they have different cultural backgrounds and communication styles.

First, through the application of Dual Perspective Theory, TechnoRise and DigiCoa can learn how to balance their own interests with those of others. This theory explains how individuals can coordinate their concerns with those of others during conflict resolution, emphasizing the importance of mutual respect and cooperation. By applying this theory, both sides can resolve conflicts more constructively and develop strategies for achieving mutually beneficial outcomes.

Next, Cultural Difference Theory greatly aids TechnoRise and DigiCoa in understanding each other's cultural values and decision-making styles. Utilizing Geert Hofstede's cultural dimensions theory, partners with different cultural backgrounds can better understand and respect each other's actions and decisions. This theory enhances cultural sensitivity and helps prevent potential issues caused by cultural differences, facilitating appropriate responses.

Relationship Coordination Theory also plays a significant role. This theory studies how the quality of communication and relationships within an organization affects work performance. Developed by Jody Hoffer Gittell, this theory demonstrates how high-quality communication and mutual respect can strengthen teamwork and enhance overall project performance. By applying this theory, TechnoRise and DigiCoa can build an effective collaborative relationship and maximize their capabilities.

Lastly, Psychological Contract Theory focuses on the implicit expectations and promises between an organization and individuals. This theory helps TechnoRise and DigiCoa clarify their expectations and carefully manage their commitments, thereby strengthening mutual trust. Denise Rousseau's research emphasizes that breaking these psychological contracts can lead to disappointment or loss of trust, which is essential for maintaining long-term partnership relationships.

By integrating and applying these psychological approaches, TechnoRise and DigiCoa can minimize conflicts and deepen trust and cooperation, ultimately helping both companies maintain a successful long-term partnership. This experience has shown both organizations the importance of a psychological approach in business alliances and laid the foundation for utilizing such approaches in similar situations in the future.

The application of psychological theories during the partnership negotiations between TechnoRise and DigiCoa provided deep insights into business negotiation and partnership building. The theoretical knowledge and practical application examples effectively managed and understood the psychological factors during the negotiation process.

The application of Dual Perspective Theory taught TechnoRise and DigiCoa how to simultaneously consider their own interests and those of the other party. Initially, each organization primarily focused on its own goals, but through this theory, they realized the importance of understanding and respecting the needs and goals of the other party. As a result, both sides engaged in more constructive conversations and successfully found mutually beneficial solutions.

The application of Cultural Difference Theory helped overcome differences in communication styles and decision-making processes between the organizations. Based on Hofstede's cultural dimensions theory, TechnoRise came to respect DigiCoa's decision-making structure and values more, which positively influenced trust building and negotiation progress. Cultural understanding and adaptation also played a crucial role in reducing misunderstandings and minimizing conflicts during negotiations.

Relationship Coordination Theory provided methods for TechnoRise and DigiCoa to maintain a cooperative relationship while effectively communicating and conducting negotiations. According to Jody Hoffer Gittell's research, high-quality communication and mutual respect were important success factors during the negotiation process. By practically applying this theory, both organizations achieved more efficient and effective cooperation.

Finally, Psychological Contract Theory played a crucial role in clarifying expectations between the parties and managing mutual commitments. Following this theory, both organizations communicated more clearly and transparently about their promises and expectations, strengthening their trust and contributing to the long-term maintenance of the partnership relationship.

By applying these psychological theories, TechnoRise and DigiCoa were able to overcome initial challenges and build a strong and sustainable partnership. This experience reminded both organizations of the importance of a psychological approach in business alliances and established a foundation for utilizing such approaches in similar situations in the future.

The partnership negotiation process between TechnoRise and DigiCoa, where psychological theories were applied, offers profound insights into business negotiations and partnership building. Exploring additional areas of psychology related to this can help negotiators and managers more effectively understand and manage the complexities of human relationships.

1. Conflict Resolution Psychology: Conflict resolution psychology studies how individuals or groups resolve conflicts. This field focuses on analyzing the causes of conflict and developing effective communication skills and negotiation strategies for conflict situations. Acquiring conflict resolution skills allows for more proactive management and resolution of issues that may arise during partnership negotiations.

2. Group Dynamics: This field studies how individuals behave within a group and how interactions occur between group members. Understanding group dynamics plays a vital role in team-based projects or complex alliances between multiple organizations. It helps develop strategies to enhance teamwork and build positive relationships among team members.

3. Motivation Theories: Motivation theories explore how individuals or organizations are motivated, maintained, and enhanced to achieve their goals. Applying motivation theories in partnership negotiations can strengthen the commitment to shared goals and increase the passion and dedication needed for long-term partnerships.

4. Emotional Intelligence: Emotional intelligence is the ability of individuals to recognize and manage their own and others' emotions. During the negotiation process, individuals with high emotional intelligence can make logical and effective decisions without being influenced by emotions. Additionally, appropriately

understanding and responding to the emotions of partners can prevent the escalation of conflicts and strengthen relationships.

These psychological fields are not only useful in addressing the challenges encountered in the partnership process between TechnoRise and DigiCoa but can also be applied effectively in all business environments. Each theory and approach helps organizational leaders and managers gain a deeper and more strategic understanding of the various human relationships and challenges they may face, ultimately contributing to the overall success and development of the organization.

3. Managing Partnership Conflicts

The Art of Reconciliation: A Psychological Approach to Managing Partnership Conflicts

Conflicts arising during the partnership process can determine the success or failure of a partnership. This chapter explores the management of partnership conflicts using psychological approaches to understand and resolve conflicts. Although conflicts are an inevitable business reality, if managed correctly, they can be transformed into opportunities to build trust and strengthen relationships. This process requires a deep psychological understanding, explained through various theories and real-life cases.

Psychology plays a vital role in identifying the roots of conflicts and understanding the complexities of human behavior that emerge in conflict situations. This allows us to find ways to constructively resolve conflicts and build more robust relationships both within and between organizations. This chapter specifically deals with conflict situations that can arise in business partnerships, exploring psychological concepts and resolution strategies in depth and investigating the potential for organizational development through conflict resolution.

Conflicts in business partnerships often arise due to unexpected issues, unclear communication, and clashes between different corporate cultures and objectives. Effectively managing these conflicts is essential not only for the success of the partnership but also for maintaining long-term partnerships. Understanding and applying conflict management techniques is a crucial skill for organizational leaders, emphasizing the importance of a psychological approach.

Now, let's explore in more detail how conflicts occur and which psychological theories can be applied in each situation. This will allow us to learn how to view conflicts not merely as obstacles but as opportunities for growth and development.

This psychological understanding will play a decisive role in managing partnership conflicts and achieving better outcomes in all relationships.

EnerTech is a company providing renewable energy solutions, currently seeking global partnerships to expand into international markets. Particularly, they are pushing forward collaborations with various regional companies to strengthen their presence in European and Asian markets. During this process, EnerTech has collaborated with companies from different corporate cultures and regulatory environments, which has presented multiple challenges.

Recently, EnerTech attempted a partnership with SolarMax, a Europe-based solar energy company. During the initial discussion phase, both companies had high expectations for technology sharing and joint marketing strategies. However, as negotiations progressed, several issues began to emerge. EnerTech's corporate culture, which emphasizes quick decision-making and execution, clashed with SolarMax's more cautious and gradual approach. Additionally, EnerTech felt that SolarMax's decision-making structure was complex and time-consuming, which slowed down project progress.

These cultural and operational differences led to mismatches in project goals and schedules, eventually leading to tensions and mutual dissatisfaction between the two companies. Particularly, a skeptical view of the partnership began to spread within each organization, negatively impacting the negotiation process. To manage the situation, both companies convened several emergency meetings, but failed to clearly align their expectations and requirements.

This situation necessitated that EnerTech and SolarMax adopt psychological approaches and strategies to effectively manage and resolve conflicts. This could be used as an opportunity for both companies to understand and adapt to their differences, constructively resolve conflicts, and build effective cooperative relationships.

The fundamental causes of the conflicts that arose in the partnership between EnerTech and SolarMax were complex and influenced by multiple factors. Analyzing these factors reveals that most stem from differences in organizational culture, communication styles, and failures in managing expectations. By deeply understanding these conflict factors, organizations can avoid similar problems in future partnerships and perform more effective negotiation and relationship management.

The first cause is differences in organizational culture. EnerTech values quick decision-making and rapid action, whereas SolarMax prefers a more cautious and gradual approach. This difference formed divergent expectations about the speed and priorities of the project, becoming a source of conflict. Such cultural differences are a common issue in international business partnerships, and if not recognized and managed, they can reduce the chances of partnership success.

The second cause is differences in communication styles. EnerTech prefers direct and goal-oriented communication, while SolarMax has an indirect and relationship-centered style. These differences can lead to misunderstandings and amplify misinterpretations, causing unnecessary conflicts during the negotiation process, especially when discussing important decisions or changes.

The third cause is the failure to manage expectations. Both sides started the partnership with high expectations, but these were not clearly aligned and managed. As the specific goals each organization hoped to achieve through the partnership were not sufficiently shared, conflicts intensified over time. Effective expectation management is essential for the success of a partnership, allowing both sides to understand and respect each other's needs and limitations.

Based on this analysis of the problem causes, EnerTech and SolarMax need to structurally resolve conflicts and develop effective negotiation strategies tailored to each organization's characteristics. This will provide a crucial foundation for overcoming conflicts and building more constructive and sustainable relationships.

The psychological theories applicable to managing and resolving the conflicts between EnerTech and SolarMax provide methods for the two organizations to understand and harmoniously cooperate despite their different cultures and operational styles. These theories allow for a deep understanding of the sources of conflict and the derivation of solutions based on effective communication and mutual understanding.

According to Morton Deutsch's conflict resolution theory, conflicts can be resolved in a cooperative or competitive manner, with cooperative approaches yielding more constructive long-term results. Through this theory, EnerTech and SolarMax can find ways to more effectively integrate each other's needs and goals by approaching conflict situations cooperatively. A cooperative conflict resolution approach establishes a foundation for building trust between the two organizations and transforming conflicts into opportunities for positive change.

Edgar Schein's organizational culture theory explains how an organization's core values and norms influence approaches to conflict resolution. If EnerTech and SolarMax clearly understand each other's organizational cultures and approach their cultural differences with respect, more smooth communication and effective conflict resolution are possible. Understanding organizational culture plays a significant role in identifying the causes of conflict and strengthening collaboration between organizations.

Denise Rousseau's psychological contract theory deals with the implicit expectations and promises that can serve as sources of conflict. By clarifying the subtle expectations each organization has of the other and improving how these expectations are actually managed and met, unnecessary misunderstandings and conflicts can be reduced. Clarifying psychological contracts is essential for maintaining a successful long-term partnership and effectively resolving conflicts when they occur.

By actively utilizing these psychological theories, EnerTech and SolarMax can more constructively manage conflicts that may arise during the partnership process and build a strong and sustainable cooperative relationship. A psychological approach to conflict resolution will significantly contribute to creating a culture of understanding and mutual respect between the two organizations.

The psychological approach to resolving the conflicts between EnerTech and SolarMax effectively addresses the fundamental causes of these conflicts, providing ways to strengthen the partnership between the two organizations. Let's examine how solutions were specifically introduced and implemented at each stage using these psychological theories.

First, according to Morton Deutsch's cooperative conflict resolution theory, EnerTech and SolarMax held joint workshops to constructively address conflicts. In these workshops, core team members from both companies participated, deeply discussing each other's cultures and work styles, and exploring communication methods based on mutual respect and understanding. During this process, both organizations were able to clarify their needs and goals, and based on this, they derived mutually beneficial solutions.

Second, utilizing Edgar Schein's organizational culture theory, EnerTech and SolarMax analyzed the impact of each organization's culture on the conflict. This analysis helped both organizations to respect and understand each other's organizational cultures more, and instead of viewing cultural differences as a source of conflict, they developed ways to use diversity as an asset to the organization. A deep understanding of organizational culture helped both organizations positively accept their differences and turn them into strengths.

Third, applying Denise Rousseau's psychological contract theory, both organizations clarified their implicit expectations of each other and redefined their actual commitments. During this process, both parties adjusted their expectations of each other and clarified what each organization expected, laying an important foundation for building trust in future partnerships. Clarifying psychological contracts prevented the recurrence of conflicts and significantly contributed to maintaining a long-term cooperative relationship.

These approaches enabled EnerTech and SolarMax to resolve conflicts and build a strong partnership that shared the goals and visions of each organization. The application of psychological theories at each stage played a decisive role in resolving the causes of conflicts and enhancing cooperation between the two organizations. This provided both organizations with ways to view conflicts as opportunities for positive change, allowing them to build stronger and more sustainable relationships.

In addition to psychological theories that aid in managing and resolving partnership conflicts, there are various psychological approaches that can be usefully applied in a business environment. These theories can deeply understand interactions within and outside the organization, prevent conflicts, and strengthen organizational culture.

1. Emotional Intelligence: Daniel Goleman's theory of emotional intelligence emphasizes the ability of individuals to recognize their own and others' emotions and manage them appropriately. This theory highlights how important emotion regulation is in conflict situations, and leaders with high emotional intelligence can more effectively mediate and resolve conflicts among team members.

2. Transformational Leadership: Bernard M. Bass's theory of transformational leadership describes the process by which leaders present a vision, motivate employees, and lead changes. This leadership style can facilitate positive changes in organizational conflict situations and increase employee engagement and cooperation.

3. Cognitive Behavioral Approach: This approach deals with how an individual's thought patterns influence behavior and emotions. Applying this to conflict resolution allows employees to recognize and modify their thinking and behavior patterns, enabling more constructive conflict management.

4. Systems Theory: Viewing an organization as a complex system of interconnected elements, systems theory explains how different conflict elements within and outside the organization interact. This theory is useful for viewing conflicts from an overall organizational perspective and understanding the balance between various elements within the system.

These psychological theories provide deep insights not only for managing and resolving conflicts but also for developing strategies for healthy organizational development. By learning and applying these theories, organizational leaders can effectively manage conflict situations and strengthen organizational culture, providing a crucial foundation for all organization members to work in a more harmonious and productive environment

4. Collaborative Negotiation and Fisher & Ury's Principles

The Mindset for Collaboration: The Impact of Fisher & Ury's Negotiation Principles on Alliances

Collaborative negotiation is an essential element for the sustainability and success of business relationships. In this chapter, we explore how organizations can find win-win solutions and build lasting partnerships through the collaborative negotiation principles introduced by Fisher and Ury in "Getting to Yes." Collaborative negotiation is not just about maximizing benefits, but a process of strengthening relationships, and making decisions based on mutual understanding and trust.

The approach to collaborative negotiation focuses on eliminating the causes of conflicts and generating outcomes that satisfy all parties involved. This is especially important when negotiating with partners from various cultures and expectations in a globalized market environment. Transparency and fairness in the negotiation process play a pivotal role in ensuring the sustainability of partnerships and are directly linked to each organization's long-term strategies.

This chapter will provide an in-depth analysis through various case studies showing how these collaborative negotiation techniques can be applied in real business scenarios. Readers will gain an understanding of the practical application of collaborative negotiation and the positive changes it can bring about. Collaborative negotiation is not just a technique, but a crucial component that shapes the culture and strategies of an organization, leading to success in business relationships. This approach will be a valuable asset for organizational managers and negotiators at all levels.

Recently, NovaTech, an international software development company, sought to expand into emerging markets by exploring a collaboration with IndoTrak, a local company. NovaTech aimed to develop customized solutions suitable for the local market through a partnership with IndoTrak. Initially, both sides started with high expectations, but as differences in their work styles and operational methods became apparent, conflicts gradually intensified.

NovaTech, which has a culture of making quick decisions and executing swiftly, faced challenges with IndoTrak's more cautious and gradual approach. This difference, especially in terms of project pace, frequently caused friction. NovaTech felt that IndoTrak's decision-making process was overly slow, which became a major factor delaying the achievement of its business goals.

Additionally, communication issues were a significant source of conflict. NovaTech's direct and goal-oriented communication style clashed with IndoTrak's indirect and relationship-centered style, often leading to misunderstandings of intentions and messages, making it difficult to reach agreements on critical project decisions.

These situations caused considerable stress and dissatisfaction on both sides, ultimately affecting the potential success of the project. Both companies faced the need to explore ways to resolve conflicts and build a successful partnership. This situation highlighted the importance of managing conflicts through collaborative negotiation techniques and psychological approaches, providing lessons for both parties.

The conflict between NovaTech and IndoTrak primarily stemmed from differences in organizational culture and operational methods. These differences became significant obstacles to effective communication and project management, hindering cooperation between the companies.

First, differences in organizational culture deeply influenced each company's decision-making and work processes. NovaTech, preferring a Western management style, values quick decisions and efficient execution, while IndoTrak, rooted in traditional Indian business culture, emphasizes mutual respect and consensus in decision-making, prioritizing a careful approach. This led to friction between

NovaTech's expectation of swift progress and IndoTrak's slower, more cautious approach.

Second, differences in communication styles affected the understanding and timing of feedback on key project issues. NovaTech's clear and direct communication style conflicted with IndoTrak's indirect and situational approach, creating potential for misinterpretation and misunderstandings, ultimately negatively impacting trust building between the companies.

Third, failures in managing expectations were another significant cause of conflict. Unclear expectations and goals set at the project's outset led to serious misalignments in adjusting project objectives later on. NovaTech and IndoTrak had different visions and expectations for the project, which became clearly apparent only midway through, further intensifying conflicts.

By deeply analyzing and understanding these issues, NovaTech and IndoTrak were able to develop effective strategies for managing and resolving conflicts. Identifying the causes of conflicts is the first step in resolution, enabling the organizations to lay the foundation for a stronger and more sustainable partnership.

Various psychological theories applicable to resolving the conflicts between NovaTech and IndoTrak play crucial roles in understanding the sources of conflict and finding collaborative solutions. Specifically, the negotiation techniques presented by Fisher and Ury in "Getting to Yes" are particularly apt for this case. They emphasize focusing on interests rather than positions and making decisions based on objective criteria.

1. Collaborative Negotiation Principles: Fisher and Ury's approach encourages parties in a conflict to find common interests and seek solutions that meet each party's needs. These principles focus on problem-solving rather than negotiating based on personal position or power. This provides a way for NovaTech and IndoTrak to collaborate beyond differences in work styles and cultural backgrounds.

2. BATNA (Best Alternative to a Negotiated Agreement): This principle involves identifying the best alternative that a negotiator can have and actively using it to achieve the most favorable outcome in negotiations. Clarifying BATNA in the

conflict resolution process between NovaTech and IndoTrak helps each organization understand the range of concessions they can make and the essential conditions from their perspectives.

3. Psychology of Conflict Resolution: Psychological approaches to conflict resolution focus on both parties understanding the fundamental causes of conflict and improving communication based on mutual respect. This is essential for NovaTech and IndoTrak to constructively resolve conflicts and maintain a long-term relationship.

The application of these theories helps NovaTech and IndoTrak overcome conflict situations, deepening their understanding of each other and enabling the construction of a more effective cooperative relationship. Collaborative negotiation techniques and psychological approaches serve as effective tools for reducing conflicts and enhancing trust and cooperation between organizations.

The process of applying Fisher and Ury's principles in the collaborative negotiations between NovaTech and IndoTrak was implemented at various stages. This approach played a crucial role in helping both companies resolve conflicts and build an effective partnership.

First, by adopting an interest-based negotiation approach, NovaTech and IndoTrak focused their discussions around common goals rather than individual needs. To facilitate this, both companies clearly defined their core interests and explored how they could be mutually complementary. For example, while NovaTech valued innovation in technology development, IndoTrak provided deep understanding and accessibility to the local market.

Second, regular joint workshops were held to foster a culture of understanding and respect for each other's work methods among team members from both organizations. These workshops allowed participants from both companies to experience each other's business environments and cultures, helping to break down communication barriers and reduce conflicts.

Third, mechanisms for early diagnosis and resolution of conflicts were established. Both companies set up processes that allowed for quick resolution of conflicts when they occurred and conducted regular mutual evaluations to identify and address potential issues during the collaboration process.

Fourth, during the negotiation process, the BATNA principle was used to clarify the limits of what each company could concede and the conditions beyond which they could not go. This helped both companies make realistic and feasible decisions at the negotiation table and provided a foundation for exploring alternative solutions when conflicts arose.

The application of psychological approaches and collaborative negotiation principles effectively managed the initial conflicts between NovaTech and IndoTrak, ultimately leading to the establishment of a successful business relationship. This experience was a significant learning opportunity for both organizations, deepening their understanding and respect for each other and laying a solid foundation for future business cooperation. This case serves as an excellent example of how psychological theories can be effectively applied in real business situations.

In addition to psychological theories related to collaborative negotiation, there are additional psychological approaches that can be utilized in business negotiations and relationship management. These theories can help develop effective communication and negotiation strategies in various situations within and outside the organization.

1. Emotional Intelligence: Daniel Goleman's theory of emotional intelligence plays a crucial role in negotiation and leadership. According to this theory, individuals who can recognize and manage their own and others' emotions can achieve better outcomes in relationships. Emotional intelligence helps negotiators maintain composure in conflict situations and consider the emotions and needs of others to derive more constructive negotiation outcomes.

2. Cognitive Behavioral Psychology: Cognitive behavioral psychology explores how an individual's thought patterns and behavior affect their emotions and interpersonal relationships. Using this approach in negotiation tasks, negotiators can identify and modify irrational thoughts or assumptions to develop more effective communication strategies.

3. Relational Systems Theory: This theory explains how relationships between individuals and groups function as interdependent systems. Applying this in negotiations allows organizations to understand and optimize the dynamics occurring not only within individual relationships but across the entire network. This is particularly useful in complex inter-organizational negotiations and contributes to strengthening strategic alliances.

4. Psychological Contract Theory: This theory deals with the implicit promises and expectations between individuals and organizations. Understanding and clarifying psychological contracts during the negotiation process is important for aligning expectations and building trust. This enables negotiators to prevent conflicts and manage partnerships between organizations more effectively.

These psychological approaches can be usefully applied not only in business negotiation situations like those between NovaTech and IndoTrak but also in everyday organizational operations and personal professional development. Each theory draws inspiration from various fields of psychology, providing strategic tools that can be effectively applied in real business situations..

5. The Psychology of Long-Term Business Relationships

Timeless Connections: Psychological Insights in Long-Term Business Relationships

Long-term business relationships transcend mere contracts and involve a complex interplay of psychological and social factors. This chapter explores the psychological principles and theories essential for maintaining and strengthening long-term business relationships. For business partnerships to be successful over time, it's crucial to look beyond mere economic benefits to trust, interdependence, and the emotional connections between individuals and organizations. These psychological elements determine the quality of the partnership and provide stability in a changing market environment.

The success of long-term business relationships begins with trust and transparency between partners. Trust is built over time through consistent behavior, fulfilling commitments, and open communication. This psychological stability becomes a strong support in times of challenges and crises that the business may face. Therefore, this chapter will delve deeply into the psychological foundations and practical strategies necessary to sustain long-term relationships.

Moreover, understanding the role of emotions in long-term business relationships is vital. Emotions significantly influence decision-making and interpersonal relationships; positive emotions can foster a cooperative work environment, while negative emotions require careful management. If organizational leaders can understand and manage these emotional dynamics effectively, they can respond more effectively to internal and external challenges.

This chapter will examine how these psychological approaches can be applied in real business scenarios, providing psychological insights and strategies needed to successfully maintain and develop long-term business relationships. Through this, readers will gain the tools and knowledge needed to reassess and strengthen their business relationships.

Creative Solutions, a digital marketing agency, has maintained long-term contracts with clients across various industries. The agency is particularly known for its decade-long partnership with a clothing brand, which has brought significant benefits to both parties. However, in recent years, rapid changes in the digital marketing environment and shifts in consumer expectations have posed a series of challenges between the brand and the agency.

Responding quickly to changing market demands has been key to maintaining a successful collaborative relationship between the two. However, Creative Solutions realized that their existing marketing strategies were no longer effective, facing the need to readjust their strategies. Additionally, the clothing brand began demanding more innovative and creative marketing approaches, prompting the need for a new collaborative model between the two.

The issues that arose in this process included some misalignments in communication styles and expectation management between the two companies. Creative Solutions conducted several internal brainstorming sessions to meet the client's needs, but when the proposed ideas did not meet the client's expectations, conflicts intensified. This eroded trust between the two parties and added tension to the long-term relationship.

This case provides an opportunity to apply psychological principles and theories to resolve conflicts and strengthen collaboration in long-term business relationships. Developing strategies based on mutual understanding and trust to achieve mutually successful outcomes in a changing market environment is crucial. Such an approach can help both parties maintain a stronger and more sustainable partnership.

The challenges between Creative Solutions and the clothing brand primarily stemmed from failures in expectation management, inadequate communication, and difficulties in adapting quickly to market changes. These factors are closely linked, and understanding how each can trigger the other is crucial.

Firstly, failure in expectation management prevented Creative Solutions from adequately responding to the client's changing needs. The agency continued to use certain marketing strategies based on past successes, but these gradually lost effectiveness over time. The client expected more innovative and creative approaches, but these expectations were not clearly communicated, and the agency was not fully aware of them.

Secondly, the inadequacies in communication led to issues where the mutual expectations were not accurately aligned. Subtle differences in communication styles meant that the ideas and proposals presented often did not match the client's needs. This lack of communication made it difficult for both sides to fully understand each other's needs and constraints, ultimately leading to unnecessary misunderstandings and conflicts.

Thirdly, the failure to adapt to market changes is a critical factor in this field. The digital marketing environment is constantly evolving, and adapting quickly to these changes is key to success. Creative Solutions' failure to promptly detect market signals and develop appropriate strategies made it challenging to meet the client's demands.

By comprehensively analyzing these issues, Creative Solutions and the clothing brand can find solutions to each problem and explore ways to improve their long-term relationship. The application of psychological approaches and theories will play a crucial role in this process.

Psychological theories play an important role in strengthening long-term business relationships, and particularly useful theories for resolving conflicts and improving relationships between Creative Solutions and the clothing brand include:

1. Daniel Goleman's theory of Emotional Intelligence emphasizes the ability of individuals to recognize and manage their own and others' emotions. This is very important in business relationships, especially in long-term partnerships where understanding and appropriately responding to the emotions of others is essential. Creative Solutions and the clothing brand can apply this theory to manage conflicts and better understand each other's emotional needs.

2. Eric Berne's Transactional Analysis divides human interactions and communications into three ego states: Parent, Adult, and Child. This theory can be used to understand and improve communication patterns within an organization and can be useful in enhancing communication between Creative Solutions and the clothing brand. Recognizing their own ego states and promoting more productive and mature communications from the 'Adult' state can facilitate more effective interactions.

3. John Bowlby's Attachment Theory explains how early childhood experiences affect an individual's ability to form relationships and regulate emotions. Applying this theory in business relationships can help understand issues of trust and dependency within the partnership. By forming a stable attachment between the agency and the client, the long-term cooperative relationship can be more effectively maintained.

These psychological approaches provide Creative Solutions and the clothing brand with the opportunity to effectively resolve conflicts and strengthen their long-term partnership through the psychological insights offered by each theory. The application of these theories in conflict resolution and relationship improvement processes restores trust between the two parties and lays a solid foundation for future cooperation.

The process of resolving conflicts between Creative Solutions and the clothing brand using psychological theories was an important step in improving the relationship. Specifically, Emotional Intelligence, Transactional Analysis, and Attachment Theory each approached the problem in their unique ways and offered solutions.

By applying the theory of Emotional Intelligence, the management team at Creative Solutions was able to better understand and manage the emotional responses between themselves and the representatives of the clothing brand. This allowed both organizations to recognize how their actions could impact each other and to have more constructive conversations even in conflict-inducing situations. This approach, which emphasizes the recognition and regulation of emotions, contributed to creating a culture of deeper understanding and respect.

Using Transactional Analysis, both organizations improved their understanding of communication styles. Members of each organization realized that their communication methods sometimes stemmed from the Parent, Adult, or Child ego states and adjusted their interactions accordingly. By strengthening communication from the 'Adult' state, clearer and more objective conversations became possible, which helped effectively resolve conflicts.

The application of Attachment Theory focused on building psychological stability and trust between the two organizations. Trust is a very important element in long-term relationships, and both organizations were able to develop deeper relations by strengthening their dependency and attachment. By forming a stable attachment, each organization explored ways to make the partnership more valuable and sustainable.

These psychological approaches provided both organizations with opportunities to cooperate and grow beyond conflicts. The application of each theory was essential not only in resolving conflicts but also in more effectively managing and strengthening the relationship between the organizations. Through this process, Creative Solutions and the clothing brand were able to build a more robust and mutually beneficial long-term business relationship.

In strengthening long-term business relationships, the following psychological approaches and theories are also worth exploring. These can provide useful insights for relationship building, communication improvement, and conflict resolution.

1. Interpersonal Theory: Developed by Timothy Leary, this theory analyzes patterns of interaction between individuals. Interpersonal Theory can be applied in business partnerships to increase predictability of each other's behaviors and develop more effective interaction strategies.

2. Social Exchange Theory: This theory approaches relationships from an economic perspective, suggesting that people seek to balance costs and benefits. In business relationships, applying Social Exchange Theory can analyze the value that the partnership provides to both parties, thereby building stronger motivation and satisfaction.

3. Psychological Contract Theory: This theory explores the subtle and implicit expectations between an organization and an individual. When psychological contracts are well managed and met, it enhances employee satisfaction and performance. Similarly in business partnerships, understanding and managing unspoken expectations and promises is important.

4. Cultural Differences and Negotiation Strategies: In negotiations with partners from diverse cultural backgrounds, cultural understanding is crucial. Understanding how each culture influences the negotiation process can lead to more appropriate and effective negotiation strategies.

These psychological approaches and theories can help deeply understand business relationships and develop strategies for long-term success. Each theory provides tools that are useful for organizations to build strong and sustainable relationships both internally and externally.

6. Network Theory and Strategic Alliances

The Power of Connection: Building Strategic Alliances through Network Theory

Network theory and strategic alliances play a crucial role in today's global business environment. This chapter explores how organizations form networks and strengthen strategic alliances from a psychological perspective. Business networks are more than mere connections; they encompass complex systems of human relationships and interactions. Within these networks, strategic alliances can significantly enhance an organization's innovation, growth, and competitiveness.

This chapter will examine how interdependent relationships between organizations are formed and maintained through network theory. It will analyze how organizations can enhance mutual benefits and secure competitive positions by sharing diverse capabilities and resources. Additionally, it will explain how psychological elements within networks, such as trust, power, and influence, contribute to the success of strategic alliances.

Strategic alliances occur when two or more organizations collaborate to achieve common goals. Psychological factors are essential for understanding how partnerships are formed, maintained, and sometimes dissolved. The success of an alliance can greatly depend on how each organization's culture, values, and goals interact.

Therefore, this chapter aims to provide a deep analysis of how organizations can collaborate more effectively and manage long-term business relationships successfully through a psychological understanding of network theory-based strategic alliances. This understanding will offer crucial insights for business leaders in making strategic decisions and provide guidelines on achieving organizational goals through networks and alliances.

TechInnovate, a global software development company, has strategic alliances with companies across various countries. It is particularly known for strengthening its global presence by forming networks with several companies in Europe, Asia, and North America. However, in recent years, global economic volatility and differences in business practices due to regional characteristics have caused difficulties in several of its alliances.

One of TechInnovate's main challenges arose in its collaboration with a partner in Asia. The characteristics of the Asian market meant significant differences in business operations and decision-making processes, often clashing with TechInnovate's Western business model. In particular, differences in communication styles and project management approaches led to miscommunications, resulting in delays and quality issues in projects.

Another issue was data security concerns with North American partners. Although TechInnovate applies advanced security protocols for data management, some partners were not fully integrated into these systems, increasing the risk of critical information leaks and leading to trust issues that strained the alliances.

These situations highlighted the need for TechInnovate to reevaluate its network management methods and strategic alliance approaches. Understanding and effectively integrating diverse cultures and business practices within its global network is crucial for the company's sustainable growth and success. This case underscores the importance of network theory and strategic alliances and provides an opportunity to explore solutions for complex challenges in a global environment.

Analyzing the causes of TechInnovate's issues reveals several key factors, primarily related to the complexities of the global business environment, cultural differences, and difficulties in technological integration.

Firstly, cultural differences were one of the major obstacles in collaboration with Asian partners. The fundamental differences between Asian and Western business cultures in communication styles, decision-making structures, and operational methods led to inefficiencies in projects. These cultural clashes triggered communication errors and complicated interactions, causing disruptions in project progress.

Secondly, failures in technological integration were prominent in data security issues with North American partners. Differences in security systems and data management protocols increased the risk of information leaks, leading to a decrease in trust within the partnerships. The inability of all partners to adopt and effectively integrate TechInnovate's advanced security protocols became a significant issue in the alliances.

Lastly, inadequate management of strategic alliances was a fundamental cause that prevented the proper prevention or resolution of these issues. TechInnovate's failure to fully understand the complexities of strategic alliances and to have a system and strategy in place for effective management exacerbated the problems. Careful preparation, continuous assessment, and adjustment are essential in managing strategic alliances, allowing for the early identification and response to potential issues.

This analysis of problem causes provides TechInnovate with important insights for more effectively managing future strategic alliances and continuing successful expansion in the global market. It also helps the organization develop specific strategies to overcome cultural, technological, and managerial challenges that can arise within a global network.

The psychological theories applicable to overcoming the challenges and issues TechInnovate faces in the global business environment provide deep insights into managing strategic alliances effectively and resolving conflicts with partners from diverse cultural backgrounds. The selected theories each offer unique perspectives, playing a crucial role in helping TechInnovate understand and find solutions to the complexities of strategic alliances.

Geert Hofstede's Cultural Dimensions Theory is extremely useful for understanding interactions between different countries and cultures. This theory provides practical ways for individuals and organizations to recognize and overcome cultural differences. Hofstede analyzed cultural traits by dimensions such as power distance, individualism versus collectivism, masculinity versus femininity, uncertainty avoidance, and long-term orientation, explaining how these traits impact business practices. TechInnovate can use this theory to understand the cultural backgrounds of each partner and develop customized strategies to manage strategic alliances more effectively.

George C. Homans' Social Exchange Theory views interactions in relationships as economic transactions, analyzing the process of assessing costs and rewards in human relationships. This theory helps TechInnovate evaluate each partnership and clarify the benefits each alliance provides to the company. By ensuring a balanced value exchange in all partnerships and securing the best return on investment, the company can pursue more favorable conditions through additional negotiations or strategically adjust alliances if necessary.

Ronald Burt's Structural Hole Theory analyzes the strategic positions within a network and their impact on an individual's or organization's access to information, resources, and influence. This theory enables TechInnovate to optimize its network position and identify and strategically utilize structural holes. By playing a significant role within the network, the company can optimize the flow of information and resources through strategic alliances, enhancing overall business performance.

The in-depth application of these psychological theories enables TechInnovate to effectively manage the complex challenges of strategic alliances and pursue successful expansion in the global market. Each theory provides the psychological insights necessary for the organization to anticipate and respond to issues arising from strategic alliances, supporting sustainable success in the global business environment.

The application of psychological theories in resolving the global business network issues faced by TechInnovate has played a crucial role in overcoming various challenges. Specifically, Cultural Dimensions Theory, Social Exchange Theory, and Structural Hole Theory have brought fundamental changes to the management of strategic alliances.

Utilizing Geert Hofstede's Cultural Dimensions Theory, TechInnovate developed strategies to effectively manage cultural differences with partners in Asia and North America. Based on this theory, the company adopted communication styles and decision-making processes tailored to the cultural traits of each regional partner, minimizing conflicts and maximizing cooperation. For example, with partners in Asian countries where power distance is significant, a more hierarchical communication structure was maintained, while with individualistic North American partners, a more open and egalitarian approach was emphasized.

Additionally, by applying George C. Homans' Social Exchange Theory, TechInnovate meticulously analyzed the costs and benefits in each partnership, striving to achieve a balanced benefit in all alliances. If the value provided by a partnership did not meet expectations, the company pursued more advantageous conditions through further negotiations or strategically readjusted the alliance if necessary.

Finally, the application of Ronald Burt's Structural Hole Theory allowed TechInnovate to occupy strategic positions within the network and optimize the flow of information and resources. By conducting network analysis to identify structural holes, the company played a more significant role within the partnership, securing strategic advantages that enhanced its ability to utilize resources and information and increase opportunities for innovation and growth through partnerships.

These psychological approaches and theories have been crucial in helping TechInnovate resolve issues in the global business environment and develop strategies for managing strategic alliances effectively. This process has taught the company how to adapt effectively to different cultures and market conditions and enhance competitiveness through strategic alliances.

For global companies like TechInnovate facing various challenges, additional psychological theories can be considered to further strengthen strategic alliances and facilitate successful interactions in the global environment.

1. Group Conformity Theory: Solomon Asch's theory explains how individuals seek conformity within a group. This theory is useful when global companies are looking to enhance team cohesion in culturally diverse environments. TechInnovate can use this theory to minimize conflicts among team members from various backgrounds and increase conformity to team goals.

2. Identity Negotiation Theory: Stella Ting-Toomey's theory deals with how individuals and groups form and negotiate their social identities. This theory can help TechInnovate manage cultural conflicts that may arise during interactions with partner companies. The organization can develop ways to recognize and respect the identities of partners from various cultural backgrounds based on this theory.

3. Interdependence Theory: John Thibaut and Harold Kelley's theory explains how individuals depend on each other in relationships, and how this dependency determines their actions and choices. This theory provides TechInnovate with a way to analyze the dynamics of each partnership and manage interdependence constructively. Through this, the company can more effectively structure and strengthen partnerships.

These psychological theories provide fundamental assistance in understanding the challenges that may arise in a global network and appropriately responding to them, allowing for the construction of more effective strategic alliances. Each theory offers psychological insights necessary for organizations to build strong and sustainable relationships, both internally and externally, in complex global environments.

7. Social Exchange Theory in Business Alliances

The Principle of Reciprocity: The Role of Social Exchange Theory in Business Alliances

Social Exchange Theory in business alliances provides an important theoretical foundation for understanding cooperation and networking between organizations. This theory views interactions in human relationships as economic transactions, analyzing the costs and rewards that individuals or organizations provide to each other through their exchanges. This chapter explores how this theory can be applied to modern business alliances and how it can help organizations build and maintain more effective strategic relationships.

In the contemporary business environment, organizations utilize their resources and capabilities to pursue mutual benefits through alliances with other organizations. In such contexts, Social Exchange Theory serves as a useful tool for analyzing the complex dynamics of interdependent exchanges that occur within these alliance relationships. Organizations can use this theory to carefully measure and evaluate the benefits and costs that partnerships must offer, enabling them to make strategic decisions.

This chapter examines real business cases to demonstrate the application of this theory, deriving lessons and strategic insights from these examples. In particular, it analyzes how Exchange Theory can provide concrete direction in organizational strategic decision-making and explores how this theoretical approach can be usefully implemented in the real business world. Through this process, readers will gain a deeper understanding of similar situations their organizations may face and develop more effective alliance strategies.

IntelliNetwork, a global IT solutions provider, has established a complex network of technology partners distributed worldwide. The company is particularly focused on expanding its business around cloud-based services and security solutions, requiring tailored strategies to meet regional characteristics and market demands. However, IntelliNetwork has faced challenges in collaborating with partners in North America and Europe due to cultural differences and discrepancies in operational approaches.

In collaborations with North American partners, there was a strong emphasis on decision speed and efficiency, while European partners preferred more in-depth analysis and cautious approaches. This often led to conflicts in project priorities and execution plans. Additionally, IntelliNetwork encountered communication issues while trying to expand into the Asian market, exacerbated by language barriers and differences in business practices.

These problems posed significant challenges in the management of IntelliNetwork's strategic alliances, reducing the efficiency of partnerships and causing obstacles in project progression. The company recognized the need to develop customized approaches that are well-suited to the cultural and business environments of each region. Managing the complexities of global alliances and maximizing the benefits from strategic alliances became a primary challenge for the company.

The root causes of the problems IntelliNetwork faced in its global partnerships stemmed mainly from cultural differences, communication discrepancies, and failures in aligning expectations between organizations.

Firstly, cultural differences caused fundamental mismatches in operational methods and decision-making processes between North American and European partners. North American partners' preference for swift decisions and actions contrasted with European partners' emphasis on careful, detailed analysis. These differences formed divergent expectations in project prioritization and progression, increasing communication barriers.

Secondly, communication discrepancies were particularly evident in the Asian market. Language barriers, coupled with a lack of understanding of local business practices, led to numerous misunderstandings and conflicts in cooperation, severely hindering effective communication and reducing efficiency in project management and execution.

Thirdly, failures in aligning expectations among organizations acted as obstacles to building balanced, mutually beneficial alliances. The business goals and strategic priorities of IntelliNetwork and its partners were not sufficiently coordinated, preventing the alliances from fully realizing the anticipated synergistic effects.

By analyzing these root causes, IntelliNetwork can more effectively manage the complexities of strategic alliances and develop customized strategies that consider the cultural characteristics and business practices of each region. The application of various psychological theories, including Social Exchange Theory, is expected to play a significant role in this process.

Several psychological theories can enhance IntelliNetwork's management of global partnerships. These theories provide in-depth insights necessary for understanding and effectively managing complex interactions between organizations.

Firstly, Geert Hofstede's Cultural Dimensions Theory is invaluable for analyzing how cultural differences impact organizational work styles and communication methods. Hofstede categorizes culture into several dimensions, explaining how these differences affect business practices in different regions. Using this theory, IntelliNetwork can develop communication and decision-making strategies tailored to the cultural traits of each regional partner, facilitating effective cooperation with global partners. For example, with partners in European countries where a detailed analysis is preferred, decisions are made through more thorough discussions, while with North American partners, a focus on quick decision-making and execution is emphasized.

Secondly, George C. Homans' Social Exchange Theory views interactions in relationships as economic transactions, explaining that individuals or organizations assess the costs and benefits to determine the value of these relationships. This theory can help IntelliNetwork evaluate the costs and benefits of each partnership, aiding in the construction of fair and sustainable business relationships. By clearly analyzing the expected benefits and costs, IntelliNetwork can establish objective grounds for making strategic alliance decisions.

Lastly, Stella Ting-Toomey's Identity Negotiation Theory explains how individuals and groups form and negotiate their social identities in interactions. This theory can help IntelliNetwork manage cultural conflicts that may arise during interactions with partners and develop ways to effectively cooperate while respecting each organization's social identity. Through a process of identity negotiation based on cultural understanding and respect, IntelliNetwork can strengthen relationships with global partners and minimize potential conflicts.

These psychological approaches and theories have been crucial in enabling IntelliNetwork to successfully expand in the global market and manage the challenges that arise in diverse cultural and market environments through strategic alliances. By enhancing global networks and pursuing long-term sustainable growth, these theories help IntelliNetwork strengthen its competitive edge in the global business environment.

In addition to the major psychological theories applied to resolve the issues IntelliNetwork faced while expanding its global business, further exploration of additional psychological theories could enhance the organization and its strategic alliances. These theories could provide deeper understanding and effective strategies for addressing various challenges that may arise during the alliance process.

1. Transactional Analysis Theory - Eric Berne: This theory analyzes individuals' behaviors and social interactions through three ego states (Parent, Adult, Child), explaining the complex dynamics in human relationships. Transactional Analysis can help IntelliNetwork analyze communication patterns with partner organizations, prevent unnecessary conflicts, and build more constructive relationships.

2. Relational Coordination Theory - Jody Hoffer Gittell: This theory describes how communication and relationship quality in work relationships impact work performance. IntelliNetwork can use this theory to optimize task coordination and information sharing within partnerships, strengthening cooperation between organizations.

3. Emotional Intelligence Theory - Daniel Goleman: This theory emphasizes the importance of an individual's emotional intelligence in human relationships and leadership success. If leaders at IntelliNetwork can better recognize and manage their own and others' emotions through this theory, it can enhance partnerships and teamwork.

These psychological theories provide IntelliNetwork with a deeper understanding of various situations that may arise through strategic alliances, supporting the organization's global expansion and business objectives. The application of each theory is crucial in enabling the organization to proactively resolve issues in the alliance process and ensure the long-term success of strategic alliances. Through these measures, IntelliNetwork can strengthen sustainable growth and enhance its competitiveness in the global business environment.

8. Psychological Stability and the Sustainability of Partnerships

Building a Sense of Stability: The Impact of Psychological Stability on the Sustainability of Partnerships

Psychological stability is one of the key factors ensuring the sustainability of partnerships. This chapter explores how to achieve and maintain psychological stability, essential for the long-term success of partnerships. Psychological stability supports organizational members to act consistently without instability during times of uncertainty and change. It plays a vital role in enhancing trust, satisfaction, and commitment in all partnership relationships.

In the global business environment, companies face the challenge of maintaining stable growth and development amidst continually changing market conditions and competition. In this context, psychological stability is particularly valuable in managing strategic partnerships. Partnerships extend beyond mere economic agreements, deeply influenced by the exchange of emotions and the quality of interactions. The psychological stability generated through these interactions lays the foundation for maintaining healthy long-term partnerships.

This chapter introduces various methods and theories to strengthen psychological stability and provides an in-depth analysis of how to overcome various internal and external challenges that partnerships may encounter. It highlights the role of psychological stability in building trust between organizations, resolving conflicts, and maintaining positive relationships, with practical examples demonstrating the application of these theories. Readers will gain concrete insights into how to improve and apply psychological stability within their organizations or partnerships.

A case that underscores the importance of psychological stability in maintaining partnership relationships is the experience of the global pharmaceutical company, MediCare Solutions. This company is engaged in various research and development projects with numerous international partners. However, MediCare Solutions faced difficulties in progressing projects due to communication issues and misalignment of mutual goals in the initial stages of the partnerships.

The problems primarily arose from cultural differences and diversity in operational approaches. For example, one of MediCare Solutions' European partners preferred a conservative approach to the pace and methodology of research and development, while an American partner demanded faster results and was more open to new initiatives. This led to conflicts over project priorities and resource allocation, increasing instability and distrust within the team.

Moreover, communication issues within the partnership significantly demotivated the team toward project goals. The lack of communication prevented a clear understanding of each partner's roles and expectations, resulting in decreased psychological stability among project team members.

These situations forced MediCare Solutions to reevaluate its relationships with each partner and take proactive measures to enhance psychological stability. The company recognized the need to strengthen partnerships based on psychological stability and foster positive team dynamics as a strategy to ensure the long-term success of partnerships.

The challenges MediCare Solutions faced in project progression stemmed from cultural differences, communication failures, and misalignment of goals. These three main causes undermined psychological stability and significantly reduced the effectiveness of the partnerships. Cultural differences led to fundamental discrepancies in work styles and decision-making processes between European and American partners. The conservative approach of the European partners and the progressive attitude of the American partners formed divergent expectations about the direction and pace of the projects, which ultimately led to conflicts and made consensus within the team difficult.

Additionally, the absence of communication was evident in various phases of the project, showing that information sharing was not properly conducted. This situation prevented team members and partners from understanding the current status and next steps of the project, which triggered unnecessary misunderstandings and diminished trust within the team. The misalignment of goals also posed a serious problem. Unclearly set common goals among partners continued to cause conflicts in resource distribution and priority setting, weakening the project's direction and reducing overall partnership efficiency.

These issues prompted MediCare Solutions to recognize the need to restructure its strategies for effectively managing partnerships and securing psychological stability. The company began efforts to overcome cultural differences, enhance communication, and clarify shared goals, aiming to establish a substantial foundation for the success of long-term partnerships. The application of psychological approaches and theories is expected to play a significant role in this process.

MediCare Solutions successfully resolved various issues in partnership management by effectively applying psychological theories. The application of these theories enabled the construction of healthy partnership relationships based on psychological stability.

Utilizing Gert Hofstede's Cultural Dimensions Theory, MediCare Solutions developed tailored communication strategies that considered the cultural characteristics and values of each partner, which significantly contributed to minimizing conflicts and respecting each partner's work style and decision-making mechanisms during interactions with partners from various countries. For example, with European partners, the company emphasized detailed project planning and thorough risk management, while with North American partners, it adopted a strategy prioritizing swift decision-making and execution.

Applying George C. Homans' Social Exchange Theory, the company was able to balance the evaluation of costs and benefits provided by each partnership. This process focused on restructuring or dismantling inefficient partnerships and concentrating on maintaining quality relationships, thereby effectively allocating resources and enhancing the overall success rate of partnerships. Moreover, this theory helped clarify the tangible benefits expected from each relationship, allowing for optimized investment and resource distribution.

Stella Ting-Toomey's Identity Negotiation Theory was used to effectively manage identity-based conflicts that arose during the cooperation process with partner organizations. By applying this theory, the organization prioritized understanding and respecting the cultural differences and individual identities, actively integrating each partner's unique values and strengths into the projects. This approach allowed all partners to gain a deeper understanding of the common goals and to accept each other's differences positively, enhancing cooperation.

These psychological approaches and theories played a crucial role in enabling MediCare Solutions to maintain and strengthen partnerships in a global environment, significantly contributing to the company's strategic goal achievement. Through this process, the company secured sustainable growth and competitive strength based on psychological stability.

In addition to the psychological theories applied by MediCare Solutions in managing partnerships, further exploration of additional psychological approaches could be valuable. These theories can enhance the interaction and quality of partnerships, providing useful insights for improving organizational relationships.

Daniel Goleman's Emotional Intelligence Theory, which centers on an individual's ability to recognize and manage their own and others' emotions, has a significant impact on communication and conflict resolution within partnerships. By applying this theory, MediCare Solutions can strengthen psychological stability within partnerships, promoting bonding and cooperation among team members.

Complexity Theory explains how organizations and systems operate through complex interactions, aiding in understanding organizational behavior and decision-making processes in environments of high uncertainty and variability. This theory could be useful for MediCare Solutions in managing its complex global partner network, providing strategies for responding to unpredictable situations.

Harry Stack Sullivan's Interpersonal Theory, which deals with the impact of human relationships on an individual's behavior and personality development, helps understand how interactions within a partnership can contribute to personal and organizational growth. MediCare Solutions can use this theory to strengthen internal and external relationships and create a healthier partnership environment.

By exploring and applying these theories, MediCare Solutions can more effectively manage partnerships and successfully overcome challenges in the global environment, securing the necessary psychological tools and strategies for long-term success. This will significantly contribute to the organization's sustainable growth and enhanced competitiveness.

9. Dissolution of Partnerships and Emotion Management

The Psychology of Separation:
The Importance of Dissolution of Partnerships and Emotion Management

Dissolution of partnerships and emotion management is an inevitable reality in the business world. As organizations grow and change, not all partnerships can be permanent, and sometimes it becomes necessary to dissolve strategic alliances. This chapter explores how to manage the emotional issues that can arise during the dissolution process and how a psychological approach can constructively navigate this phase.

When alliances are dissolved, strong emotional reactions often occur. Disappointment, feelings of betrayal, anxiety, and stress can surface, impacting both individual and organizational performance negatively. Thus, managing these emotions effectively during the dissolution process is crucial. Effective emotion management is essential to maintain trust among team members, protect long-term business relationships, and preserve the organization's reputation.

This chapter will define clear situations that necessitate the dissolution of a partnership and develop strategies to minimize the emotional issues that may arise during the process. It will also introduce psychological theories and practical applications to manage the variety of emotional reactions that can occur during the decision and execution of dissolving a partnership. Through this, readers will learn how to achieve the best outcomes in unavoidable dissolution scenarios.

The complex task of managing the psychological impacts of partnership dissolution is illustrated through the experiences of TechBridge, a global technology company. TechBridge has been rapidly growing through its partnerships with various corporations worldwide, providing innovative technological solutions. However, due to economic volatility and changes in market strategy, TechBridge faced the necessity to end several key partnership relations.

Particularly, TechBridge decided to dissolve a long-standing alliance with a European-based technology partner. Although the partnership was initially very successful, diverging business directions made it difficult to maintain common goals. The decision to dissolve caused significant controversy within TechBridge, particularly within the associated project teams, heightening feelings of disappointment and instability.

After the announcement of the dissolution, motivation within the team waned, and stress and uncertainty increased. Complaints about insufficient information regarding the dissolution decision arose among team members, leading to a decline in trust. Additionally, tensions escalated in the relationship with the partner company, complicating cooperation in the final stages.

This case demonstrates that the dissolution of a partnership signifies more than just the end of a contract, impacting both the internal and external environments psychologically and emotionally. TechBridge's experience underscores why it is crucial to anticipate and manage psychological issues that can arise during the dissolution process effectively.

The problems TechBridge encountered during the dissolution were primarily due to a lack of communication, psychological instability, and inadequate management. These three main factors increased the complexity of the dissolution and triggered various emotional and psychological reactions internally and externally.

Firstly, the lack of communication led to unnecessary misunderstandings and anxiety by failing to adequately convey the decisions and reasons for the dissolution to both internal team members and external partners. The absence of transparent communication during the process left employees unsure about their future and the direction of projects, increasing stress and disappointment and negatively affecting team motivation and performance.

Secondly, psychological instability stemmed from the uncertainty and changes brought about by the dissolution affecting the team members' work environment.

As the alliance was dissolved, fears of job loss, career uncertainty, and stress over new work alignments increased among team members. This psychological instability triggered internal conflicts and worsened the overall work atmosphere.

Thirdly, inadequate management meant that after making the dissolution decision, the executive management of TechBridge failed to provide the necessary meticulous management and support during the actual execution. This compounded the complexity of the dissolution, leaving team members to manage the changes on their own without necessary adjustments and support, exacerbating the issues.

These three causes highlight how crucial it is to effectively manage the psychological and emotional impacts of a dissolution. Adequate communication, psychological support, and effective management strategies are essential to overcome the various psychological challenges that arise during the dissolution process and to maintain the health and performance of the organization.

The psychological approaches and theories that can be managed during TechBridge's dissolution process include various strategies focused on resolving conflicts, maintaining psychological stability, and managing change within the organization.

Conflict Resolution Theories can help manage conflicts that arise during the dissolution effectively. Martha Selman, an American psychologist, emphasizes the importance of communication in the conflict resolution process, providing ways to understand and respect different perspectives. This theory can play a crucial role in making and effectively communicating dissolution decisions and minimizing conflicts at TechBridge.

Change Management Theories offer strategies to manage psychological resistance that can occur during organizational changes and encourage a positive acceptance of changes. John Kotter's 8-Step Change Model is particularly useful in this context. Each step of the model describes preparing for, implementing, and solidifying changes, providing a structured approach suitable for managing significant organizational changes like a dissolution.

Psychological Stability Theories provide a theoretical framework for minimizing instability and maintaining psychological stability among employees. This theory is crucial for managing the uncertainties and stresses that can arise during the dissolution process, supporting employees to better adapt to changes.

These psychological theories and their application can help TechBridge manage the dissolution process more constructively and protect the emotional and psychological well-being of its members. This is essential for maintaining the overall health of the organization and laying the groundwork for long-term success.

The psychological theories applied during TechBridge's dissolution process played a significant role in effectively managing the various psychological challenges and minimizing conflicts within and outside the organization. The process, particularly centered around conflict resolution, change management, and psychological stability theories, was conducted.

Through the application of Conflict Resolution Theories, TechBridge was able to prevent potential conflicts within and outside the organization during the dissolution process and effectively resolve any that had already occurred. The organization ensured transparent information sharing through regular meetings with all involved parties, clearly understanding each party's concerns and expectations. This reduced uncertainties and negotiated more equitable and reasonable dissolution terms from each partner's perspective.

By utilizing Change Management Theories, TechBridge approached the dissolution as a strategic change for the entire organization. Following John Kotter's 8-Step Change Model, the company communicated the necessity of the change to employees and demonstrated strong leadership. Additionally, various training and workshops were provided to help employees accept and adapt to the new situation. This approach was successful in alleviating employees' anxieties and securing organizational support for the change.

The application of Psychological Stability Theories focused on protecting employees' psychological stability during the dissolution. The organization provided regular psychological counseling services and operated stress management programs to support employees' emotional health. Additionally, to address the career uncertainties that could arise from the dissolution, the company enhanced its career development support and repositioning programs.

These psychological approaches and strategic actions significantly helped TechBridge minimize the negative impacts of the dissolution and support the organization's long-term stability and growth. This process provides a valuable case study for other organizations on the psychological factors to consider and the appropriate management strategies during a dissolution.

In situations of dissolution and emotion management, further psychological theories and approaches can provide deep insights into overcoming the changes and emotional challenges faced by organizations and individuals. These theories offer a broader methodology for managing the dissolution process, enhancing organizational resilience, and ensuring employee satisfaction and stability.

1. Trauma Psychology - The dissolution of a partnership can act as a type of organizational trauma. Trauma psychology provides ways to understand and treat the psychological responses of individuals and organizations after significant shock events. This theory can be used to manage organizational shock responses that may appear after a dissolution and support the recovery process.

2. Resilience Theory - This theory studies the ability of individuals and organizations to overcome difficulties and challenges and become stronger as a result. It is important to develop strategies to enhance an organization's resilience in change situations like a dissolution. Resilient organizations are more flexible in accepting changes and can adapt quickly and successfully move forward.

3. Emotional Intelligence Theory - Emotional intelligence is the ability of individuals to recognize and manage their own and others' emotions. Properly managing the various emotions that can arise during the dissolution process and maintaining team cohesion and cooperation through emotional intelligence is crucial. Leaders and team members with high emotional intelligence can maintain positive interpersonal relationships even through the process of change.

By considering and applying these additional psychological theories, organizations like TechBridge can more effectively manage the psychological and emotional issues that arise during the dissolution process. This allows organizations to develop ways to healthily and productively manage changes, promoting long-term success and stability.

10. International Alliances and Cross-Cultural Psychology

The Bridge of Culture:
The Role of Cross-Cultural Psychology in International Alliances

International alliances have become an essential strategy in today's global economy. However, differences between cultures often complicate these alliances significantly. The success of international partnerships depends not only on economic or technical cooperation but also heavily on mutual understanding and psychological harmony between partners from diverse cultural backgrounds. This chapter explores how cross-cultural psychology plays a crucial role in international alliances and how it can manage the challenges and opportunities that arise.

Operating in global markets inherently involves the potential for clashes between diverse cultural values and expectations. These clashes frequently manifest in business practices, communication styles, decision-making processes, and expectations of organizational hierarchies. Organizations pursuing international alliances must recognize and appropriately manage these differences. Cross-cultural psychology serves as an essential tool in overcoming cultural barriers at every stage of an alliance, building strong cooperative relationships based on mutual respect and understanding.

This chapter introduces methods for applying cross-cultural psychology to successfully manage international alliances, offering strategic insights on how organizations can effectively navigate challenges in the global environment. This approach minimizes psychological and cultural conflicts during the alliance process and is a key element in fostering growth and innovation in global markets.

BioPartners, a global pharmaceutical company, has recently sought alliances with various regional companies to expand into the Asian market. During this process, the company experienced significant cultural differences and related challenges, particularly during negotiations with Japanese and Chinese companies.

BioPartners' management found that negotiations with their Japanese partner were much more cautious and procedural than anticipated. The decision-making process with the Japanese company was collective, involving a broad consensus among all stakeholders. In contrast, negotiations with the Chinese partner required direct communication and rapid decision-making. These differences conflicted with BioPartners' Western business practices, leading to issues in several negotiations.

These situations caused considerable turmoil within BioPartners. The cultural differences increased stress and instability among team members, leading to delays in project timelines and decreased efficiency. Not only did this reduce the likelihood of successful alliances, but it also risked affecting the company's international reputation long-term.

Separately, during the development of partnerships in Indonesia and Malaysia, BioPartners underestimated the decision-making styles of the local companies. In these regions, relationship building and personal trust significantly impact business decisions, but BioPartners' approach was too mechanical and result-oriented. As a result, from the initial discussions, the company faced mistrust and cool responses from partners, encountering unexpected obstacles.

These cases clearly illustrate that the success of an alliance process is not limited to contract terms or financial benefits but heavily depends on cultural sensitivity and psychological harmony. BioPartners recognized the need for additional strategies and investments to manage these cultural differences and minimize conflicts. This realization prompted a reevaluation of the company's overall international business strategy and the adoption of a more comprehensive cultural approach.

The challenges BioPartners faced in developing international alliances in the Asian market can primarily be summarized as a lack of cultural understanding, differences in communication styles, and inadequate internal preparation. These issues interacted to hinder the efficiency and success of the alliances.

A lack of cultural understanding was one of the most significant problems. BioPartners' management and negotiation teams did not sufficiently understand the business cultures and communication styles of various countries. Negotiations in Japan and China particularly highlighted stark cultural conflicts. While decision-making in Japan was cautious and collective, it was rapid in China. These differences led to unexpected delays and misunderstandings, complicating the negotiation process.

Furthermore, differences in communication styles varied according to each country's culture, causing serious issues during negotiations. In Indonesia and Malaysia, using a direct Western business approach without considering the importance of informal meetings and personal trust building made the negotiation partners uncomfortable.

Inadequate internal preparation also played a significant role. BioPartners was not sufficiently prepared internally for international alliances, lacking training and resources to overcome cultural differences. Particularly, the lack of cultural sensitivity training for management and negotiation teams exacerbated the problems. This inadequacy led to insufficient capacity to adequately respond to the various issues arising during the alliance process, resulting in project delays and reduced efficiency.

These complex causes highlight key elements that BioPartners must consider when pursuing international alliances, emphasizing the importance of cultural sensitivity and internal preparedness. Adopting a systematic and culturally sensitive approach can smooth the alliance process and ensure successful expansion in international markets.

BioPartners successfully applied psychological theories to overcome these challenges during the expansion of international alliances in the Asian market. The company provided training programs based on Geert Hofstede's cultural dimensions theory to help employees understand the cultural characteristics of each alliance country, particularly focusing on differences between collectivism and individualism, which greatly aided in developing more effective communication strategies during negotiations with Japanese and Chinese partners.

As a next step utilizing David Livermore's concept of cultural intelligence, BioPartners formed teams of employees from various cultural backgrounds to simulate real situations and practice responses in different cultural contexts through workshops. These practical exercises helped team members understand each other's cultural backgrounds and constructively respond in conflict situations, teaching them practical methods to overcome cultural differences in actual negotiation scenarios.

Using William Ury's conflict resolution theory, the company proactively built mechanisms to intervene and resolve conflicts when they arose. Mainly through workshops and team-building sessions among employees, this mechanism taught them how to control emotions and foster mutual understanding in conflict situations. This training helped employees develop skills to transform conflicts into positive outcomes and effectively manage issues that could arise during the alliance process. This approach also enhanced the organization's overall cultural sensitivity and preemptively prevented problems that could arise in alliance relationships.

The lessons learned from BioPartners' experience with international alliances provide a basis for further exploring psychological theories that can significantly contribute to the success and sustainability of alliance relationships. These theories are particularly useful in international business environments where understanding and harmonizing each other's values and goals beyond cultural differences is crucial.

1. Emotional Bonding Theory - This theory focuses on the quality of relationships and the role of emotions. Strong emotional bonds enhance trust and loyalty, crucial elements in an alliance relationship. Understanding and applying ways to build strong emotional connections between partners during the alliance process can be key to maintaining successful long-term cooperation.

2. Cultural Adaptability Theory - This theory deals with how individuals and organizations can effectively adapt and integrate into various cultural contexts. Enhancing cultural adaptability during the alliance process is important for ensuring smooth interactions between partners with diverse values and belief systems. Developing and implementing strategies to enhance cultural adaptability

can minimize friction in international alliances and more effectively integrate each partner's business practices and communication styles.

3. Application of Organizational Psychology - Organizational psychology studies the interaction between human behavior and organizational structures and processes. Applying organizational psychology in the context of international alliances helps understand and manage the complexities of human relationships and motivation issues within alliance relationships. An organizational psychological approach can play a crucial role in resolving people-centered issues and effectively integrating organizational cultures during the alliance process.

By further exploring and applying these psychological theories, BioPartners can more effectively execute global expansion strategies through international alliances and proactively manage and resolve the various problems that can arise during the alliance process. This equips the organization with the psychological tools needed to support its global business activities and promote sustainable growth and innovation through partnerships.

VII. Financial Management and Psychology

Exploring Human Psychology at the Heart of Behavioral Finance

In the realm of financial management, while numbers and data are traditionally viewed as the primary elements in decision-making, the influence of human behavior and psychology on financial decisions is an indispensable factor. This chapter delves into the psychological aspects surrounding financial management, explaining how economic decision-making transcends mere logical and calculative processes. Behavioral finance, particularly, challenges traditional financial theories, revealing how economic behaviors are often swayed by irrational and emotionally driven decisions.

Human emotions play a significant role in financial decision-making. Emotions such as fear, greed, and hope can significantly distort investment decisions, and understanding the role of these emotions is crucial for financial managers. By analyzing psychological responses during economic crises, we can see how individuals and organizations may act irrationally under stress. Additionally, when designing diversified investment portfolios, considering human psychological traits allows for a broader management of risk and the development of strategies to mitigate the fear of potential losses.

Financial stress management is another key area of study within this field, highlighting how financial instability impacts individuals' psychological health and daily lives. By integrating financial planning with psychological approaches, financial advisors and planners can provide personalized advice based on an understanding of their clients' psychological factors. This helps individuals and organizations pursue long-term financial stability and tune their economic behaviors more rationally.

This chapter provides an in-depth exploration of how financial management and psychology interact, and how the integration of these two fields can aid in understanding and improving the financial world. By understanding the psychological aspects of investment behavior, we can make better financial decisions, enhance economic stability, and promote overall financial health. This is particularly crucial in a rapidly changing economic environment, where psychological insights allow financial professionals to respond more effectively to challenges.

1. Financial Decisions and Behavioral Finance

Financial Decisions and Behavioral Finance: Reevaluating Economic Choices Through the Lens of Psychology

In the realm of financial management, it is often assumed that numbers and statistics dominate. However, various psychological factors deeply influence the backdrop against which these decisions are made. 'Behavioral finance' analyzes these psychological elements to explain why people often make economically suboptimal choices or why markets do not always react in predictable ways. This field diverges from the traditional economic theory of the rational actor model to explore the real, often irrational behavior patterns of humans.

This section examines how behavioral finance can be applied to the financial decision-making process, highlighting its importance through theoretical insights and practical examples. In making financial decisions, investors are often significantly influenced by past successes, personal emotions, and the current market mood. These factors can lead investors to act independently of the market's fundamental values, sometimes leading to market inefficiencies.

Behavioral finance introduces various psychological theories to explain human economic behaviors. For example, 'confirmation bias' describes the tendency of people to selectively gather information that supports their beliefs and ignore opposing information. This tendency is commonly observed in the investment decision process and can lead to incorrect market valuations. Additionally, 'loss aversion' explains the psychological tendency for people to take greater risks to avoid losses, which can lead to excessively risky behaviors.

Through this understanding, readers will grasp the various psychological factors that can arise during financial decision-making, and explore practical ways to identify and manage these factors. Furthermore, the insights provided by behavioral finance will establish a foundation for making more rational and effective financial decisions. This is invaluable not only for individual investors but also for organizational financial managers.

A case in point for the application of financial decisions and behavioral finance is the recent investment failure experienced by the large investment bank, Metropolitan Investments. The bank had injected substantial capital into high-risk, high-return emerging tech startups. Initially, there was significant market optimism; however, the invested startups encountered major obstacles in technology development and commercialization, failing to perform as expected.

This investment decision was driven by Metropolitan Investment's previous successful investment experiences and excessive optimism about technological innovation. Analysts overestimated the market potential of the invested companies and did not sufficiently consider the risks associated with technological development. Moreover, despite the uncertain economic outlook and fierce competition, the investment was pursued, ultimately leading to substantial losses.

Internally, this high-risk investment decision also sparked significant controversy within Metropolitan Investments. While some executives advocated for a more cautious approach, the company's decision-making structure prioritized expanding investments in the new technology sector. This internal decision-making hindered the objectivity of investment analysis and resulted in flawed financial decisions.

The case of Metropolitan Investments clearly illustrates how psychological factors, particularly overconfidence in past successes and optimistic projections about market trends, can distort financial judgments. This serves as a crucial example of how behavioral finance interprets and understands the role of human psychology in financial decisions, emphasizing that psychological factors should not be overlooked when making financial decisions. This case analysis provides a basis for making more balanced decisions in similar high-risk investment scenarios in the future and assists financial professionals in developing strategies to recognize and address these psychological errors.

Metropolitan Investment's investment failure can be analyzed through various psychological theories, including the theory of cognitive dissonance, developed by Leon Festinger. This theory explains the psychological discomfort people experience when their actions and beliefs do not align, prompting individuals to distort or ignore information to maintain their existing beliefs. When market data contradicting initial optimistic forecasts emerged, Metropolitan Investment's analysts overlooked this and continued with their initial decisions to avoid cognitive dissonance, leading to the persistence of faulty investment decisions.

Additionally, the theory of loss aversion, developed by Daniel Kahneman and Amos Tversky, highlights that people prefer to avoid losses more strongly than achieving gains. This theory is useful in explaining why investors might continue to pour more capital into failing investments to prevent potential losses. In the case of Metropolitan Investment, when initial investments turned sour, analysts decided to invest more capital to avoid greater losses, a decision based on emotional motivations rather than economic logic.

The theory of emotional contagion, researched by Hatfield, Donald, et al., also plays a crucial role. This theory describes how emotions can spread within a group, and how positive or negative feelings can quickly influence group members and affect group decision-making. In Metropolitan Investment's scenario, the company's internal optimistic atmosphere justified taking excessive risks in the decision-making process. This emotional spread contributed to the investment team ignoring market warnings and continuing with excessive investments.

By analyzing Metropolitan Investment's investment failure through these psychological theories, financial professionals can gain a deep understanding of the significant role human psychology plays in financial decisions. Theoretical insights allow financial professionals to make more careful and balanced investment decisions and develop strategies to manage and minimize the influence of psychological biases and emotions. This will ultimately enhance the company's financial health and competitive edge in the market.

In light of Metropolitan Investment's case, several psychological interventions could improve the investment decision-making process.

Firstly, to reduce cognitive dissonance, the company should identify cognitive biases that can arise during the decision-making process and introduce training programs to address these. This encourages employees to recognize discrepancies between their beliefs and actions and to focus on making decisions based on objective data.

Secondly, to manage loss aversion tendencies, the company should strengthen risk management protocols during investment decisions. This helps prevent investors from continuing aggressive investments unnecessarily out of fear of potential losses. For example, implementing procedures that require regular risk analysis of each investment decision and evaluation by an investment committee can prevent these overly risky decisions.

Thirdly, considering the theory of emotional contagion, the company should develop strategies to minimize the impact of emotional motivations on decision-making. By conducting regular emotional management workshops, employees learn how to manage their own and others' emotions more effectively, supporting the maintenance of objectivity and rationality during decision-making processes.

These approaches can help Metropolitan Investment reduce decision-making errors due to psychological factors and develop more robust and sustainable investment strategies. This contributes to enhancing the company's financial soundness and strengthening its competitiveness in the market. By successfully integrating the principles of behavioral finance into actual financial management, Metropolitan Investment can maximize the positive impact of psychological insights on financial decisions.

Further research and theories in the psychology of financial decisions can provide crucial insights for companies like Metropolitan Investment to make more effective investment decisions. Here are some key topics for further exploration in this field:

1. Behavioral Finance: This field combines traditional financial theories with psychological insights to explore why people make irrational financial decisions. Understanding how investors process market information and which psychological biases affect their investment behavior is crucial.

2. Emotions and Decision-Making: Researching how emotions affect individuals' investment decisions can help investors avoid being swayed by strong feelings such as anxiety, fear, or greed. Understanding the role of emotions can help develop strategies to regulate emotional responses and promote more balanced investment decisions.

3. Social Influence and Investment: Exploring the impact of social influence on individual and group investment decisions can also be beneficial. This helps understand how investors are affected by the behaviors and opinions of those around them, and how these influences are reflected in investment outcomes.

4. Psychological Stability and Investment Performance: Studying how psychological stability affects investment performance provides important insights for financial professionals. Analyzing whether a stable mental state leads to better financial decisions or whether an unstable state increases financial risks can be included in this research.

By exploring these additional topics, financial professionals can gain a deeper understanding of the broad impacts of human psychology on financial behavior, based on which more effective financial management strategies can be developed. This also plays a crucial role in ensuring that companies maintain better financial health and competitiveness over the long term.

2. Risk-Taking and Financial Management

The Adventure of Finance: A Psychological Approach to Risk-Taking and Financial Management

One of the core elements of financial management depends on how effectively risk-taking is managed. Identifying the various risk factors that can arise when making financial decisions and appropriately adjusting them is a decisive factor in determining a company's financial stability and growth potential. In this risk management process, psychological factors also play a crucial role, as they significantly influence how individuals and organizations perceive risks and the decisions they make in response.

When examining financial management related to risk-taking, it involves more than just calculating the potential for loss. Risk management, including psychological elements, should be understood in multiple dimensions—from investor behavior and market psychology to economic forecasting volatility. For instance, understanding why investors prefer high-risk investments during periods of economic uncertainty requires a behavioral finance approach, rather than simple yield calculations.

From this perspective, this chapter explores how psychological factors affect financial management and risk-taking decisions, and seeks strategies to make better financial decisions. We will particularly apply psychological theories related to risk to explore how financial managers can integrate these theories into the actual financial decision-making process. Through this, financial professionals can develop the ability to manage risks more effectively and make stable decisions even in financial crises.

BlueWave Capital, a global investment bank, has faced significant difficulties in managing its investment portfolio amid the rapidly changing uncertainties of the global financial market in recent years. The bank has particularly aimed to expand its investments aggressively in emerging markets and high-tech startups, targeting high returns. However, the unpredictable volatility of these markets has unexpectedly impacted BlueWave Capital's financial soundness.

The bank's management has sought to adapt to various changes in the global economy, but unforeseen factors like interest rate hikes, changes in economic policies of major countries, and heightened trade tensions have negatively affected the bank's investment performance. Particularly, interest rate increases in the U.S., instability in the European economy, and slowdowns in China's economic growth have been significant variables. These global economic trends have severely compromised the validity of BlueWave Capital's initial investment strategy, and the company has had to devise appropriate risk management strategies in response.

The situation at BlueWave Capital highlights the importance of a strategic approach to managing high-risk investments in an uncertain economic environment. The management needs to re-evaluate its existing investment strategy and make more cautious investment decisions based on new economic forecasts to secure the company's long-term financial stability and minimize investment losses. In this process, recognizing the influence of psychological factors and considering various psychological biases that can occur during investment decision-making is essential.

In this context, BlueWave Capital is considering developing a risk management framework that can effectively manage high-risk investments and systematically check financial risks. Developing such a framework would provide a foundation for the company to actively respond to market volatility and global economic uncertainties, and support financial professionals in performing risk-taking and financial management more effectively.

BlueWave Capital's investment failures have stemmed from several factors: Firstly, excessive market optimism was one of the root causes. Overly optimistic expectations for economic growth clouded investment decisions, inducing higher risk-taking regardless of actual market conditions. This optimism was particularly pronounced in areas where high growth was expected, such as emerging markets and technology startups.

Secondly, failures in internal communication and information asymmetry had a significant impact. Inadequate sharing of information within the investment bank led to insufficient consideration of all relevant data and risk factors during the decision-making process, causing some departments to fail to respond to market changes in time and overlook potential risks.

Thirdly, rapid changes in the external economic environment played a role. Inevitable external factors such as global financial crises, interest rate fluctuations, and trade wars directly influenced the bank's strategy. In particular, interest rate hikes in major economies unexpectedly increased capital costs, negatively affecting investment returns.

Fourthly, psychological factors also played an essential role. The phenomenon of groupthink among investors distorted risk assessments. Collective optimism about certain investments suppressed critical thinking and failed to adequately incorporate opposing views, ultimately leading to poor decisions.

These various issues collectively led BlueWave Capital to experience unexpected investment losses, requiring a serious reevaluation of the company's overall financial strategy. This case has prompted financial management professionals to deeply consider how to respond to external market changes and strengthen internal decision-making structures while taking psychological factors into account to make more balanced investment decisions.

Among the various psychological theories that could be applied to BlueWave Capital's situation, Behavioral Finance is crucial. This theory revises the traditional financial theory's rational investor model to explain the irrational behaviors and decision-making of actual investors. Behavioral Finance explores how psychological factors and cognitive biases operate in financial markets, analyzing why investors sometimes make irrational decisions to prevent losses.

A notable theory is the Prospect Theory proposed by Daniel Kahneman and Amos Tversky. Prospect Theory explains that investors react more heavily to losses than gains. That is, investors prefer to avoid losses more than they prefer equivalent gains. This theory helps understand the collective optimism and groupthink that appeared in BlueWave Capital's investment decision-making process.

Additionally, the Nudge Theory developed by Richard Thaler and Cass Sunstein is also important. This theory presents ways to adjust the structure of choices through simple interventions (nudges) to help people make better decisions. For example, during the investment decision-making process, structuring choices to induce safer options or emphasizing risk-related information corresponds to this. Nudge Theory can be useful in resolving the issues faced by the investment bank, guiding investors to make more information-based decisions.

Other psychological research exploring the role of emotions is essential in understanding how investors are influenced by emotional factors, especially in high-stress market environments. Through these theories, BlueWave Capital can reestablish its financial management strategy and lay the foundation for making more effective investment decisions based on psychological insights. This would reduce financial risks and support the company's long-term success.

BlueWave Capital has found improvement measures by integrating psychological theories into its approach to risk management issues. The company has particularly used Prospect Theory to analyze investors' tendencies to avoid losses and incorporated this understanding into the investment decision-making process. While reviewing the investment portfolio, the bank identified investment options where investors might overreact to potential losses and established a clear management strategy for these. This helped improve the warning system for high-risk investments, assisting investors in making more cautious decisions. These measures have induced investors to make more balanced investment decisions without being swayed by emotions.

During the application of Nudge Theory, small changes were introduced to the decision-making structure to encourage investors to make more rational choices. Adjusting the composition of information provided during the investment process allowed investors to recognize risks more clearly and consider long-term profitability. For example, emphasizing investment risk information and simultaneously providing information about long-term profit potential helped investors move away from a tendency to avoid short-term losses. This created an environment where investors could make investment decisions from a more balanced perspective.

This approach is based on the fact that investor behavior is significantly influenced by psychological factors. By applying psychological theories to financial management strategies, BlueWave Capital has established a foundation for making more robust investment decisions, minimizing psychological errors that can occur in the decision-making process. This has enhanced investors' psychological stability, reduced financial risks, and ultimately supported the company's long-term financial health and growth. This strategic psychological approach has significantly improved the efficiency of financial management and allowed the investment bank to respond more flexibly to market volatility and global economic uncertainties.

Based on the effective application of psychological theories in BlueWave Capital's case, the use of psychology in financial management can significantly contribute to better understanding and optimizing investors' decision-making processes. Several additional psychological approaches that could be further explored include:

1. Cognitive Dissonance Theory: This theory explains the discomfort individuals experience when they have conflicting beliefs, attitudes, or behaviors. Applying this theory in financial decision-making can help understand the tendency of investors to justify their investment choices after experiencing losses. This can be useful in developing strategies to support more rational decision-making.

2. Confirmation Bias: This describes the tendency for people to pay more attention to information that supports their existing beliefs and ignore contrary information. Understanding the tendency of investors to continue defending their initial investment decisions can be helpful and important in devising strategies to manage and overcome this bias.

3. Hursh's Law: This law, a principle of behavioral economics, explains the relationship between the size of a reward and the effort performed. Applying this law in investment decision-making can analyze how investors take risks to maximize rewards (returns). This can help design mechanisms to prevent investors from taking excessive risks.

By further exploring and applying these theories, financial managers can better understand investor behavior and develop more effective investment strategies and risk management approaches. Psychological approaches go beyond simple numerical analysis to comprehensively address the complexity of human behavior and decision-making, a trend that is becoming increasingly important in the finance sector.

3. The Role of Emotions in Financial Decision-Making

How Do the Waves of Emotion Shape Financial Decision-Making?

Financial decision-making is often perceived as being based on numbers and data, but in reality, emotions play a significant role. Especially in the high-pressure financial markets, the emotions of investors often act as an undeniable factor in the decision-making process. Not understanding the role of emotions can put companies and individuals at risk of making decisions that may unknowingly lead to financial loss. Therefore, exploring the relationship between emotions and financial decision-making has become a critical challenge and a necessity for financial professionals.

In this chapter, we will delve deeply into the impact of emotions on financial decision-making and explore psychological approaches to manage them. Specifically, we will examine how uncertainty and stress in the financial markets affect investor behavior, and how these emotional factors can enhance the effectiveness of financial decisions. We will analyze how investors can recognize and regulate their emotions, and how this ability can bring about positive changes in actual financial outcomes. This will provide financial managers and investors with methodologies for understanding and managing emotions to make superior financial decisions.

InvestWave, a prominent investment firm, has recently been severely affected by the influence of emotions in its decision-making process amid the volatile stock market. The company primarily invests in the technology and biotechnology sectors, which are particularly susceptible to the influence of market news and press releases. Recently, excessive positive media coverage of certain tech stocks has induced overheated emotions among investors. In such situations, emotions can escalate, and investors often tend to make excessive investments, regardless of the fundamental value of the stocks.

These overheated emotions can also lead to excessive panic selling during sharp market downturns, resulting in significant losses to the company's portfolio and hindering long-term investment strategies. InvestWave's management is deeply contemplating how to identify and manage the negative impacts of emotional upheavals on the financial decision-making process. The company is working on strategies to stabilize investors' emotions and help them make more rational investment decisions.

This situation is a clear example of how market information can trigger emotional reactions and subsequently affect financial decision-making. When emotions are heightened, the decisions made by investors are often based on emotional motivations rather than calm analysis, potentially leading to irrational investment behaviors. With this awareness, InvestWave is exploring various approaches to minimize the impact of emotional factors on investment decision-making.

The issues InvestWave is experiencing are deeply rooted in emotional decisions and market psychological trends. Market information spreads rapidly among investors, and the flow of this information amplifies emotional responses, acting as a primary factor in emotional reactions. Investors tend to overreact to positive or negative news, which often distorts their financial decisions.

The first major cause is the influence of the media. Powerful media coverage shapes investors' expectations about specific stocks or markets, and these expectations can inflate or deflate stock prices regardless of actual market value. In such cases, investors often base their investment decisions on the information provided by the media, leading to decisions based on emotional responses rather than the quality of the information.

The second cause is collective behavior. Emotional contagion in the market is facilitated through collective behavior. When investors observe the actions of others and begin to follow them, this creates a phenomenon known as 'herd behavior.' This is particularly evident in unstable market conditions, where emotions play a strong role and can lead to more adverse decisions.

The third cause is the intensity of emotions. When making investment decisions, investors are often significantly influenced by their current emotional state. For example, excessive optimism or fear can lead investors to take greater risks or, conversely, make overly conservative decisions. These emotions can obscure objective analysis of the market's future and prevent proper assessment of potential risks.

All these factors combine to create the issues faced by companies like InvestWave, and solving these problems requires understanding and effectively managing the role of emotions. This is essential for making the investment decision-making process more rational and securing long-term economic stability.

By applying important psychological theories to InvestWave's situation, particularly Cognitive Dissonance Theory, Confirmation Bias, and Emotional Decision-Making Theory, it is evident that these can significantly impact investors' decision-making processes. These theories provide deep insights into the psychological mechanisms that influence how investors interpret information and make decisions.

Cognitive Dissonance Theory, introduced by Leon Festinger, explains the psychological discomfort that occurs when an individual holds contradictory beliefs, knowledge, or behaviors simultaneously. This theory is crucial for understanding the psychological motivation to resolve cognitive dissonance when investors make decisions that exclude information inconsistent with their belief systems and selectively accept congruent information. This cognitive dissonance can lead to overlooking excessive risks or justifying incorrect decisions in the investment decision-making process.

Confirmation Bias describes the tendency for investors to pay more attention to information that confirms their existing beliefs and ignore information that contradicts them. This bias causes investors to unconsciously process information selectively in the financial market's interpretation and decision-making process, potentially underestimating risks and fostering excessive confidence. As a result, this can amplify extreme market volatility.

The Emotional Decision-Making Theory, developed by researchers including Daniel Goleman, explores how emotions can aid or hinder rational thinking in the decision-making process. In investment decisions in the financial market, while often overlooked, strong emotional reactions can lead investors to make decisions based on emotions rather than technical market analysis or financial indicators. For instance, when investors experience economic instability or personal fear, their investment choices can often be irrationally aggressive or overly defensive.

By integrating these psychological theories into InvestWave's investment decision-making process, the company can develop strategies to better understand and adjust investors' emotions and cognitive biases. This helps investors make more rational and consistent investment decisions in the long term, fostering the financial stability and growth of the company.

The situation at InvestWave provides a crucial point about the role of emotions and the application of psychological theories in financial decision-making. While financial decision-making is commonly thought to be based on numbers and data, emotions actually play a very significant role. Especially in uncertain and volatile financial markets, emotions are an undeniable factor in the decision-making process. Without proper understanding and management, companies or individuals may risk making decisions that could lead to financial loss.

At InvestWave, recent investments in the rapidly changing technology and biotechnology sectors have been greatly influenced by market news and press releases. Positive media coverage of specific tech stocks has raised expectations among investors, inflating stock prices regardless of market value. However, these excessive expectations have led to excessive panic selling when the market declined, causing significant losses to the company's portfolio and hindering long-term investment strategies.
To solve these problems, InvestWave has started applying several psychological theories to the decision-making processes of its investors.

Firstly, using Cognitive Dissonance Theory, investors were educated to evaluate information more objectively. This allowed investors to be more open to information that contradicted their beliefs, leading to a more balanced consideration of various market data.

Secondly, to manage Confirmation Bias, a team of experts was assembled to analyze investments, allowing for the sharing and discussion of different opinions. This environment prevented investors from relying on a single perspective and enabled them to make more balanced decisions.

Thirdly, training programs were introduced based on Emotional Decision-Making Theory, teaching investors how to recognize and regulate their emotions.

These approaches helped investors maintain composure and make rational decisions amidst the uncertainties and stress of the financial market. As a result, InvestWave reduced emotional responses among investors and enabled more rational and consistent investment decision-making, significantly contributing to the company's financial stability and profitability improvement. In this process, the company learned methodologies for understanding and managing emotions to make superior financial decisions, which became an essential factor in strengthening the company's competitiveness in the long term.

When seeking a deeper understanding of the role of emotions in financial decision-making, there are many psychological theories and topics to explore. These theories can provide deep insights not only into investor behavior but also into general business decision-making processes. Here are some topics that can offer a deeper understanding of emotions and financial decision-making:

Emotional Accounting
Proposed by Richard Thaler and Hersh Shefrin, Emotional Accounting theory explains how emotions can distort financial judgments when people make decisions related to money. This theory deals with how the emotional connections that investors have with specific investments or expenditures influence their financial decisions. For example, investors have a strong tendency to avoid losses, which can often lead to irrational holding or selling decisions.

Framing Effect
The Framing Effect shows how people's reactions and decisions can change depending on how information is presented. Research by Daniel Kahneman and Amos Tversky explains how investors' responses can differ when the same

information is presented from the perspectives of loss or gain. This theory significantly influences marketing, advertising, product design, and the way financial products are offered.

Risk Perception

Risk Perception is a topic that deals with how individuals perceive and handle risks, with a significant role played by emotions. Investors can react very differently to the same risk, depending on their experiences, inclinations, and emotional states. This is an important factor not only in investment decisions but also in financial planning and risk management strategies.

Behavioral Finance

Behavioral Finance studies irrational human behaviors and psychological factors that traditional financial theories do not address. This field helps explain why investors make certain financial decisions and why markets do not always move in predictable ways. It includes the effects of various emotional factors such as fear, greed, and groupthink on economic decisions.

Emotional Intelligence

Emotional Intelligence is the ability of an individual to recognize, understand, manage, and regulate their own emotions and those of others. In financial decision-making, emotional intelligence helps investors manage their emotions and make rational decisions even under the stress of financial markets. It also plays a significant role in the broader business world, including leadership, teamwork, and customer management.

Exploring these psychological theories and concepts can provide a deeper understanding of how emotions operate in financial decision-making and how they can be managed. This can offer important insights not only to individual investors but also to financial institutions, companies, and policymakers.

4. Economic Crisis and Psychological Response

The Mind in Crisis: Economic Crisis and Psychological Response Strategies

Economic crises often arrive unexpectedly and can dramatically shake the fate of a company. These sudden events affect not just financial losses but also deeply impact the psychological environment within the company, affecting employee motivation, work efficiency, and overall organizational culture. In times of crisis, how a company responds can be a critical factor determining its long-term survival and success in the market. Therefore, understanding the psychological stress experienced by companies during times of economic uncertainty and their responses is crucial in developing strategies to overcome crises.

In this chapter, we will closely examine the various psychological challenges companies face during economic crises and explore how these can be effectively managed. Based on psychological theories and empirical research, we will analyze how real businesses navigate crises and which psychological approaches and strategies actually work. We particularly focus on managing employees' emotions, maintaining motivation, the role of leadership, and various strategies to enhance organizational psychological resilience and flexibility. Through these psychological approaches, companies overcoming economic crises can develop strategic plans not just for survival but for sustainable growth, providing deep insights and practical lessons for both executives and all employees.

By understanding the psychological challenges and responses of each company when an economic crisis hits, we aim to analyze in depth how organizational leaders and employees can cope more effectively and what psychological mechanisms are at play. This process will offer a broader perspective on how organizations and individuals can become stronger beyond economic uncertainty and what psychological preparations and improvements are needed.

AutoParts Global, a company manufacturing automotive parts, is currently facing serious challenges amid global economic instability. With declining demand in the European market, rising raw material costs, and stringent trade regulations, AutoParts Global's profitability is increasingly under pressure. These external pressures are also causing numerous problems internally, particularly reducing production efficiency and increasing anxiety among employees, eventually leading to the departure of some key talent.

The management has adopted cost reduction and resource optimization as the main strategies to overcome this crisis, but these measures have had the unintended side effect of negatively impacting employees' motivation and job satisfaction. For example, to cut costs, management decided to lay off temporary employees and reduce overtime. These decisions might have succeeded in reducing costs in the short term but significantly harmed employees' loyalty and productivity in the long run, ultimately hindering the company's overall performance recovery.

Furthermore, operating in the volatile technology and automotive industries, AutoParts Global has been significantly affected by market emotional reactions driven by news and press releases. Whenever negative market news was released, fear spread among investors and employees, leading to capital and talent outflows. Management had to explore various strategies to manage these emotional reactions and restore trust and stability within the organization.

This case illustrates how economic crises and global market trends interact with the psychological environment inside companies. Analyzing how external factors lead to internal unrest and staff turnover, and their impact on the entire organization, is crucial. In the case of AutoParts Global, economic uncertainty increased fear and stress among employees, affecting their ability to perform daily tasks. If employees feel insecure and continuously worry about job instability, their focus and commitment to their work naturally decline.

Understanding how the decisions of AutoParts Global's management trigger employees' psychological reactions, and how this, in turn, affects the company's strategic direction and performance, is crucial. To effectively manage changes in the external environment and minimize internal employee anxiety and stress, management needs a more careful and strategic approach. This is vital for companies facing economic crises to analyze both internal and external factors comprehensively and develop responsive strategies. Through such analysis, companies can establish stronger and more sustainable responses, contributing to enhancing long-term organizational resilience.

Several theories relevant to understanding organizational and individual responses in economic crises can be applied to the case of AutoParts Global, providing insights into how these theories can be utilized in real business settings.

First, Richard Lazarus's Stress and Coping Theory offers an important framework for understanding how organizations and employees react to stress situations like economic crises. Lazarus argued that the way individuals perceive and evaluate the situation they face dictates their coping methods. In the case of AutoParts Global, if employees perceive economic uncertainty and workplace changes as threats, their stress levels may increase, and productivity may decline. Coping strategies might include strengthening internal communication and providing employees with sufficient information to reduce anxiety.

Second, Daniel Kahneman's Loss Aversion Theory explains why employees and management tend to prefer conservative decisions in crisis situations. According to Kahneman, people are inclined to take greater risks to avoid losses, which can mean missing potential opportunities. Applying this theory at AutoParts Global helps understand the likelihood of management making conservative decisions like excessive cost-cutting or investment reductions during a crisis. While these decisions may provide short-term stability, they can limit the company's long-term growth opportunities.

Third, Carl Rogers' Person-Centered Theory emphasizes the importance of fostering an environment that encourages personal development and growth even in times of crisis. By applying Rogers' theory, AutoParts Global's management can enhance organizational resilience by actively soliciting employee feedback and providing opportunities for personal growth and training. This helps employees develop their skills and job satisfaction even during crises.

These psychological theories enable AutoParts Global to maintain employee motivation and develop strategies for long-term organizational survival and growth during economic crises. These approaches go beyond mere crisis management to establish a foundation for the organization to transform into a stronger, more adaptable entity, positively affecting all employees. This strategic approach can provide important lessons in psychological coping methods during crises for other companies as well.

Additionally, I want to further explore psychological concepts related to economic crises. This will help understand how psychological factors influence employees' reactions and decision-making processes when companies face economic difficulties.

Psychological Impact of Economic Crises
Economic crises not only cause financial losses but also deeply affect the psychology of organizations and individuals. Stress, anxiety, and uncertainty directly impact employees' work performance, which in turn reflects on the overall performance of the organization. Understanding and managing these psychological impacts is crucial for organizations to overcome crises and achieve long-term success.

The Role and Management of Stress
Stress is one of the most common psychological responses observed in economic crisis situations. Job insecurity, wage cuts, and increased workloads all contribute to increasing stress among employees. To effectively manage stress, organizations should support their employees through mental health programs, stress management training, and providing adequate rest periods to help them overcome this stress.

Emotional Intelligence and Crisis Management
Emotional intelligence includes the ability to recognize one's own emotions, manage them appropriately, understand others' emotions, and respond to them. In economic crisis situations, leaders and employees with high emotional intelligence can better manage anxiety and stress, maintaining effective communication and cooperation even in crisis situations. Therefore, organizations should focus on

enhancing emotional intelligence through leadership development programs and employee training.

The Importance of Leadership
The role of leadership is even more emphasized in economic crises. An effective leader maintains trust among employees, unites the team, and provides clear vision and direction even in crisis situations. Leaders shape organizational culture through their actions and decisions, which significantly影s the organization's crisis response capabilities.

Utilizing Positive Psychology
Positive psychology focuses on recognizing and using individual and organizational strengths to overcome difficulties. By adopting a positive approach even during economic crises, organizations can enhance their long-term resilience and growth potential. This gives employees hope and motivation and boosts the overall resilience of the organization.

By adopting these psychological approaches and theories, organizations can establish the psychological foundation needed to overcome economic crises, playing a crucial role in ensuring long-term success and stability. These psychological insights also facilitate tangible changes within the organization, equipping all employees with the tools and knowledge needed to overcome crises.

5. Investment Portfolios and Psychological Diversity

Beyond Emotions: Strategic Investment

The composition and management of investment portfolios are not solely based on financial analysis and forecasts. In reality, the psychological diversity of investors plays a significant role and can determine the success or failure of investment decisions. Understanding this psychological diversity and applying it appropriately in portfolio management is crucial for diversifying risk and maximizing potential returns. This chapter aims to explore in-depth how individual psychological traits can influence investment behaviors and how these can be effectively managed.

We will first examine a real case from 'Global Investment Solutions', a large investment firm. This firm manages a broad investment portfolio across various sectors, with a recent focus particularly on emerging markets and the technology sector. However, this investment strategy comes with high volatility and considerable market uncertainty, which are major factors inhibiting profitability. Particularly, the instability in the global economy and escalating geopolitical tensions have increased psychological instability among investors.

This situation often leads to investors overreacting to potential market risks or, conversely, making hasty investment decisions due to excessive optimism. These psychological factors directly impact portfolio performance and sometimes necessitate a revision of the entire investment strategy. 'Global Investment Solutions' is seeking new approaches that consider investors' psychological diversity to address these issues.

For this company, understanding how economic uncertainty and market volatility trigger internal psychological reactions, and how these affect the entire organization's investment strategy, is crucial. Managing the anxiety and stress that arise among employees and investors, and effectively regulating these, are essential for ensuring the organization's long-term success and stability. The organization needs a more meticulous and strategic approach, which is crucial for companies facing economic crises to analyze both internal and external factors comprehensively and develop responsive strategies.

Through such analysis, companies can establish more robust and sustainable response strategies, contributing to strengthening long-term corporate resilience.

'Global Investment Solutions' manages an extensive portfolio in the global investment market, with particular interest in the emerging markets and technology sectors. Recently, the company has faced rapid changes and instability in the international financial markets. These conditions were triggered by economic and political issues worldwide, introducing significant uncertainty across the investment landscape.

Especially, the emerging markets that 'Global Investment Solutions' focuses on are particularly sensitive to these global issues. For example, the trade war between China and the USA, political instability in the European Union, and escalating geopolitical tensions in the Middle East have significantly shaken the value of assets managed by this company. This has led to extreme reactions among investors, such as panic selling or excessive investment holding.

Moreover, investments in the technology sector have experienced rapid growth in recent years, but this comes with high volatility. Rapid technological advancements and the resulting quick changes in the market provide great opportunities for investors but also pose significant risks. For instance, innovative developments in areas like artificial intelligence, blockchain, and renewable energy are underway, but the commercialization process of these technologies can encounter unexpected obstacles, or intensified competition can increase the uncertainty of investment returns.

These external market conditions pose significant challenges to the portfolio management strategies of 'Global Investment Solutions'. The unstable psychological state of investors and the global economic uncertainty combine to require the company to readjust its investment strategies and actively respond to various market conditions. This creates a complex and challenging situation for the investment management team, which must continuously monitor market trends, manage risks, and seek ways to maintain investor trust.

Now, let's analyze the specific causes of the problems faced by 'Global Investment Solutions'. The company's main issues can be divided into two categories: external factors related to global economic uncertainty and internal investor psychological instability.

Firstly, global economic uncertainty has been triggered by various international events such as international trade wars, political instability, and geopolitical tensions. These factors directly affect the investment market, particularly increasing the volatility of the emerging markets and technology sectors that 'Global Investment Solutions' heavily relies on. For example, the trade war between the USA and China led to increased tariffs and the establishment of trade barriers, negatively impacting the value of the assets that the investment company operates in the Chinese and US markets.

Secondly, the internal psychological instability of investors is a major cause that makes them overreact to market volatility. Economic uncertainty amplifies anxiety and fear among investors, leading to fear-based investment decisions, such as excessive selling or underestimating investment opportunities. This psychological state of investors significantly impacts the overall performance of the portfolio and can often conflict with long-term investment goals.

These two problem sources interact with each other and present complex challenges to the investment strategies and performance of 'Global Investment Solutions'. Global economic uncertainty influences investor psychology, and investors' psychological instability, in turn, destabilizes the company's investment decisions and market response strategies. This causes the company to continuously adjust and adapt strategies to manage changing market conditions and investor expectations.

Several psychological theories useful when applying a psychological approach to the situation faced by 'Global Investment Solutions' will be introduced and explained in detail for their importance.

Firstly, an essential theory is the Prospect Theory developed by Daniel Kahneman and Amos Tversky. Prospect Theory explains that investors show a significantly greater psychological response to losses than gains. That is, investors tend to avoid excessive risks to prevent potential losses, which is more pronounced when market instability is high. This theory can help 'Global Investment Solutions' understand investors' psychological responses and develop investment strategies based on this.

Secondly, the Emotional Decision-Making Theory deals with how emotions influence the investment decision-making process. According to this theory, investors do not make decisions based solely on logical and rational information; emotional factors can significantly distort their decisions. This provides important insights for understanding how investors cope with economic uncertainty and for developing investment education and counseling programs that minimize the influence of emotions.

Thirdly, the Cognitive Dissonance Theory explains the psychological process where investors distort or ignore information to resolve the discomfort when they experience cognitive dissonance related to their investment decisions. This theory is useful for understanding how investors react when confronted with information that challenges their belief systems, helping to improve investment education programs or communication strategies.

By integrating and applying these psychological theories, 'Global Investment Solutions' can more effectively understand and manage investors' psychological diversity and response patterns. This plays a crucial role in strengthening risk management for the investment portfolio and building trust with investors. Such a psychological approach will help prevent potential issues in the investment decision-making process and contribute to optimizing investment performance even in economic crisis situations.

Now, let's take a detailed look at the actual resolution process based on the psychological theories applicable to the situation of 'Global Investment Solutions'. We will analyze the specific strategies and measures taken by this company to manage investor psychology and optimize portfolio performance.

Firstly, using an approach based on Prospect Theory, 'Global Investment Solutions' has strengthened its investor education program and supported investors in understanding and managing their emotional responses. The company conducts regular webinars and workshops to explain to investors how excessive fear of losses can harm long-term investment goals and visually demonstrates the expected losses and gains in various market scenarios to aid understanding. This education encourages investors to adopt a more logical and rational approach in responding to market volatility.

Secondly, based on the Emotional Decision-Making Theory, the company provides tools and resources to reduce investors' emotional impulses and help them make more balanced decisions. For example, the investment portfolio management platform includes automated alert features that reduce emotional impulses, giving investors an opportunity to reconsider before making emotionally driven decisions. These tools particularly help investors maintain composure during rapid market changes.

Thirdly, applying the Cognitive Dissonance Theory, the company has improved its response strategies for market information that investors find difficult to accept. The company conducts transparent and continuous communication to reduce the discrepancy between investors' beliefs and current market conditions. Regular market analysis reports, investment briefings, and Q&A sessions help investors accurately understand market realities and make more informed investment decisions based on this understanding.

Through these measures, 'Global Investment Solutions' has been able to consider investors' psychological diversity and maximize the performance of the portfolio even amidst economic uncertainty, maintaining investor trust. This has enhanced investors' psychological comfort and strengthened long-term investment relationships, a success made possible because the company's strategic approach was based on psychological theories.

Exploring deeper psychological concepts related to investment portfolio management and psychological diversity is crucial for understanding how this knowledge can be applied in investment decisions and management. Psychological factors in the investment world are often overlooked, but they actually have a decisive impact on investor behavior and market outcomes.

Cognitive Biases and Investment
Cognitive biases play a crucial role in the investment decision-making process. For example, confirmation bias explains the tendency of investors to selectively collect and pay attention to information that supports their beliefs. This can lead investors to process market information unevenly, potentially making incorrect investment decisions. Additionally, the availability heuristic indicates the tendency for people to make decisions based on the most recently accessed information or the most easily recalled examples. This can cause overreaction to short-term market fluctuations.

The Role of Emotions
Emotions significantly influence investor behavior, especially during abrupt market changes. Emotional investing refers to cases where investors make investment decisions based on emotions rather than logical and systematic analysis. For example, fear and greed are two major emotions that operate in the stock market, potentially leading to excessive market fluctuations.

Social Influence and Group Behavior
Investment decisions are often influenced by social impact and conformity within a group. Groupthink is commonly seen in investment clubs or institutions, where there is a tendency to agree without critical thinking, which can often lead to negative investment outcomes.

Understanding and applying these psychological concepts is important for both individual investors and investment management companies. Through this, investors can better understand their investment styles and minimize potential risks arising from biases and emotional factors. Additionally, investment management companies can use this knowledge to develop investment education programs or design more effective risk management strategies for investment portfolios. This psychological approach will ultimately contribute to optimizing investment performance and building long-term trust relationships with investors.

6. Managing Financial Stress

psychological strategies for managing financial stress

Financial stress poses serious challenges for both organizations and individuals. For businesses, financial pressure extends beyond mere numbers, impacting employees' daily work, job satisfaction, and the overall health of the organization. This chapter explores the effects of financial stress on businesses and approaches from a psychological perspective how organizations can effectively manage it. We will present strategies for turning financial challenges into opportunities and fostering long-term stability and growth for employees and the organization.

In today's rapidly changing global economy, the IT company "TechLeaders" is experiencing severe financial pressure due to economic downturns and abrupt technological shifts in the market. Despite investments aimed at developing new technologies and expanding markets, unexpected increases in competition and volatility in consumer demand have significantly affected the company's profitability. These external environmental changes have amplified anxiety and stress within the company, negatively impacting not only employee performance but also the organizational culture.

This chapter will examine in-depth how "TechLeaders" handles this financial stress. By utilizing psychological theories, we will explore strategies for managing financial stress within the organization and analyze how these strategies can positively affect employee well-being and overall organizational performance. Managing financial stress involves more than just adjusting financial numbers; it is a crucial process that enhances organizational sustainability and boosts employee job satisfaction. Through this process, companies like "TechLeaders" can learn how to overcome economic difficulties, maintain competitiveness, and grow even in a shifting market environment.

"TechLeaders" is currently facing severe financial stress due to rapid market changes and internal cost increases. The company has made substantial investments in technological development but has not achieved expected returns due to unforeseen market shifts. Additionally, new regulatory demands and increased pressure from competitors are causing operating costs to continually rise. These external and internal pressures are heightening tensions across the company, spreading anxiety and uncertainty among employees.

This situation is placing significant stress on "TechLeaders'" management and employees, particularly affecting daily work performance and job satisfaction. Employees are anxious about the company's future, leading to decreased focus and reduced productivity. The management must find ways to reduce this stress and restore stability within the organization. This involves identifying financial stressors, analyzing their causes, and developing strategies to address them, where psychological theories and approaches can be immensely beneficial.

"TechLeaders" is under serious pressure from two main factors: challenges in the volatile technology market and rising internal costs.

Firstly, the instability of the technology market is directly impacting "TechLeaders'" profitability. The tech industry experiences high volatility due to rapid changes and innovations, making investment and revenue forecasting challenging. For instance, the emergence of new competitors in artificial intelligence and big data is quickly shifting market share, negatively affecting the investment return rates expected by "TechLeaders."

Secondly, the increase in internal operating costs has been another cause for concern. Continuous investments in research and development and the expansion of technological infrastructure have increased the financial burden on the company. Moreover, intensified regulations and changes in environmental standards in the global market have added additional cost pressures. These rising internal costs are exacerbating liquidity issues, limiting financial flexibility, and becoming obstacles to executing long-term growth strategies.

These two major issues are placing extensive stress on "TechLeaders'" operations and amplifying anxiety and uncertainty among employees, leading to reduced work performance and lower job satisfaction. Therefore, accurately understanding and effectively managing these causes are crucial for ensuring the organization's long-term stability and success.

We will explore psychological theories that can be applied to manage the financial stress situation faced by "TechLeaders." These include several key theories essential for understanding stress response mechanisms.

Firstly, Richard Lazarus's Stress and Coping Theory is crucial. Lazarus argued that stress occurs based on an individual's appraisal of an event. This theory can help understand how "TechLeaders'" employees perceive the company's financial situation and respond to it. Based on this theory, the company can provide accurate information to employees and develop communication strategies to alleviate their concerns.

Secondly, Carol Wright's Stress Overcoming Theory is also beneficial. Wright emphasized that an individual's ability to cope with stress depends on their resources and support systems. "TechLeaders" can use this theory to enhance employee support programs and activate social support networks within the workplace to reduce stress.

Lastly, Daniel Kahneman's Prospect Theory explains how risks and rewards are perceived in financial decision-making. This theory can help "TechLeaders" understand employee decision-making patterns in financial stress situations and mitigate potentially irrational responses. For instance, the company can use this theory to educate employees on managing economic uncertainty and making decisions from a long-term perspective.

By integrating and applying these psychological theories, "TechLeaders" can minimize the impact of financial stress on employees and the organization, and develop strategies to support organizational health and growth. This involves not only solving financial issues but also strengthening organizational culture, enhancing employee well-being, and laying a foundation for long-term organizational success. This approach is especially crucial in an era of frequent changes and challenges, as it strengthens the organization's capacity to adapt and grow sustainably.

Exploring a broader psychological perspective in managing financial stress in investment portfolios and organizational contexts is highly beneficial for both organizations and individuals. This approach deepens the understanding of the impact of financial stress on organizational performance and individual well-being and helps develop necessary strategies to cope with it.

Psychological resilience and organizational success correlation

Psychological resilience refers to an individual's ability to recover from stress, crises, or failures and to grow from these experiences. In an organizational context, psychological resilience is particularly crucial, especially for organizations facing financial challenges. Measures to enhance psychological resilience include improving employees' stress management skills, fostering a positive workplace culture, and strengthening ongoing education and communication.

The role of emotional intelligence

Emotional intelligence (EQ) involves the ability to recognize and manage one's own and others' emotions. In an organization, leaders and members with high EQ are more emotionally stable in financial stress situations, effectively leading and motivating teams. EQ training and workshops help employees manage stress more effectively and adapt to changing market environments.

Organizational psychology and cultural change

Organizational psychology studies human behavior within the workplace, including aspects related to organizational culture, structure, and leadership. A positive and supportive organizational culture helps employees better manage stress, leading to higher productivity and job satisfaction. Change management strategies enable organizations to respond flexibly in financial stress situations, contributing to overall organizational success.

These psychological approaches allow organizations like "TechLeaders" to effectively manage financial stress, promote organizational health, and foster growth. The application of psychological insights within the organization goes beyond simple problem-solving, contributing to sustainable development and enhancing employee welfare, ultimately playing a crucial role in the organization's long-term success.

7. Financial Planning and Psychological Approaches

Deep Understanding of Financial Planning: A Psychological Approach

Financial planning plays a crucial role for both companies and individuals. In particular, financial planning that considers psychological factors is vital not only for achieving long-term financial goals but also for managing stress in daily economic activities. This chapter aims to explore how effective financial management strategies can be developed by combining financial planning with a psychological approach. Such an approach will help individuals and organizations understand the psychological factors involved in making financial decisions and manage them effectively, thereby creating a healthier and more efficient financial environment.

We will first look at a tech startup called "FutureTech Industries." This company is growing rapidly through innovative technological development but is experiencing financial stress due to high research and development costs and barriers to market entry. The company's new product development requires significant capital, and pressure from investors and challenges from competitors require ongoing adjustments to the company's financial plans. This situation also causes significant stress to employees, affecting their work efficiency and creativity.

This chapter will explore in depth how "FutureTech Industries" manages this financial stress and how psychological theories can help in this process. By integrating psychological approaches into financial planning, the company can minimize the psychological impacts of financial decisions on individuals and organizations, and develop strategies to ensure long-term financial soundness. These strategies will positively affect job satisfaction and overall organizational health.

The specific situation faced by "FutureTech Industries" involves rapid growth due to innovative technological development and the financial stress caused by high research and development costs and market entry barriers. The company is investing substantial capital in developing and introducing new technologies to the market, which requires continuous financial support from investors. However, market uncertainties and challenges from competing firms make this fundraising even more difficult.

Moreover, "FutureTech Industries" incurs significant costs in marketing and product deployment necessary for successful product launches. The expenses incurred during this process burden the company's liquidity, which in turn increases financial stress. Especially if product development is delayed or market acceptance falls short of expectations, this stress can increase sharply.

Additionally, within the company, this financial pressure affects the daily work and creativity of employees. In particular, the research and development team involved in new product development is trying to balance between limited resources and high expectations, increasing the team's stress level. Moreover, the management team must make extra efforts to maintain relationships with investors and secure funding, which also causes significant stress.

This situation emphasizes the need for "FutureTech Industries" to consider psychological elements in establishing and executing their financial plans. Understanding how financial stress affects various levels within the organization is crucial for developing effective management and resolution strategies.

"FutureTech Industries" intends to introduce several psychological theories applicable to its financial stress situation. These theories can help the company understand the financial challenges and stress it faces and find solutions.

The first important theory is the Cognitive Appraisal Theory, developed by Richard Lazarus and Susan Folkman. This theory focuses on how individuals perceive and evaluate situations where they experience stress. According to this theory, the degree of stress varies depending on how an individual interprets a situation. "FutureTech Industries" can use this theory to train employees to evaluate the company's financial situation from a more realistic and positive perspective, providing ways to alleviate their stress.

The second theory, Emotion Regulation Theory, explains how individuals manage and regulate their emotions. Developed by James Gross, this theory includes strategies for recognizing and expressing emotions, which can help find effective coping methods in stressful situations. The company can base its training for employees on this theory, supporting them in handling the negative emotions associated with financial instability.

The third, Psychology of Organizational Behavior, provides important insights into the behavior of individuals and groups within an organization. Research in this field explores how organizational culture, team motivation, and leadership styles affect employees' performance and well-being. "FutureTech Industries" can use this theory to develop strategies that reduce stress levels within the organization and increase productivity.

These psychological theories will contribute to "FutureTech Industries" managing financial stress more effectively and supporting the organization's health and long-term success. Psychological stability and well-organized financial planning can maintain the company's growth momentum and protect it in potential crisis situations.

"FutureTech Industries" will examine in detail the process of managing and resolving financial stress based on the psychological theories applied. The company is implementing specific strategies through these psychological approaches to effectively overcome financial challenges and improve employee welfare.

Firstly, using Cognitive Appraisal Theory, "FutureTech Industries" helps employees reinterpret the company's financial situation positively. To do this, the company holds regular information sessions where management explains the current financial status and future plans, answering employees' questions and concerns to reduce uncertainty and increase transparency. Additionally, workshops with psychologists support employees in effectively coping with stressful situations.

Secondly, by applying Emotion Regulation Theory, the company provides emotion management training to employees. This training is particularly targeted at employees in finance-related departments, helping them recognize and regulate the pressures and stress they experience during work. The training includes mindfulness meditation, emotion diary writing, and breathing techniques to control stress responses.

Thirdly, based on the Psychology of Organizational Behavior, the company enhances leadership training and team-building activities. These activities improve communication within the team and help leaders better understand and support team members' emotions and stress. In particular, leaders are trained on how to motivate team members and create a positive work environment.

These strategies are effective for "FutureTech Industries" in managing financial stress and improving the overall welfare of the organization. The company is using this approach to enhance the psychological stability and satisfaction of its employees, simultaneously improving financial performance and supporting the organization's long-term success. These psychological approaches bring positive changes to the organization, maintaining its health and growth even in the face of economic challenges.

In addition to integrating psychological approaches into financial planning, various psychological theories and concepts can be further explored to address financial stress and enhance the financial health of individuals and organizations. In this regard, we will examine several important psychological concepts further.
Behavioral Finance
Behavioral finance studies how psychological factors affect financial decision-making processes. This field analyzes cognitive biases and emotional factors that lead investors to make irrational decisions. For example, loss aversion bias explains the tendency of individuals not to take excessive risks to avoid potential losses, which can often result in missing financial opportunities. Organizations like "FutureTech Industries" recognize these biases and offer training programs to help employees make more balanced financial decisions.

Stress Theories

Stress theories describe how individuals experience and respond to stress. In particular, the Yerkes-Dodson Law of stress suggests that a certain level of stress can enhance performance, but too much stress can reduce it. Organizations can understand this law and manage employees' stress levels to induce optimal work performance.

Motivation Theories

Motivation theories explore the internal and external factors that drive individuals to perform specific actions. Edwin Locke's Goal Setting Theory suggests that clear and challenging goals can enhance an individual's performance. Organizations apply this theory to set clear financial goals for employees and motivate them to achieve these goals.

These psychological concepts play an essential role in helping "FutureTech Industries" effectively manage financial challenges and enhance the financial health of the organization. By integrating insights from psychology into financial planning, organizations can reduce employees' stress, maximize work performance, and improve overall organizational health. This approach goes beyond solving financial problems, contributing to the sustainable development of the organization and enhancing employee welfare.

8. Economic Behavior of Individuals and Organizations

The Psychology of Economic Behavior: Decision-Making Analysis in Individuals and Organizations

Economic behavior is a fundamental activity for both individuals and organizations, observed across various dimensions from micro-level personal choices to macro-level organizational strategies. This chapter explores the complex psychological factors in economic decision-making, particularly how these factors are directly linked to the financial health of individuals and organizations. The psychological approach to economic behavior plays a crucial role in understanding that financial decisions are not made solely based on economic logic. This approach explains how various non-economic factors such as personal emotions, cognitive biases, and social influences impact economic decisions.

We will specifically examine the case of 'Economica International,' a global company that has achieved significant success in selling various products in the global market but has faced several economic challenges in recent years due to economic uncertainty and market volatility. Notably, the cultural differences and uncertainties in consumer behavior encountered while attempting to enter new markets significantly impact the company's global strategy.

This chapter will deeply cover how 'Economica International' perceives and manages these challenges, exploring how psychological theories can be applied and how they can lead to better economic decisions. Understanding economic behavior through a psychological approach can critically contribute to improving the decision-making process within organizations and establishing strategies for long-term success.

The specific challenges faced by 'Economica International' relate to entering new markets, with cultural differences and market volatility playing crucial roles. Recently, the company has been attempting to enter markets in Asia and South America, struggling to understand and adapt to the unique consumer behaviors and expectations in these regions. For example, in the Asian market, there is a high expectation for product quality, but price sensitivity is also significant. These characteristics suggest that 'Economica International' needs to adjust its pricing and marketing strategies.

In the South American market, political instability and economic volatility present additional challenges. Consumers in this region react sensitively to economic uncertainties, significantly reducing consumption when uncertainty increases. This reaction has led to lower sales volumes for 'Economica International,' impacting the company's overall profitability.

The company is also facing complexities in the global supply chain and rising raw material costs, which increase production costs and ultimately affect the pricing of the final products. 'Economica International' faces difficult choices in managing these cost increases and deciding how to reflect them in product prices.

These complex situations have a significant impact on 'Economica International's strategic decisions and long-term financial planning, indicating a need for careful and systematic approaches to sustain growth and maintain competitiveness in the market. This situation serves as an opportunity for the company to reassess its market entry strategies and develop tailored approaches that fit the characteristics of each region.

Now, it's time to analyze the problems faced by 'Economica International' using psychological theories and introduce these theories. Through this, we can gain a deeper understanding of the complexities of economic behavior and how organizations can effectively manage these challenges.

The first important theory involves cultural differences and consumer behavior. Geert Hofstede's Cultural Dimensions Theory explains how the cultural values of different countries influence consumers' purchasing decisions and brand perceptions. For instance, in cultures with a high uncertainty avoidance index, consumers may exhibit high brand loyalty and slow acceptance of new products. This suggests that 'Economica International' must carefully consider cultural elements to successfully introduce products in new markets.

Secondly, Richard Thaler and Cass Sunstein's Nudge Theory addresses the psychological factors influencing economic behavior. This theory argues that small 'nudges' can improve consumer choices and can be very useful in marketing strategies. For example, adjusting product placement or pricing strategies can naturally guide consumer purchasing decisions.

Thirdly, Daniel Kahneman's Prospect Theory explains how humans perceive risk and uncertainty and make decisions accordingly. This theory can help 'Economica International' understand and predict consumer purchasing patterns in economically uncertain markets. Particularly, considering that consumers are likely to make conservative purchasing decisions due to economic instability, pricing policies and promotional activities need to be adjusted accordingly.

These theories enable 'Economica International' to establish customized strategies considering the cultural and economic characteristics of each region. These strategies will play a crucial role in facilitating successful expansion in the global market and maintaining long-term competitiveness.

Now, let's examine the specific resolution process applied through the psychological theories used to address the problems faced by 'Economica International'. This approach will clearly demonstrate how the company overcomes cultural differences and market uncertainties and makes strategically successful decisions.

Firstly, using Hofstede's Cultural Dimensions Theory, 'Economica International' has developed customized marketing strategies based on the cultural characteristics of each region. For instance, in Asian countries with high uncertainty avoidance indices, advertising campaigns emphasize product reliability and quality assurance, and detailed information and support for product use are provided to alleviate consumer anxiety. This approach has contributed to increasing the acceptance of new products and enhancing brand loyalty.

Secondly, applying Nudge Theory, the company has implemented several measures to influence consumer purchasing decisions. For example, improving packaging design to enhance product visibility and offering small discount coupons or additional bonus products to facilitate consumer purchasing decisions. Additionally, the company has focused on actively collecting consumer feedback and reflecting it in product improvements to increase customer satisfaction.

Thirdly, through Prospect Theory, 'Economica International' has understood consumer behavior in response to uncertain economic conditions and adjusted its pricing strategy accordingly. In regions with high economic instability, price reduction strategies are implemented to reduce the purchasing burden on consumers, and more accessible product lines are developed to maintain market share.

These strategies have helped 'Economica International' effectively overcome the various challenges it faces in the global market. The application of psychological theories not only solves problems but enriches the strategic decision-making process of the company and lays the foundation for sustainable growth. This approach serves as a useful case for other organizations, emphasizing the importance of integrating psychological elements into economic decision-making.

Expanding the use of psychological perspectives beyond managing investment portfolios and financial decisions related to psychological diversity is immensely beneficial for both organizations and individuals. This broader approach helps in deeply understanding the impact of financial decisions on organizational performance and individual well-being, and assists in formulating effective response strategies.

Application of Behavioral Economics

Behavioral economics focuses on understanding and predicting irrational behaviors in economic decision-making. When companies like 'Economica International' face economic uncertainties and volatility in the global market, applying this theory can help identify irrational consumer behavior patterns and psychological triggers, enabling the development of more sophisticated marketing strategies and product pricing.

Utilization of Decision Theory

Decision theory provides methodologies for making optimal choices under uncertainty. When 'Economica International' analyzes various market conditions and internal data, utilizing this theory can significantly aid in managing risks and assessing potential opportunities. Especially, it helps in effectively balancing risks and expected returns during the strategic decision-making process.

Application of Information Processing Theory

Information processing theory deals with how information is collected, interpreted, and utilized in the decision-making process within an organization. This theory assists organizations like 'Economica International' in effectively managing information overload and making quick and accurate decisions based on critical information. Particularly, in a global environment, the quality and speed of information processing are key elements in securing a competitive edge.

These strategies have helped 'Economica International' effectively overcome various challenges faced in the global market. The application of psychological theories not only solves problems but also enriches the company's strategic decision-making process and lays the foundation for sustainable growth. This approach serves as a valuable example to other organizations, emphasizing the importance of integrating psychological elements into economic decision-making.

9. Pursuing Financial Stability

Pursuing Financial Stability: The Impact of Psychology on Financial Health

Financial stability is a crucial element for the sustainable growth and prosperity of a company. Achieving this stability involves more than just maximizing profits and managing costs; it is vitally important to understand and appropriately manage the psychological factors of organizational members. A psychological approach can explain the various human elements that may occur when financial decisions are made and help develop more effective financial management strategies. This chapter will explore in depth how a psychological approach can aid in the pursuit of a company's financial stability. We will examine various psychological factors such as emotions, cognitive biases, and social influences that affect financial decisions, and analyze how managing these factors can strengthen an organization financially.

The case study of 'Global Tech Solutions', a large technology company active in the global market, illustrates this point. Despite its high growth potential, the company faces several financial challenges due to market volatility and intense competition. In particular, the company experiences financial pressure due to high financing costs associated with significant investments in new technology development and the uncertain return on these investments. This uncertainty threatens the company's financial stability and increases anxiety and stress among employees, which in turn negatively impacts the organization's overall performance. Through the experience of 'Global Tech Solutions', we will demonstrate how economic decisions are influenced by various psychological factors and how managing these factors can enhance financial stability.

This chapter will detail how 'Global Tech Solutions' manages these financial challenges and the role that related psychological theories play in this process. By understanding and appropriately managing psychological elements in the financial decision-making process, organizations can more effectively handle crises and establish strategies for long-term financial stability. This approach not only provides deep insights for organizations and individuals but also contributes to solving financial issues, supporting the sustainable development of the organization, and improving employee welfare.

Financial stability is essential for the sustainable growth and prosperity of a company. Achieving this requires more than just maximizing profits and managing expenses; it is crucial to understand and appropriately manage the psychological factors affecting organizational members. A psychological approach helps explain the various human factors that may occur during financial decision-making and aids in developing more effective financial management strategies. This chapter will deeply explore how a psychological approach can assist in pursuing a company's financial stability. We will examine various psychological factors such as emotions, cognitive biases, and social influences affecting financial decisions, and analyze how managing these factors can strengthen an organization financially.

'Global Tech Solutions', chosen for our case study, is a large technology company active in the global market. Despite its high growth potential, the company faces several financial challenges due to market volatility and intense competition. Particularly, the company experiences financial pressure due to high financing costs associated with significant investments in new technology development and the uncertain return on these investments. This uncertainty threatens the company's financial stability and increases anxiety and stress among employees, which in turn negatively impacts the organization's overall performance. Through the experience of 'Global Tech Solutions', we will show how economic decisions are influenced by various psychological factors and how managing these factors can enhance financial stability.

This chapter will detail how 'Global Tech Solutions' manages these financial challenges and the role that related psychological theories play in this process. By understanding and appropriately managing psychological elements in the financial decision-making process, organizations can more effectively handle crises and establish strategies for long-term financial stability. This approach not only provides deep insights for organizations and individuals but also contributes to solving financial issues, supporting the sustainable development of the organization, and improving employee welfare.

The specific financial challenges faced by 'Global Tech Solutions' stem from high costs of technological development and the unpredictable market conditions. The company is particularly investing heavily in research and development (R&D) related to new technologies, and the high financial costs involved are increasing the financial pressure. Additionally, with intensifying global competition, substantial marketing and sales expenses are necessary to maintain and expand market share. These circumstances have complex effects on various financial aspects such as investor relations, corporate creditworthiness, and cash flow management.

The company also faces the need for continuous innovation and market adaptability to maintain competitiveness in the rapidly changing tech market, which poses an additional financial burden. The unpredictability of market conditions and the risk of technology development failures make it difficult to predict returns on investment, thereby increasing financial risk. Furthermore, changes in global trade policies or political instability also directly impact the company, requiring constant adjustments to its financial planning and strategy.

These issues threaten the financial stability of 'Global Tech Solutions' and increase anxiety and stress among employees, negatively impacting workplace performance and satisfaction. This situation necessitates a more strategic and psychologically informed approach, suggesting the need to integrate various psychological theories into financial decision-making and policy formulation. Based on this analysis, we will explore how the application of psychological theories can help overcome the challenges faced by the company and restore financial stability.

We will analyze the financial challenges faced by 'Global Tech Solutions' and explore psychological theories that can be applied to help the organization navigate through these challenges effectively.

The first critical theory is cognitive dissonance theory, developed by Leon Festinger. This theory explains the psychological discomfort individuals experience when there is a discrepancy between their beliefs, knowledge, and actions. In the case of 'Global Tech Solutions', a gap may occur between the company's objectives and actual financial outcomes, increasing cognitive dissonance among management and employees. To manage this dissonance, the company may need to reset its goals or adjust the expectations of its employees. Additionally, enhancing education and communication to help employees better understand the company's financial status and strategic directions is crucial.

The second theory, loss aversion, explains how the tendency to avoid losses influences economic decisions. Developed by Daniel Kahneman and Amos Tversky, this theory suggests that people feel losses more acutely than an equivalent gain, which can lead to excessive risk aversion in investment decisions. The financial managers of 'Global Tech Solutions' need to understand this theory and establish a balanced risk management strategy to ensure that excessive conservatism does not lead to missed opportunities.

The third theory, social comparison, deals with the emotional and behavioral changes individuals experience when they compare themselves to others. This theory suggests that within an organization, employees may feel dissatisfied when they compare their rewards and performance with their colleagues. This can negatively impact workplace motivation and satisfaction, so 'Global Tech Solutions' needs to maintain a fair and transparent reward system and reinforce the perception that all employees are contributing to the company's success.

These psychological theories can help 'Global Tech Solutions' effectively manage its financial challenges and develop strategies to enhance its financial stability. By utilizing insights from psychology, not only can economic decisions be influenced, but also positive changes in employee behavior and attitudes can be fostered, improving overall organizational performance and welfare.

We will examine in detail the process of pursuing financial stability based on the psychological theories applied at 'Global Tech Solutions'. This approach will show how the organization can overcome economic challenges and achieve financial stability.

Firstly, applying cognitive dissonance theory, 'Global Tech Solutions' has introduced a transparent communication strategy to reduce the gap between management and employee expectations and reality. The company has implemented regular financial updates and strategic meetings to ensure that all teams understand the company's financial status and strategic direction and are involved in the financial decision-making process. This has helped employees feel a greater sense of belonging and responsibility towards the company's financial goals and reduced potential anxiety and stress.

Secondly, utilizing loss aversion theory, the company developed a training program to mitigate the tendency towards excessive risk aversion in investment decisions. This program provided employees with a deeper understanding of the balance between risk and reward, aiding in making more balanced investment decisions. Additionally, various scenario planning and risk management workshops were conducted to help employees rationally assess and manage potential risks.

Thirdly, through social comparison theory, 'Global Tech Solutions' completely reviewed its performance evaluation and reward system. This involved introducing a new reward policy based on fairness and transparency, ensuring that employees felt their efforts were adequately recognized. Additionally, by strengthening a corporate culture that emphasizes collaboration and teamwork over competition, the focus was shifted towards mutual support and growth within the workplace.

These strategic approaches have significantly contributed to 'Global Tech Solutions' overcoming its financial challenges and securing long-term stability. The application of psychological theories has enriched the organization's strategic decision-making process and simultaneously improved employee welfare and performance. This serves as a valuable example to other organizations, emphasizing the importance of integrating psychological elements into economic decision-making.
In pursuing financial stability, there are deeper psychological concepts that organizations should consider in addition to a psychological approach. These concepts can help organizations and individuals more clearly understand the psychological motivations and behavior patterns displayed when making financial decisions. We will explore additional psychological theories and their impact on financial behavior.

Behavioral Finance

Behavioral finance explores the various psychological factors that influence economic decision-making. This field challenges the 'rational actor' model assumed by traditional finance theories, showing that people often act in irrational or unpredictable ways. For example, overconfidence—where investors overestimate their knowledge or control—can lead them to take excessive risks. 'Global Tech Solutions' can use this recognition to identify potential biases in internal investment decisions and establish more cautious investment review procedures.

Stress and Decision-Making

The impact of stress on economic decision-making is a critical topic in both psychology and finance. Stressful situations can significantly impair an individual's decision-making ability, leading to poor financial decisions. Establishing stress management programs within the organization and supporting employees in making effective decisions even under high stress is crucial. To this end, 'Global Tech Solutions' provides mindfulness, stress management workshops, and relaxation spaces to support employees' emotional stability.

Motivation and Financial Behavior

Motivation theories explain the fundamental reasons why individuals perform certain actions. Intrinsic and extrinsic motivations can greatly influence financial behavior. For example, if employees receive sufficient extrinsic motivation through a reward system, they are more likely to actively contribute to achieving the company's financial goals. Conversely, employees with strong intrinsic motivation may find greater satisfaction in their work and value long-term career development and loyalty to the company.

Integrating psychological concepts into financial management plays a vital role in enhancing an organization's financial stability. This goes beyond merely solving financial problems, supporting the overall health and growth of the organization, and improving employee welfare and satisfaction. Such psychological approaches are very useful for organizations in effectively overcoming financial challenges and establishing strategies for long-term success.

10. Investment Behavior and Psychological Traits

The Psychology of Investing: The Connection between Investment Behavior and Psychological Traits

Investment behavior extends beyond mere numbers and economic predictions; it is deeply rooted in the psychological traits of investors. This chapter will deeply explore the psychological traits associated with investment behavior and examine how these traits influence the decision-making process in investing. Psychology plays a crucial role in how investors interpret market information, perceive risks, and make decisions, understanding the various psychological motives and biases that can arise during this process is key to investment success.

This chapter's case study will focus on 'Financial Wealth Investment,' a global investment company managing portfolios across various asset classes. In recent years, the company has faced unexpected losses due to rapidly changing market conditions and high volatility. We will analyze how psychological factors have contributed to these outcomes. In particular, we will examine how excessive optimism or fear among investors can drive collective market behaviors and how this has impacted the overall performance of the portfolio.

We will also delve into how 'Financial Wealth Investment' recognizes and manages these challenges and which psychological theories they apply. By integrating psychological elements into their financial decision-making process, the organization aims to better understand investment behaviors and base strategic decisions on this understanding. This approach offers deep insights not only to the organization but also to individual investors, helping them make more rational and successful investment decisions by understanding the psychological underpinnings of investment behaviors.

Through this chapter, we will focus on developing strategies to optimize investment performance by understanding and effectively managing the psychological traits of investors and market psychological trends. We will also explore in depth how to enhance individual investors' management of emotions and recognition of biases, which are essential for making better decisions in the market.

'Financial Wealth Investment' faces specific challenges stemming from high volatility and increasing competition in the global financial markets. Managing a diversified portfolio across various countries, the company must adapt to different market conditions and economic cycles. The growing uncertainty in the global economy over recent years has made investment returns unpredictable, significantly affecting the company's investment strategies. Psychological reactions of investors, particularly hypersensitivity to sharp market declines and rises, have presented additional challenges in portfolio management.

In these situations, investors are sometimes influenced by cognitive biases that occur during the information processing phase. For example, confirmation bias leads investors to selectively accept information that supports their beliefs while ignoring contrary data. This can cloud objective market analysis and sometimes lead to poor investment decisions. Additionally, the representativeness bias causes investors to overestimate the representativeness of a sample when predicting the future based on past events, which can lead to incorrect predictions about market fluctuations.

Investment behavior is deeply influenced by complex psychological factors beyond simple numerical analysis or market predictions. Investors' decisions often vary based on their inner beliefs, emotions, and social circumstances, which can determine the success or failure of their investments. Through the case study of 'Financial Wealth Investment,' a global investment company, we will examine the major psychological theories affecting investment behavior and explore how these theories can be applied in real investment decision-making processes.

Behavioral economics focuses on explaining irrational behaviors of investors and scholars like Richard Thaler and Cass Sunstein emphasize the cognitive biases and emotional factors that humans often experience when making economic decisions. For example, loss aversion bias explains the tendency of investors to take on greater risks to avoid losses, which can lead to irrational decisions in the market. 'Financial Wealth Investment' recognizes these biases and provides investors with education and tools to overcome them, promoting more rational investment decisions.

Moreover, cognitive dissonance theory deals with the psychological discomfort that investors might experience when they encounter information that contradicts their investment choices. According to this theory, investors may attempt to minimize dissonance by justifying their decisions, which could lead to holding onto wrong investments or selling at inappropriate times. The company prevents this by encouraging investors to periodically reevaluate their portfolios in response to market changes and emphasizing the importance of making investment decisions based on objective data.

The role of emotions is also a significant factor in investment decisions. Particularly, sharp rises and falls in the market can trigger strong emotional responses among investors, leading emotions such as fear or greed to dominate their investment decisions. 'Financial Wealth Investment' provides regular market analysis reports and psychological coaching to help investors recognize and manage these emotions, supporting them in making more composed and reasoned investment decisions.

To manage these challenges, 'Financial Wealth Investment' has invested in the psychological training and education of its employees. The training programs, particularly aimed at investment analysts and portfolio managers, focus on recognizing biases and developing skills to overcome them. These educational efforts help employees process information through more objective and analytical approaches, minimizing psychological errors in the investment decision-making process.

Additionally, the company has strengthened communication with clients to manage investors' emotional responses. Regular market analysis reports and updates on investment strategies provide investors with clear and in-depth information about market conditions, alleviating their anxieties and encouraging a long-term investment approach. This approach prevents investors from overreacting to short-term market fluctuations and promotes more stable investment behaviors.

These strategic approaches have significantly helped 'Financial Wealth Investment' effectively manage the psychological traits associated with investment behaviors and establish a solid foundation for long-term investment success. The company's efforts have optimized investment performance and enhanced investors' trust, serving as an important role in the broader financial industry. This serves as a valuable example to other organizations, emphasizing the importance of integrating psychological elements into economic decision-making.

Through these psychological approaches, 'Financial Wealth Investment' has successfully understood the complexities of investment behavior and based its effective investment strategies on this understanding. This provides valuable insights not only to individual investors but also to the entire organization, laying an important foundation for investment success. These insights are essential for all investors to make better decisions in the market, highlighting the importance of integrating psychological elements into economic decision-making.

We will further explore psychological theories related to investment behavior and investigate how organizations and individuals can improve their investment actions through these theories. These psychological approaches are crucial for understanding investors' behaviors and effectively managing the various psychological factors that can arise during the investment process.

The Psychology of Self-Control in Investment

Self-control in investment refers to an investor's ability to resist short-term temptations to achieve long-term goals. In the investment process, self-control is a crucial element, allowing investors to remain steadfast in their long-term investment plans without being swayed by short-term market fluctuations. As demonstrated in Walter Mischel's marshmallow experiment, the ability to willingly forgo a smaller present reward for a larger future reward can lead to investment success. 'Financial Wealth Investment' applies this principle in its investor education programs, emphasizing self-control skills and helping investors apply these skills in real life.

Groupthink and Investment Decisions

Groupthink is a phenomenon that occurs within a group where strong cohesion leads individual members to suppress critical thinking and conform to the group's opinion. This can also be observed in the investment field; if groupthink occurs within an investment team, there is a high likelihood of overlooking potential risks and making overly uniform decisions. To prevent this, 'Financial Wealth Investment' implements policies that promote diversity and openness in the investment decision-making process and regularly holds investment review sessions to gather a variety of opinions and critical perspectives.

Risk-Taking Propensity and Investor Psychology

The risk-taking propensity related to investment is closely linked to an individual's psychological traits, indicating how prepared an investor is to take on risks. Various psychological theories and research show that an investor's risk-taking propensity can vary based on their personality, experiences, and even emotional state. The company recognizes these individual differences and offers customized portfolios to each investor, crafting investment strategies that align with each investor's risk tolerance and financial goals.

These psychological approaches help 'Financial Wealth Investment' establish more effective investment strategies that consider the behaviors and psychological traits of investors. These strategies optimize investment performance for both individual investors and the organization as a whole and minimize psychological errors that can occur in the investment decision-making process. This is essential for all investors to make better decisions in the market, emphasizing the importance of integrating psychological elements into economic decision-making.

Conclusion

1. The Importance of Psychology in Management Practices

The Hidden Psychological Elements
in Management: Secrets to Organizational Success

Emphasizing the importance of psychology in management practices is becoming increasingly vital in modern management. Understanding human behavior and psychology is not just an option but a necessity for the successful operation of an organization. This applies both internally in managing employees and externally in interactions, such as customer relations. Psychology aids managers in making more effective decisions and achieving organizational goals across all these areas.

The application of psychology in management varies. For instance, psychological theories can be used to enhance employee motivation and satisfaction. Understanding and fulfilling employees' basic and growth needs through policies inspired by Maslow's Hierarchy of Needs or Herzberg's Motivation-Hygiene Theory contributes to employees feeling more satisfied and engaged with their work. Additionally, psychological approaches can develop programs to manage employee stress and promote mental health, playing a crucial role in enhancing overall productivity and efficiency.

Psychology also plays a crucial role in customer relations. Understanding the decision-making process of customers, and accurately identifying their needs and preferences is essential. Various theories and models of consumer psychology can be applied to comprehend how emotions affect customers' choices and integrate this understanding into marketing strategies, which can increase customer loyalty and build long-term relationships. Analyzing and predicting customer behaviors on new platforms like social media also requires a psychological approach.

Moreover, psychology significantly contributes to resolving internal conflicts and improving organizational culture. Analyzing the causes of conflicts psychologically and developing strategies that facilitate effective communication among organizational members is essential for organizational health and growth. This helps create a more positive and productive work environment, which can be a critical factor in long-term organizational success.

Overall, the importance of psychology in management practices lies in enabling organizations to adopt a human-centered approach, effectively meeting the needs and expectations of all organizational members while achieving organizational goals. This approach goes beyond short-term gains to foster sustainable growth and development, emphasizing the importance of managers being well-versed in psychology and actively using this knowledge. It enables effective decision-making at all organizational levels and creates an environment where all members can feel satisfied and engaged.

2. Sustainable Management Through Psychological Approaches

Sustainable Management Strategies:
A Psychological Perspective on Future Organizational Culture

Sustainable management extends beyond financial profits to include the social and environmental responsibilities of an organization. A psychological approach is essential in laying the foundation for long-term prosperity, as it helps understand and predict various human behaviors and interactions within and outside the organization. This section will explore how a psychological approach can contribute to sustainable management and positively impact organizational strategy.

Psychology and Organizational Social Responsibility

Effectively undertaking Corporate Social Responsibility (CSR) requires that the attitudes and behaviors of internal members align with CSR goals. Psychological theories, especially theories of motivation and attitude change, can be used to motivate employees to actively participate in an organization's social responsibility activities. For example, when an organization participates in environmental conservation efforts, it is crucial to educate employees on the personal significance of these activities and their positive impact on the organization and the environment. This helps employees value these activities more and participate voluntarily.

Strengthening Organizational Culture Through Psychological Approaches

For sustainable management, a strong and positive organizational culture is essential. Organizational culture consists of the values, beliefs, and norms shared among members, which can be shaped and strengthened through a psychological approach. Activities that enhance belonging and camaraderie within the organization, policies that promote employees' psychological safety, and systems that encourage open communication all contribute to employees feeling valued as part of the organization and actively contributing to its sustainable growth. This environment fosters creativity and innovation among employees, enhancing the organization's long-term competitiveness.

Leadership Development Using Psychology

Leadership for sustainable management requires a deep psychological connection with team members, going beyond traditional leadership styles. By applying psychological theories to leadership, leaders can better understand how their actions and decisions affect employees' emotions and attitudes. For example, transformational leadership theory provides ways for leaders to intrinsically motivate employees and build consensus around organizational visions and goals. This type of leadership helps employees integrate their personal goals with those of the organization, energizing and unleashing the creativity needed to achieve organizational objectives.

Managing Change Through Psychological Approaches

Managing the inevitable changes that come with pursuing sustainable management is crucial. Integrating a psychological approach into change management can help organizations reduce resistance to change and enable members to adapt more quickly and effectively to new situations. It is important to understand and address employees' anxieties and fears, with clear communication and support. Educating members about the necessity and benefits of change is also critical.

Using a psychological approach to drive sustainable management provides organizations with the flexibility to overcome challenges and respond effectively to changing market and societal demands. This not only benefits the organization but also has a positive impact on society at large, bringing advantages to all stakeholders involved in the organization's long-term prosperity.

3. Future Prospects for Management Strategies Utilizing Psychology

Innovative Management Strategies and Psychology:
Preparing for Tomorrow

The future outlook for management strategies that utilize psychology is very promising. As organizations face complex challenges and seek sustainable growth in the contemporary management environment, the role of psychology is becoming increasingly crucial. This is due to the deep understanding of human behavior and the predictive power of psychology, which are instrumental in making strategic decisions in various aspects of an organization. Psychology will continue to expand its significance in future management strategies in several ways.

Increased Emphasis on Integrated Approaches

Future management strategies will require an integrated approach, and psychology will be a key component of this. With advancements in technology, the field of psychological data science, which combines data analysis with an understanding of human psychology, is expected to grow significantly. This will allow organizations to more precisely analyze and predict consumer behavior, providing customized solutions for marketing strategies, product development, and customer service improvements. It will also contribute significantly to optimizing personnel management and team composition by analyzing employee behavior and performance.

Emphasis on Sustainability and Ethical Management

Sustainability and ethical management will become crucial values for future corporations, and the role of psychology in these areas will expand. Organizations will take their social and environmental impacts seriously and can use psychological approaches to effectively communicate and motivate their internal and external stakeholders. For instance, psychology can provide motivational techniques and strategies that organizations can use to promote sustainable behaviors among employees, which can also influence consumers to choose environmentally sustainable products.

Challenges of Globalization and Cross-Cultural Management

As globalization progresses, understanding and managing employees and customers from diverse cultural backgrounds becomes a critical management challenge. Psychology is essential for understanding cultural differences and analyzing how these differences impact interactions within and outside the organization. This enables organizations to develop effective communication and collaboration strategies as they expand globally. Psychological approaches can also optimize the performance of global teams and foster an environment that stimulates the creativity and innovation of employees from various cultural backgrounds.

Interaction with Technology

The advancement of technologies like artificial intelligence, robotics, and virtual reality will play a significant role in the future work environment, and psychology will play a key role in these interactions. Psychological knowledge will be crucial in managing the stress employees may experience when using technology, resistance to technology adoption, and new forms of workplace relationships that arise from technology interaction. This will help organizations effectively integrate technology and find ways for employees to positively embrace these changes.

Innovative Psychological Approaches in Management Strategies

Management strategies that utilize psychology will continue to evolve, enabling organizations to respond more agilely to changes in their internal and external environments and manage complex challenges effectively. By integrating psychological elements into decision-making processes, organizations can adopt more human-centered and ethical approaches, which are crucial for achieving sustainable growth and fulfilling social responsibilities. These approaches will promote the well-being of all organizational members and ensure the overall success of the organization.

To our readers...

We sincerely hope that the psychological insights shared in this book with a global readership from various cultural backgrounds will provide rich inspiration for your management practices. In modern management, human behavior and psychology are as important as numbers and data, and this book explores their importance in depth. We especially hope that readers from countries with distinct cultural characteristics, such as the United States, United Kingdom, Korea, and Japan, will find great assistance in understanding the importance of psychological approaches in management and applying them effectively.

For American readers, we hope this book provides a deep understanding of how to respect diversity and innovation and manage them effectively within organizational cultures. Approaching cooperation with people from diverse backgrounds psychologically in a melting pot society like the United States can enhance organizational inclusiveness and ensure that all members are valued. This promotes innovative thinking and creativity within the organization, aiding success in the changing global business environment.

For British readers, we hope this book integrates sophisticated psychological approaches into traditional management methods, helping to enhance organizational flexibility and global competitiveness. Considering the UK's deep historical background and complex international business environment, the psychological insights provided by this book offer ways for organizational leaders and team members to interact more effectively and innovatively resolve challenges faced.

For readers in Korea and Japan, we hope this book proves to be a valuable resource in emphasizing human-centered management amidst rapid economic growth and technological innovation, focusing on employee well-being and creativity in management strategies. Managing the psychological health of organizational members and supporting their potential to be fully realized, even in a high-tech and industrially advanced environment, will play a crucial role in the sustainable growth of organizations.

Finally, we hope the psychological insights presented in this book will provide practical help to organizational leaders worldwide, contributing to creating an environment where all organizational members can pursue organizational goals and personal growth simultaneously. Promoting the psychological well-being of individual members and the sustainable growth of organizations in the global business environment is becoming increasingly important. We hope this book provides profound insights into your management journey and contributes to effective decision-making and positive organizational culture formation at all levels of your organization.